John Griswold

HERRIN

The Brief History of an Infamous American City

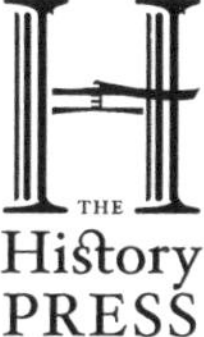

Published by The History Press
Charleston, SC 29403
www.historypress.net

First published 2009
Second printing 2013

Manufactured in the United States

ISBN 978.1.59629.797.5

Library of Congress Cataloging-in-Publication Data

Griswold, John.
Herrin : the brief history of an infamous American city / John Griswold.
p. cm.
Includes bibliographical references and index.
ISBN 978-1-59629-797-5
1. Herrin (Ill.)--History. I. Title.
F549.H56G755 2009
977.3'993--dc22
2009045618

Notice: The information in this book is true and complete to the best of our knowledge. It is offered without guarantee on the part of the author or The History Press. The author and The History Press disclaim all liability in connection with the use of this book.

For Thomas W. Haney II,

and for Herrinites everywhere.

The mine whistle throws a rocket of steam into the
air,
Top-men pick up their lunch pails and saunter to
the wash hydrants,
They sit in the shade of a concrete tipple and eat
sandwiches,
They smoke corncob pipes and discuss the shooting
at Herrin.

—*Stanley J. Kimmel, "Noon"*[1]

CONTENTS

LIST OF ILLUSTRATIONS

FOREWORD

If Illinois has a metaphorical pulse, it isn't in Springfield, where the state's blood pressure is artificially stimulated and the government tourniquet pinches all creatures great and small. Nor is it in Chicago, a megalopolis so vast and clotted by culture and commerce that it throbs day and night.

No, the real pulse of Illinois is located in places like Herrin, where the rhythm of the prairie heart beats just below the topsoil. Given the history of "bloody" Williamson County, the horrors of the Massacre that put Herrin on the national map, the Prohibition-era violence that pitted zealous Klansmen against opportunistic gangsters and the ubiquitous coal that fueled the economy, powered our cities and attracted thousands of immigrants to "Egypt," it is not surprising that the Illinois odyssey can be told so well within such narrow confines.

It takes an excellent, scholar, researcher and storyteller to take us on such a journey, and John Griswold has all the requisite qualifications. John's passion for history and his deep roots in Williamson and Franklin Counties make him the natural narrator for this adventure into our collective past. Whether you are from Chicago or Cairo, Quincy or Paris, you will recognize your Illinois past in these pages. Refreshingly, Griswold makes only two brief references to Abraham Lincoln, which in the bicentennial year of the state's favorite son is itself worthy of a footnote.

I am delighted to welcome *Herrin: The Brief History of an Infamous American City* to the Illinois history bookshelf. It's always nice to find your pulse nearby.

William Furry
Executive Director, Illinois State Historical Society

ACKNOWLEDGEMENTS

My sincere thanks go to the following.

Those at University of Illinois at Urbana-Champaign: John Hoffmann, head of the Illinois Historical Survey; Cheri Chenoweth, Scott Elrick and David Morse at the Illinois State Geological Survey's Coal Section; T.L. "Tommy" Phillips, Plant Biology; Anne Huber, ISGS librarian; Thomas E. Emerson, director, and Laura Kozuch, curator, Illinois Transportation Archaeological Research Program (ITARP); John McKinn, assistant director, American Indian Studies Program; J. Fred Giertz, head of the Department of Economics; Curtis Perry, head of the Department of English; and Lisa Bayer, marketing director at the UI Press.

Doug Lederman, Scott Jaschik and Kathlene Collins at *Inside Higher Ed*; Gary Metro and Chuck Novara at the *Southern Illinoisan*; Peter Johnson, Mining Media; and Geoffrey Ritter, the *Independent*.

Brian Butler, SIU-C; Ron Blakey, Northern Arizona University; Steve Titus, American Resources Group Ltd.; and William Furry, Illinois State Historical Society.

Donnie Allen and the Williamson County Historical Society; the staffs of the Lincoln Presidential Library, the Chicago History Museum and Special Collections, SIU-C; French Studio, Ltd.; and Michael Keepper, library director, Herrin City Library. Special thanks to Linda Banks for her time, deep knowledge, hard work and patience as our high school librarian and as curator for the Linda Jennings Banks History Room at the Herrin Library.

The Southern Illinois writers Gary DeNeal, Jeff Biggers, Taylor Pensoneau, James Ballowe, Herb Russell and Gordon Pruett.

Bill Tonso, in whose home my grandparents were married; Herrin mayor Vic Ritter; Richard Pisoni; Arma Raski; Rex Epperheimer, my oldest friend, for transport and security detail; Dan Eisenhauer, who walked all those miles with me so many years ago; and Gene and Nancy Eisenhauer, my other set of parents.

Jonathan Simcosky, commissioning editor for this book; Julie Foster, managing editor; Ryan Finn, project editor; and the rest of The History Press crew.

Charlie S. Jensen and Gardner Rogers, the only ones who know what the will and ninety days can do, for their invaluable input; James P. Leveille, for holding a room of my own; Steve Davenport, for the false claim that he's from Southern Illinois, which helped me define what it means to be from there; Peter Mortensen and Mike Finke, two swell cats; and John Balaban, upon whom I rely for the news that stays news.

Most of all, thanks and love to my sister, Ellen, and her family; my mother-in-law, Margaret; my beautiful boys, Jack and Julian; and my wife, Fiona.

INTRODUCTION

My mom loved to tell the story of how my aunt Ruby once drove the wrong way up a highway in St. Louis, Missouri. When oncoming cars swerved and honked in an attempt to save her life, Ruby leaned out her window, shook her fist at them and bellowed, "I'm from Herrin, by God!"[2]

That was in the 1950s, but strong feelings about her hometown, before and since, have not been unusual. In October 1924, at the height of the Prohibition war raging in Herrin, Illinois, Charles Lamb, twenty, and Edgar Hamby, twenty-five, were arrested in Cincinnati for carrying pistols.

"We're from Herrin, and we're not ashamed of it," one said in court. "It might have a black eye with the rest of the world, but it is home, sweet home and God's country to us."

"Do you walk around in Herrin with murderous-looking revolvers strapped to your waist?" the judge asked.

"No sir. Herrin is a peaceful little town."

The judge wasn't impressed, and when they couldn't pay the $100 fine, he sent them to jail.[3]

Herrin was, for nearly a century, alternately touted for its industry and pilloried for its crimes. When both subsided, the city was largely ignored again by the rest of the country. For those from there, it's always been a place for hard work, accomplishment, struggle and a strong sense of community—everyday life in America.

I grew up in Herrin, on East Stotlar Street, halfway between Southside Elementary and the Herrin Cemetery,[4] and graduated from Herrin High School. My mom lived in Herrin most of her life; her father moved to Herrin from Franklin County as a young man and became a state senator, as well as the United Mine Workers of America Sub-district 10 president, posts he held concurrently at the time of the Herrin Massacre of 1922.[5] Despite all this, I knew few details of Herrin's history, so I lacked context for the pride, defiance and guilt implied in Ruby's story.

Certainly none of the troubles Herrin has endured—mine riot, Prohibition war, coal depression—is what I think of first when I remember my hometown. I remember instead its landscape and its smart, funny people, as positively imprinted on me as those of nearby Hannibal, Missouri, were for that other writer. My natural sympathies are with the place I've known so well, but that doesn't preclude a desire to understand what happened and why it happened as it did.

There are a handful of well-known works on Herrin, Williamson County and Southern Illinois history, such as Milo Erwin's *The History of Williamson County, Illinois* (1876), Hal Trovillion's *Old Times in Herrin* (1922), Barbara Burr Hubbs's *Pioneer Folks and Places* (1939), Paul M. Angle's *Bloody Williamson* (1952), John W. Allen's *Legends & Lore of Southern Illinois* (1963), Gary DeNeal's *A Knight of Another Sort* (second edition, 1998) and Taylor Pensoneau's *Brothers Notorious* (2002), to which any subsequent writer must be indebted.

Anyone with an Internet connection can find free digital versions of materials in the Illinois State Historical Survey at the University of Illinois at Urbana-Champaign, such as *Williamson County, Illinois, in the World War* or *Life and Exploits of S. Glenn Young, World-Famous Law Enforcement Officer*. Other publications of interest available locally include Gordon Pruett's photo-essay compilations, such as *One Hundred Years of Herrin, Illinois* (2002), commemorative editions of newspapers, HerrinFesta souvenir booklets and church bulletins.

One of the best resources of all is the Linda Jennings Banks History Room at the Herrin City Library, which needs more funding and labor to ensure continued preservation of irreplaceable materials. The same goes for the Williamson County Historical Society Museum and resource room in the historic county jail in Marion.

In doing research for a novel set in Herrin,[6] I found other sources, such as the Oldham Paisley scrapbooks of national media coverage after the Herrin Massacre; the working files of writer Paul Angle; and the archives of Herrin editor Hal Trovillion. For the book you're holding I found many more: other books, articles, dissertations, photos and physical artifacts, including new scholarship on everything from indigenous peoples to the rise and fall of the Ku Klux Klan in Williamson County in the 1920s. Because this book must be a brief history for a general readership, it should be viewed as a stroll among these many sources. If you want to know more, the bibliography at the end of this book will point you in the right direction.

I understand, too, that there are those who don't want more—or any at all. As I was working on this book one day this summer, I met the elderly daughter of a civic leader famous for decades in Herrin. She was very sweet, but despite the fact that her father had been an avid historian and that she and I met in the Herrin History Room, where she'd gone to look at old yearbooks, she told me tartly, "None of that should be dredged up."

Milo Erwin, a lawyer and state representative, says in the nineteenth century that he met with disapproval when he wrote about the county's Bloody Vendetta. Paul Angle says that in the 1920s "a resident still had to be careful of what he said about the Bloody Vendetta, although half a century had passed."[7] Hal Trovillion reportedly helped Angle with *Bloody Williamson* in the 1950s but wanted that association kept quiet for fear of reprisal. The Herrin Lions Club passed resolutions in 1951 that these historical matters "should be…forgotten by our own press as un-American and undemocratic."[8] And just this summer an editor-in-chief of a big newspaper e-mailed to say that a friend of his who taught high school history locally had planned to do a unit on the Massacre but got a death threat at home. He changed his syllabus.

In one respect, the silence is understandable—there's something elemental in the history of Herrin that has loomed large in America's consciousness, something alive and powerful that has resisted being made harmless, let alone ridiculous, the way the bad reputation of "Bang-Bang Chicago" was converted to gangster-themed restaurants and walking tours. But if Chicago can make peace with its history, surely Herrin can, too.

Besides, the past won't stay buried any more than the coal did. The only question is how it gets used once it is dug up. We need books, not silence—something I knew as a reader long before I became a writer or teacher. Growing up in Herrin in the 1960s and '70s, I always wished I'd had something to clarify the sources of strong feelings about the place.

Someone has suggested that Illinois is the most representative state of the United States, not only for its geographical position in the heart of the country but also because it's a microcosm of the country's promise, problems and divergent opinions. The easy story of American democracy is, as the *Herrin News* once wrote, "not discord, but harmony, and not suspicion, but brotherly reliance and confidence."[9] But while difference often does make us stronger, some places become in their times cauldrons, not melting pots, and for this reason, too, Herrin is a very American city and needs to be understood.

In Herrin, what lies under the surface has always been as important as what's visible. I hope you'll find this brief discovery of interest.

CHAPTER 1

GEOLOGY

Few places illustrate the saying "Geography is destiny" better than the city of Herrin. Nestled between two great rivers, situated on the border between northern plains and southern hills and underlain with one of the world's great energy deposits, Herrin's fate has long been tied to the land.[10]

Herrin rides on a rock called Laurentia, which makes up much of North America. This craton, as it's called in geology, has sailed around with its keel deep in the earth's mantle for some 1.5 billion years and is one of the older rocks on the planet. But since the craton moves, the earth's climate changes over time and rain and wind wear away rock, the landscape has looked vastly different in different epochs.

Approximately 500 million years ago, Laurentia was a desert island at about the latitude of present-day Australia. The spoon-shaped depression in its center, called the Illinois Basin, was flooded by shallow seas countless times over hundreds of millions of years, as the world's sea levels rose and fell from the collision of tectonic plates and the formation of glaciers.[11] Tropical corals and other marine organisms in these seas formed reefs of calcium carbonate, which eventually became the fossil-bearing limestone of Southern Illinois.

Approximately 400 million years ago, when the first fish began to walk on land, Herrin was just south of the equator. Laurentia was welded to two other cratons, and mountains thousands of feet tall pushed up at their sutures. Over time, these eroded and deposited layers of sand and silt on the limestone. Seed-bearing plants grew profusely since there was little to eat them or diseases adapted to them, and for the first time on earth, great forests of trees (with little or no bark) rose up.

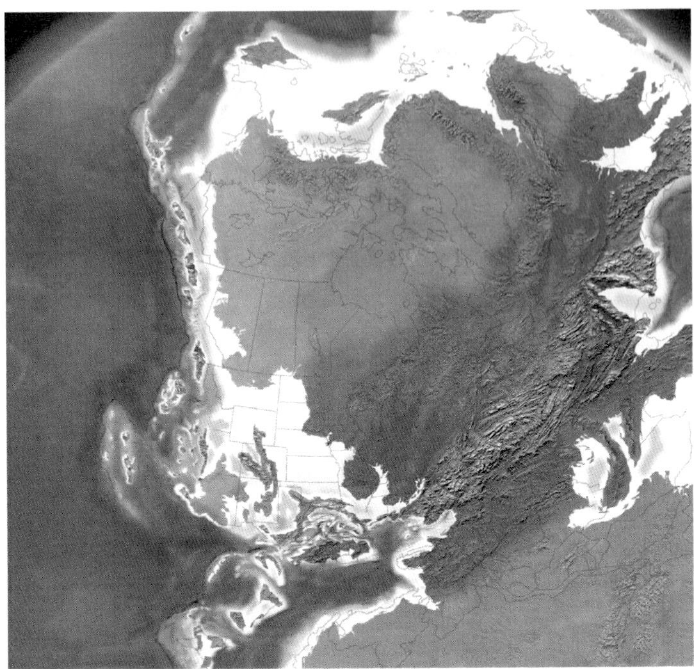

Approximately 300 million years ago, Southern Illinois was on the equator and flooded by the sea. *Courtesy Ron Blakey.*

By 300 million years ago, Herrin sat on the equator as all the cratons on earth came together in a single landmass called Pangaea. The Appalachian Mountains rose fifteen thousand feet or higher in the slow-motion collision, and the runoff from their slopes deposited more sand and mud in the water that filled the Illinois Basin. These successive layers became the sandstone and shales seen now at Giant City and Ferne Clyffe State Parks, which sit at the rim of the basin.

Conditions were right to start making good coal at this time, called the Pennsylvanian subperiod of the Carboniferous period. Much of Pangaea's landmass was located south of the equator, where glaciers formed readily. And when there was a lot of ice, which locked up water, the seas dropped, exposing the basin and allowing plants to grow in huge mires on the land surface.

The swamps required just the right amount of water at the right times, however, to make conditions ideal for growth. In addition to lowering sea levels, the glaciers helped create a band of moisture at the equator called the Intertropical Convergence Zone, which created daily rain rather than monsoonal or seasonal rains with dry spells between. Plants grew lush and thick, and their roots held sediment in place. (Good coal isn't split with other contaminants.) The Illinois State Geological Survey describes the swamp like this:

> *The deciduous trees and flowering plants that are common today had not yet evolved. Instead, the jungle-like forests were dominated by giant ancestors*

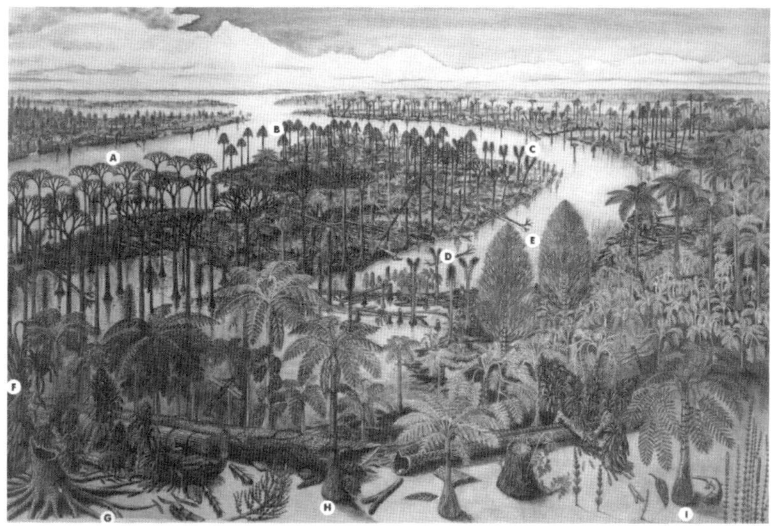

A coal swamp of the kind that made Herrin coal. *Illustration by Alice Prickett, courtesy Geological Society of America.*

> *of present-day club mosses, horsetails, ferns, conifers, and cycads. The undergrowth also was well developed, consisting of many ferns, fernlike plants, and small club mosses...Many of the Pennsylvanian plants, such as the seed ferns, eventually became extinct.*[12]

As the plants died, they fertilized the swamp and encouraged new growth under the tropical sun. Trees evolved heavy bark to help support their weight and protect themselves from plant-eating insects, and the bark's lignin—which few things can digest—as well as low oxygen levels in the swamp water, discouraged decay and acted as a preservative. A thick mat of dead plants accumulated, which we call peat. Elsewhere in the world it is burned as fuel itself.

It takes ten to twenty feet of peat to make one foot of coal. In the Herrin area, the peat was perhaps 150 feet thick. But one other thing has to happen to peat for it to become coal: it must be covered over quickly, or it oxidizes away. Coal, the rock that burns, is also a fossil.

At this time, an ancient river the size of today's Mississippi ran through the center of Illinois. Its headwaters were probably located in Canada, its mouth was southwest of Illinois and its watershed included the Appalachians and the Canadian Shield. What remains of it, the Walshville Channel, is deep underground now, 230 miles long and 1 to 5 miles wide. Plants didn't grow in the river's bed, so there was no peat in the channel and therefore no coal. But the river helped keep the swamp wet and promoted growth. More importantly, during floods the mouth of the river stopped acting like a river

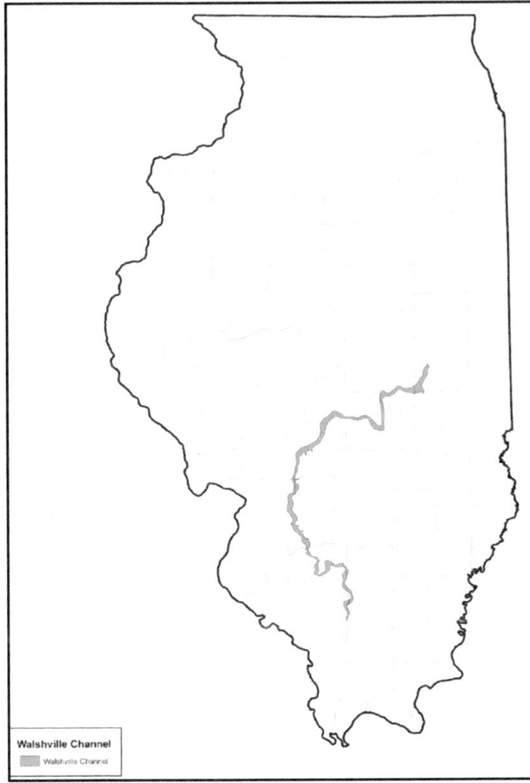

The Walshville Channel, the underground bed of an ancient river that once watered the coal swamp. *Courtesy Illinois State Geological Survey.*

and became an estuary instead. Alluvial deposits that had eroded off the Appalachians, especially gray shale, spilled out into the swamp and smothered the peat, sealing it against oxidation and natural sulfur in the sea. (Gray shale is also lower in sulfur than black shale, which was once organic material, too.)

While Herrin (No. 6) Coal lies under most of the Illinois and Appalachian Basins, these local conditions—a swamp with just the right water, lush plant growth with little sediment, peat preservation, a twenty-foot-thick (or more) cap of the right kind of shale—led to what's called the Quality Circle in Williamson, Franklin and Jefferson Counties. And it was this relatively low-sulfur,[13] high-BTU bituminous coal, which lay in a flat seam up to twelve feet thick at relatively shallow depths from the surface, that made the city of Herrin boom in the early decades of the twentieth century.[14]

Conveniently for the pace of our story, Illinois is missing 300 million years of its geologic record after the coal-bearing Pennsylvanian interval, due to erosion, and the next big thing known to have come to town was the glaciers, which shaped the visible landscape.

Approximately 2 million years ago, the climate began to cool (up to a dozen degrees colder than now), and between 1.6 million years ago and 300,000 years ago, ice sheets flowed down over the northern parts of North America at least four to eight times, scraping the surface of what by now was twelve thousand feet of sedimentary rock on top of the craton.

Each glaciation overwrote previous ones, but two of the best-known periods are the Illinoisan (300,000 years ago to 125,000 years ago) and the Wisconsin (100,000 years ago to 10,000 years ago). The Illinoisan

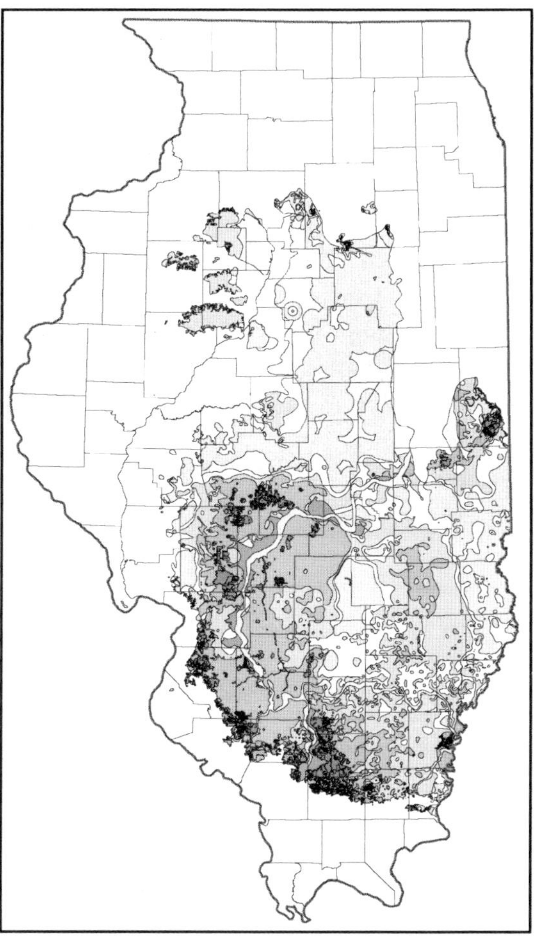

Shortly after the time of the Herrin coal swamp, about 300 million years ago. Shaded areas alongside the ancient river channel are peat beds where plants grew most thickly. The black patch at the southern end of the channel is the Quality Circle, where the river overflowed and sealed the peat with alluvial deposits, making better, lower-sulfur coal. *Courtesy Illinois State Geological Survey.*

glacier's southern limit was the bottom of Williamson County, and Herrin would have been covered in hundreds, maybe thousands, of feet of ice mixed with debris. When the glacier retreated, it left a mix of clay, silt, sand and boulders called diamicton that covers the entire state, except for the exposed rocks of the southern tip and a single county in the northwest. These gently rolling hills are what you instantly notice driving south in Illinois toward Herrin, last stop on the Southern Till Plain before the Shawnee Hills.

When the ice melted back and everything dried, dust from the glacial rivers called loess (rhymes with "bus") blew across the land. It is thickest near the beds of the big rivers—Illinois, Mississippi and Ohio—where there's up to twenty feet of it, but under Herrin there's less than five feet.[15]

The land around Herrin was spared during the Wisconsin period. That glacier only came into the northeast quadrant of Illinois, but much of Southern Illinois coursed with streams and rivers from its melt water. Finger lakes that pointed back from the big rivers' confluence left silt and clay, accounting for the composition of Herrin's soil, with which you'll be familiar if you've ever had to bury a dead cat in it. In fact, Herrin's nickname used to be Buckhorn, for the spidery weed that some thought was the only thing that would grow in the hardpan.[16]

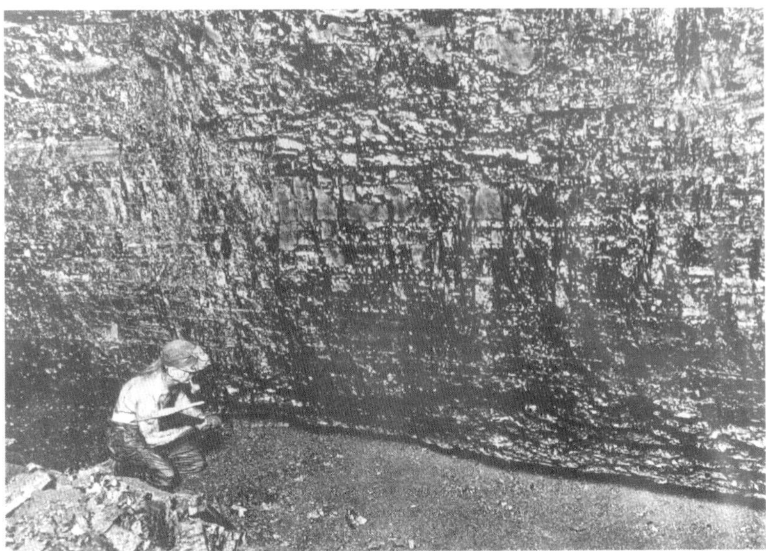

Quality Circle coal, ten feet thick, in Old Ben No. 9, about 1915. Miner is undercutting the face by light of an open-flame carbide headlamp while smoking a corncob pipe. *Courtesy Illinois State Geological Survey.*

The Herrin area is home to post-oak flatwood forests, upland forests, wetlands and remnants of prairie. Native plant species include elm; wild black cherry; wild blackberry; the vines trumpet creeper and poison ivy (in profusion); and the herbs ragweed, common dogbane and common goldenrod. Invasive nonnative species include the white mulberry tree; the shrub autumn olive; the vines Japanese honeysuckle and multiflora rose; the herbs crown vetch, English plantain, hedge parsley, curly dock and mullein; and the grasses red top, hairy chess, fescue, Kentucky bluegrass and common bristlegrass. Two plants found by scientists in 2002, just east of town on Herrin Street, had never been found in Illinois before: the Oklahoma sedge and the small-awned sedge.[17]

This region, known as Egypt,[18] has borders that are sometimes disputed for reasons both good (people up around St. Louis want to be included) and bad (when blame needs to be placed). I like the definition of archaeologist Brian Butler, who says that it should include the drainages of the Saline, Big Muddy and Mary's Rivers and that the "northwest frontier" should be the Kaskaskia River. This encompasses an area of nineteen counties and 6,600 square miles, which provided a "rich and varied landscape" for the first people, with its five major rivers, a coastal plain, Southern Till Plain and rocky uplands. Herrin lies at the heart of this Egypt.

As the continents slowly float back together again, one thing is sure: 250 million years from now, Herrin's weather and landscape will have changed yet again, and it'll be a lot easier to drive to Paris.

CHAPTER 2

INDIANS

Milo Erwin writes, "When our fathers came here, they found these vast, silent, virgin plains unclaimed, untouched, untilled, hedgeless, free to all...[There were] no monuments of past greatness; no Coliseum lay in a pile of ruins; no Obelisk of Sesostris pointed its alabaster finger to the eternal source of light; no Pyramids frowned down upon them; no battlescars were seen." Similarly, the landscape had not been cultivated: "There were no towering evergreens, Oriental bowers, or statuary. It was a virgin land...It was a new land. Her greatness was all in the future,—her history yet to be made and written."[19]

While it's true that indigenous peoples[20] left little durable architecture or writing to mark their cultures, the land had plenty of human history, long before the first white settlers arrived.

The Wisconsin glacier and the enormous quantity of water running off it probably blocked human habitation in the Herrin area before the year 15,000 BC, but recent archaeological finds suggest that small nomadic bands of Paleo-Indians began living and hunting throughout the Americas, including in the Midwest, not long afterward, a couple of thousand years before previously thought.[21]

Southern Illinois at the end of the last ice age was much cooler in summer than it is now, though not greatly colder in winter, and was covered with spruce, balsam and poplar seen now in alpine regions. Giant ground sloths the size of oxen, saber-toothed cats, mastodons, mammoths and many other large mammals lived in the area. Then, about 9000 BC, thirty-five genera of mammals suddenly went extinct in North and South America and, to a lesser degree, in Europe, Africa and Asia. The people known as the Clovis culture disappeared, too.[22] Theories on why this happened include catastrophic overhunting, climate change,[23] "hyperdisease" and, most recently, a comet impact.[24] ("The entire continent was on fire," a lead researcher says.[25]) The theories, like the cultures, rise and fall.

Limited archaeological study has been done on Indian sites in Southern Illinois, and none in Williamson County, but the closest known site to Herrin is a rare rock shelter on the Till Plains, the Little Muddy Rock Shelter in Jackson County, which dates from 10,000 BC to 9200 BC. Fewer found sites does not necessarily mean that there were fewer Paleo-Indians about, since their early camps may have been small and temporary and since strip mining, farming, roads, railroads and towns have no doubt erased some of the evidence.[26]

By 4500 to 3500 BC, the Herrin area was probably mixed hardwood forest with pockets of developing prairie (technically a savannah[27]), inhabited by recognizable animals. Along waterways and in the uplands of Southern Illinois the Indians were making bigger, long-term base camps of "lightly built wigwamlike structures" with a few more durable single-post structures. Groups left to hunt, gather and do other jobs according to the seasons and then returned. Probably their only cultivated foodstuff was gourds, and their main sources of protein were nuts, white-tailed deer and fish. Archaeologists have found evidence of trading by these people—of high-quality Cobden chert, used for stone tools, for instance—and other social contact over large distances.

By 600 to 300 BC, local Indians were still hunter-gatherers, but their population was growing, which meant that they began to be limited to territories and had to make better use of local resources. They cultivated Goosefoot (chenopodium), maygrass, knotweed, squash and little barley and collected local seeds, nuts and fruits.[28] Because many of these foods grew on the prairie pockets or in the scrub zone between them and the forest, the Indians would have moved through what came to be known as Herrin's Prairie.

From AD 650 to AD 1400, Cahokia, 120 miles away, and other mound-building societies dominated the eastern half of what is now the United States. At Cahokia alone, the people moved fifty-five million cubic feet of earth to make their mounds, a feat that required enormous resources and organization. Trade, hunting and maybe even herding would have brought them through the Herrin area. No one knows exactly what happened to the culture, though it's long been suspected that the land became exhausted and couldn't support a large population. Spanish explorers in Arkansas in the 1540s heard mention of Cahokia, but it had collapsed and disappeared by the time of the French arrival, 150 years later.[29] Chief Jean-Baptiste Ducoigne, for whom the town of

PERIOD	HORIZON	DIAGNOSTIC BIFACES
MISSIPPIAN	Missippian	Madison
LATE WOODLAND	Late Woodland II Late Woodland I (AD 790±90) Crab Orchard III	Late Woodland Arrow Points Jamestown Raymond Lowe/Steuben
MIDDLE WOODLAND	Crab Orchard II (AD 20±90)	Affinis/Snyders North
EARLY WOODLAND	Crab Orchard I (470±70 BC) (470±70 BC)	Adena/Waubesa
LATE ARCHAIC	Terminal Archaic (1040±80 BC) Late Archaic IV (1710±80 BC) Late Archaic III (1720±70 BC) Late Archaic II (2020±90 BC) Late Archaic I (2490±150 BC) (2590±150 BC)	Cypress Table Rock (Merom/Trimble) Etley Karnak Saratoga Matanza
MIDDLE ARCHAIC	Middle Archaic (3890±60 BC)	Godar
EARLY ARCHAIC	Early Archaic (5310±210 BC)	Kirk Dalton Thebes

Chronology of rock tools found at Little Muddy Rock Shelter, Jackson County, shows human habitation for seven thousand years. *Courtesy American Resources Group Ltd., Carbondale, Illinois.*

Du Quoin is named,[30] said that his ancestors built the mounds, but most of the Indians the Europeans encountered had no idea of Cahokia's greatness.

In fact, it seems that Illinois may have been without a dominant Indian presence for two hundred years after Cahokia collapsed. The Illini, a confederation of as many as twelve distinct bands in the Algonquian language group, had established themselves throughout the state by 1655, with numbers perhaps as high as twelve to fourteen thousand. But by the time the Frenchmen Marquette and Joliet made contact with the Illini in 1673, the Fox, Sauk, Kickapoo and other Great Lakes tribes were pushing down from the north, the Shawnee were moving in from Ohio to the southeast and the Iroquois and Miami had been periodically raiding from the east. The Illini often retreated west across the Mississippi to escape their enemies, only to run into hostile Sioux. When they returned to Illinois, they found the remnants of even more eastern tribes pushing into their former territory to avoid white expansion and tribal conflict.

Disease, alcoholism, acceptance of Christianity (with the idea of monogamy), limited resources (especially in constant movement) and warfare continued to shrink the tribes of the Illini. By the end of the so-called Beaver Wars in 1701, only six of the original tribes remained—the Cahokia, Kaskaskia, Peoria, Michigamea, Moingwena and Tamaroa—about 6,700 people in villages at Kaskaskia, Cahokia and Starved Rock. Above all, the tribe's reliance on the French for protection and income led to faster decline for the Illini than for more defiant tribes.

In 1736, the French counted 2,500 Illini. By the time of the American Revolution (in which they provided aid), there were 480. In 1803, the Kaskaskia tribe ceded their lands east of the Mississippi in the Treaty of Vincennes; in 1818, the Peoria did the same via the Treaty of Edwardsville. By 1818, the Illini had moved to Missouri and by 1832 to a reservation in eastern Kansas; by 1854—when the remnants merged with others to become the United Peoria, Kaskaskia, Wea and Piankashaw—there were just 84 members. They moved finally in 1867 to northeast Oklahoma. The Peoria began to grow again slowly, with current enrollment at nearly 2,000.[31]

So Indians had traversed the Herrin area for thousands of years before white settlers were also drawn by the wealth of resources of its forest, prairie and waterways: game, fish, nuts, berries, thatch for houses, medicinal herbs and more.[32]

But even though Erwin was writing in 1876, when Indians had not lived in the region for decades, he betrays mixed feelings for them. First he imagines their way of life in a Victorian prose so overheated it burns the ears:

> *This was a lovely home for the Red Man, where the dews of Egypt kindled roses and vines for him, and Nature, with her sweet influence, taught him to*

> *love and adore the Great Spirit in this fair haven of happiness and repose, too pure and stainless to be sullied by immorality.*

He stops to admire the Kaskaskia (a tribe of the Illini) because they "were friendly with the whites" and, correspondingly, "these were Indians in whom the peculiar characteristics of the race had given place to some of the courtesies and confidences of civilized man." He also pays tribute to Shawnee leader Tecumseh, even though he fought the whites, because he "was a human Indian and was never known to ill-treat or murder a prisoner, and denounced all who did, and employed all his authority and eloquence to protect the helpless." Yet most of those who resisted white encroachment, such as the other Shawnee, "were hated and feared by the whites."

And so Erwin gives a perfect example of the conflicted tone of so much American writing on Indian life:

> *They once claimed this county* [Williamson] *as their own, and the light bark canoe* [actually heavy dugout canoes] *swam on the silver bosom of the Saline...They pushed aside the thickly trailing vines and then the canoe would disturb a perfect surface of the most marvelous mirror, reflecting countless forms of leaves and twigs. How intense was the silence, broken only by the splash of a single blue heron, who, wondering at the intrusion, gazed, and then spreading his great wings, rose and slowly disappeared. Such were the scenes of these dirty, greasy, filthy Indians.*[33]

The last big fight between Indian tribes in Southern Illinois took place in 1802, fifteen miles from Herrin. It was a running battle, along the Shawneetown-Kaskaskia Trail, with members of the Kaskaskia tribe in retreat from Shawneetown, where they'd gone for provisions, and the Shawnee in pursuit. One mile west of West Frankfort, on Illinois 149, several were killed (probably Kaskaskia). Two miles farther west, where 149 crosses the Big Muddy at Plumfield, more of the Kaskaskia were killed trying to cross the river. The rest continued on, and the final slaughter came at the flooded Little Muddy River, just west of Reece Cemetery, north of Mulkeytown, where the Shawnee killed everyone who didn't get across the river. The few surviving Kaskaskia, including Chief Jean-Baptiste Ducoigne, limped back to their village, the tribe destroyed.[34]

One reads through what Milo Erwin says and senses the Indians' fear and misery at this time. A white named Thomas Griffee lived on the Saline River and "had a character for killing every Indian he could catch in the woods, and they were afraid to go down there." An elderly Indian man had a white wife, whom he never left alone on Sundays, when whites came to visit the Indian camp, "for fear the white boys would steal her." Game was scarce enough by then that Indian hunters would "go quite often to farmers' houses for something to eat."[35]

The first white man to settle on Herrin's Prairie, Hibbins, settled on the west side of the prairie in 1811 but "was compelled to leave it the next" year, presumably due to threat of Indian attack. Erwin says that in 1818 a man "doubtless murdered by the Indians" was found "at the Stotlar place" (which it was later, presumably) by a friend of Isaac Herrin[g]," the first permanent settler.[36]

Erwin says that "a very large number" of Indians camped on Phelps' Prairie, the next prairie-island south of Herrin's Prairie, in 1813. And some of the Kaskaskia were around Williamson County as late as 1828, sent out by a trader from the town of Kaskaskia to hunt and trap. They came in the fall and camped along the Big Muddy River, Hurricane Creek, Crab Orchard Creek and other streams and ponds. Erwin mentions artifacts that could still be seen in 1876, such as mounds two feet high and twenty feet across on which Indians built wigwams to keep the floors dry, north of Herrin near Pond Creek.

It's no puzzle how, when or why the Indians disappeared in the Herrin area. Erwin says that there was a "long catalogue of violent deaths, ushered in by the keen crack of the savage Indians' rifle, and ending with the hollow thud of the murderous shot-gun in this county."[37]

Far more efficient than settlers' shotguns in driving out the remaining Illini and Shawnee were new laws of the land. A Supreme Court decision in 1823, *Johnson v. M'Intosh*, traced how the Dutch, Spanish, French and British had justified land rights in North America, when the Indians were obviously there before them, and applied the concept to disputed property titles in Southern Illinois. Chief Justice John Marshall found that "it has never been doubted, that either the United States, or the several States, had a clear title to all the lands…subject only to the Indian right of occupancy, and that the exclusive power to extinguish that right, was vested in that government which might constitutionally exercise it."[38] The case established a national precedent for denying Indians possession of their traditional lands.[39]

President Andrew Jackson signed the Indian Removal Act on May 28, 1830, which authorized giving "unsettled" lands west of the Mississippi to Indians in exchange for their land in existing states. Many tribes resisted, but it was futile. During the fall and winter of 1838–39, fifteen thousand Cherokees forced from their lands in eastern Tennessee and northwest Georgia were marched west by the U.S. government toward the Oklahoma Territory. In groups of one thousand at a time, they crossed Southern Illinois twenty-eight miles south of Herrin, on what's now Illinois 146. Four thousand died from disease, starvation and exposure in the especially freezing winter that year along the eight-hundred-mile-long forced march known now as the "Trail of Tears."[40]

CHAPTER 3

SETTLEMENT

Some people scoff at the word "Midwest," implying that the area's too flat, too tame and too far east to compare with the popular myth of the American West. But Herrin sits in what was once the frontier—the farthest corner of the Northwest Territory of 1787. As recently as two hundred years ago, when the first permanent white settlers, Isaac Herring and his son-in-law David Herrin, built on their unnamed prairie, it was a hard country that required hard people.

My favorite story to illustrate this is about naturalist and artist John James Audubon. In 1811 or 1812, he was commuting on foot from Ste. Genevieve, Missouri, where he had business interests, to Henderson, Kentucky, where he lived. He probably walked the Shawneetown-Kaskaskia Trail, which would have brought him just to the north, at some point in his journey, of Herrin's Prairie.

He writes, "The weather was fine, all around me was as fresh and blooming as if it had just issued from the bosom of nature. My knapsack, my gun, and my dog were all that I had for baggage and company. But, although well moccasined, I moved slowly along, attracted by the brilliancy of the flowers, and the gambols of the fawns…to all appearances as thoughtless to danger as I felt myself."

It began to grow dark. When he saw firelight he headed for it, assuming it to be the "camp of some wandering Indians." Instead it was from a small log cabin with a tall woman inside.

"Her voice was gruff," Audubon says, "and her attire negligently thrown about her." Audubon asked for shelter and food, and she said to come on in.

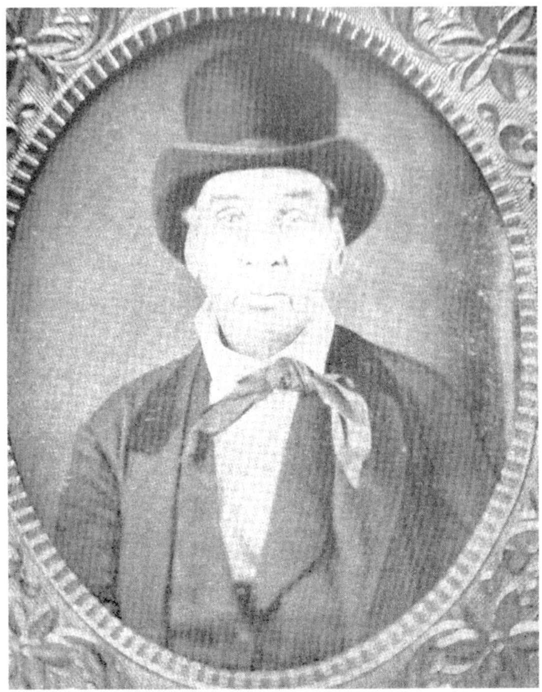

David Herrin (1793–1870), son-in-law of first permanent settler Isaac Herring.

The first thing Audubon saw was "a finely formed young Indian, resting his head between his hands, with his elbows on his knees...He moved not; he apparently breathed not." Audubon kept asking him questions, but when the man finally looked up to respond, his face was covered with blood. He didn't speak much English or French, but Audubon was able to understand he'd been shooting a coon in a tree when his arrow split on the bowstring and put his right eye out.

There was bread baking in the ashes on the hearth and plenty of venison and jerked bison meat, and Audubon was welcomed to sleep on a pile of bear or bison hides in the corner. Before he ate, he made the mistake of pulling out his pocket watch to check the time. Suddenly the big woman "was all ecstasy, spoke of its beauty, asked me its value, and put the chain around her brawny neck, saying how happy the possession of such a watch would make her."

The Indian caught Audubon's eye after supper and seemed to warn him of danger. The man pulled his knife out of its scabbard, felt its edge, put it away and filled his pipe—built into a tomahawk—with tobacco. Audubon got his watch back and went outside, pretending to check the weather, reloaded his gun and came in and pretended to go to sleep.

In a short while the woman's two grown sons came in carrying a stag between them on a pole. They started to drink whiskey, and when they asked who the two visitors were, mom told them to be quiet, said something about Audubon's watch and took them into a corner to whisper. She boozed with her boys, and they all got a little rowdy. Audubon writes:

> *Judge of my astonishment when I saw this* [devil] *incarnate take a large carving knife, and go to the grindstone to whet its edge. I saw her pour the water on the turning machine, and watched her working away with the*

> *dangerous instrument, until the cold sweat covered every part of my body, in despite of my determination to defend myself to the last. Her task finished, she walked to her reeling sons, and said, "There, that'll soon settle him! Boys, kill yon ——, and then for the watch."*

But just as Audubon was about to shoot the woman—knowing the sons would then kill him—two new travelers entered. Audubon jumped up and explained his predicament, and they helped him disarm and tie up the woman and her sons. Audubon and his new friends sat up talking through the night, and in the morning, "we marched them into the woods off the road," Audubon says, "and having used them as Regulators [vigilantes] were wont to…we set fire to the cabin, gave all the skins and implements to the young Indian warrior, and proceeded, well pleased, towards the settlements."[41]

And this guy was a *watercolorist*. You can imagine how tough the average settler must have been.

Europeans often traveled the rivers in their early explorations, and Hernando de Soto, in 1541, came as close to Herrin as northeast Arkansas.[42] Others may have come inland from the rivers three hundred years ago, starting with French trappers and hunters in the wake of the 1673 Mississippi River expedition of Louis Joliet and Father Jacques Marquette.[43]

The hunters would have found a wildness almost unimaginable to us now, more like Virginia in the sixteenth century when the English arrived. Deer, bears, wolves, cougars, wildcats, otters and minks lived in the river bottoms and woods; "hundreds of rattlesnakes… their huge scaly bodies… shining…in folds upon hill-sides…would throw open their mouths in a daring and reckless manner"; and bison[44] and elk roamed the prairie islands in grass higher than a man's head. By 1702, there was a French hide and wool tannery near

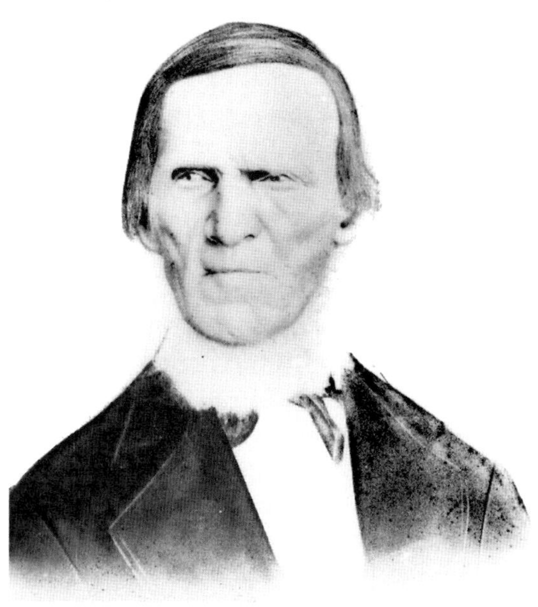

John D. Sanders (1801–1875), first sheriff of Williamson County. He was so tough even the camera couldn't catch all of him.

present-day Cairo, estimated to have processed thirteen thousand hides from bison across Southern Illinois, in about a year, before it folded.[45]

Historian Barbara Burr Hubbs mentions that French traders bought pelts from Indians camped near present-day Blairsville, just west of Herrin, on the Big Muddy and even established a crude trading post there called Au Vase, for their name for the Big Muddy River, Riviere au Vase, or "river of mud." And Eight Mile Prairie, southwest of Herrin, made French hunter-traders exclaim "Fredonne!" ("it hums") when they saw swarms of bees pollinating Spanish needle blossoms. The word became "Fredonia," the post office that opened there in 1837.[46]

A Frenchman, Renault, left France in 1719 with two hundred lead miners, bought five hundred slaves at San Domingo and set himself up for business in St. Phillip, a village near Fort Chartres, Illinois, in 1720. He stayed in business for more than twenty years and spent a great deal of money, and Erwin believes that his company must have traversed Williamson County in the search for ore.

The next time white men came into the county, according to Erwin, was in 1766, when four men who had been exploring in Kentucky crossed into Illinois at the mouth of the Tennessee, headed north and were "lost sight of forever. It is likely they were killed by the Indians in this county."[47]

Soon afterward came the era of log stockades in the wilderness, built for group safety and for symbolic control. The French built Fort De L'Ascension in 1757 on the Ohio, near Metropolis, to defend against Britain and its allies in the French and Indian War, later changing the name to "Massiac" after the French minister of colonial affairs. But when the war ended in 1763, they abandoned the fort, and Chickasaw Indians burned it down. The British took control and anglicized it to "Massac" but never rebuilt. This allowed Colonel George Rogers Clark and his "Long Knives" regiment to steal into Illinois at Massac Creek in 1778, march to the then British fort at Kaskaskia—traditionally crossing Herrin's Prairie en route—and take the Illinois Territory for the State of Virginia, which ceded it after the Revolution to the new federal government.[48]

Early settlers also built stockades and blockhouses. Jordan's Fort was built in 1804, two and a half miles southeast of Thompsonville, at Pond Creek in Franklin County, on an old Indian encampment. Hubbs says that it was the first settlement by Americans west of Equality, the old French saltworks. The fort wall enclosed several cabins, and the Jordan brothers and a few others "lived on the country with no attempt to farm." In 1812, James Jordan and William Barberry were gathering wood outside the stockade wall and were attacked, presumably by Shawnees. Barberry was killed and scalped.

The first local road in Williamson County led from Jordan's Fort, through Herrin's Prairie, to a small blockhouse built by Charles Humphreys in

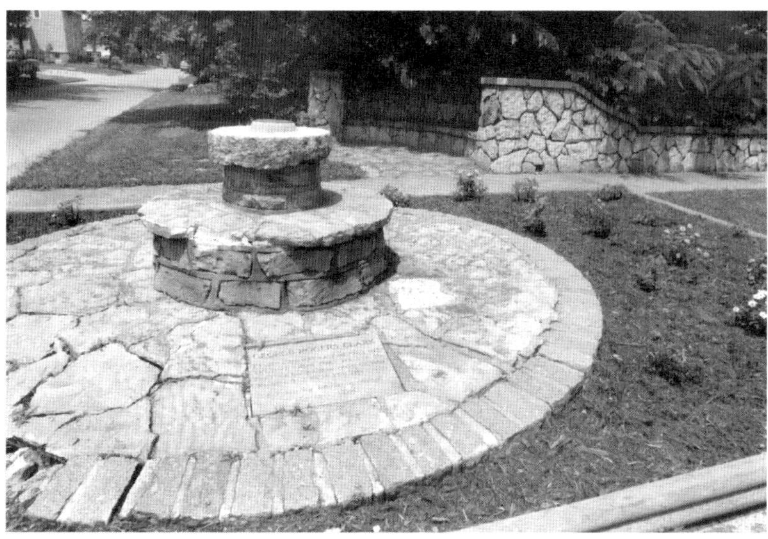

Marker placed by editor Hal Trovillion on his property to commemorate George Rogers Clark's passage in 1778 through the prairie that would become Herrin. *Courtesy Herrin City Library.*

1808, in Blairsville Township, at Humphreys' Ford on the Big Muddy River. The river ford was on the main route for travelers coming from anywhere south of Shawneetown and was the site of the French-Indian trading post in the eighteenth century. Humphreys, his wife Mary (known as Polly) and a young cousin, John Boles, ran the gravity ferry, raised hogs and a cow and traded with Indians. Polly is said to have nursed a Shawnee to health, who then helped the settlers defend the blockhouse against an attack by three Kickapoos. The Humphreyses abandoned their settlement for a time during the War of 1812, when "Indian hostilities increased."

The blockhouse between Phelps' Prairie (the old Bainbridge) and Poor Prairie (now Marion) was built in 1811 in response to instruction by Illinois Territory governor Ninian Edwards that settlers defend themselves against Britain's Indian allies. It was twenty feet square, made of hewed logs and had a slab roof. It's telling that by 1817 a horse-powered corn mill had been set up nearby, as well as a shingle-roofed house—both firsts in the county—since they wouldn't have been risked if danger had still been high.[49]

Most of the early settlers were of Anglo-Scots-Irish-German descent and came over the Ohio River from Kentucky, Tennessee and the Carolinas, bringing with them a southern Appalachian culture that still persists and that was nearly exclusive until immigration for the mines began at the end of the nineteenth century. The hunter-trappers, even in American times, distrusted the prairie, thinking that nothing would grow on it, not even scrub brush, let alone trees. Erwin still reveals this bias in 1876 when he says the northern and southern parts of Williamson County were "well-timbered; but the central was a vast barrens, without a shrub, except on the streams."[50]

Except for hunting, settlers stuck to the woods or its margins, as the Indians had done, where there was shelter, shade, water and wood for fuel and building. One could make a slit in the deep prairie sod with an axe and drop in a few corn seeds—the stalks were called sod corn—but large-scale farming would have to wait for the 1837 invention of the steel-tipped plow by John Deere, an Illinois transplant, and anyway these men were not the farmer type.[51]

Milo Erwin is also ambivalent about the American woodsmen of 1810–35, who "produced no change in the country—neither improving it nor destroying the game, but lived like the Indians, mostly in the woods." In doing so, they had a sort of wisdom that came from intimacy with nature; they "knew every rock, stream, lake, shoal, and valley in the county… They were conversant with the character of every animal, fish and bird in the county."[52]

But the early "rangers of the woods," as Erwin calls them, "idled away their aimless lives on the fertile plains that lay untilled before them." As game became more scarce,[53] this "hunting class…were mostly idle and unoccupied" and turned to "dissipation…whiskey shops [and] profanity," and in a generation or two, they were the "men who lave[d] in the lecherous sea of prostitution." "[T]hey never made anything," Erwin says; "those who stuck to the farm are the wealthy ones now."[54]

The ancient animal traces and Indian trails were soon deepened by those other settlers who came to the county by 1815 and made a web of connections across the bottom third of the state. Three significant trails passed through Herrin's Prairie alone: the Jordan's Fort trail (east–west, along Pond Creek to the Big Muddy); the old French Grande Trace (northwest–southeast, probably a French military road from Kaskaskia to Fort Massac and Lusk's Ferry); and the post road of 1839 (southwest–northeast).

During this time, Shawneetown, on the Ohio River, had the regional land office and the first banks in the state of Illinois. Self-excoriating legend has it that when investors came, hats in hands, looking for capital to build a new town called Chicago, they were turned down as a bad risk because everyone knew that Southern Illinois would not only continue to grow and prosper, but would also always serve as the seat of government, money and power. The first Illinois capital was in Kaskaskia, after all, south of St. Louis; the second was in Vandalia.

Whether it was the relative wealth of the farmer-merchants that permitted the record of their own history, or whether the "hunting class" became extinct or were assimilated into the changing society, it's mostly those permanent settlers whose names still exist in Herrin-area histories and in the names

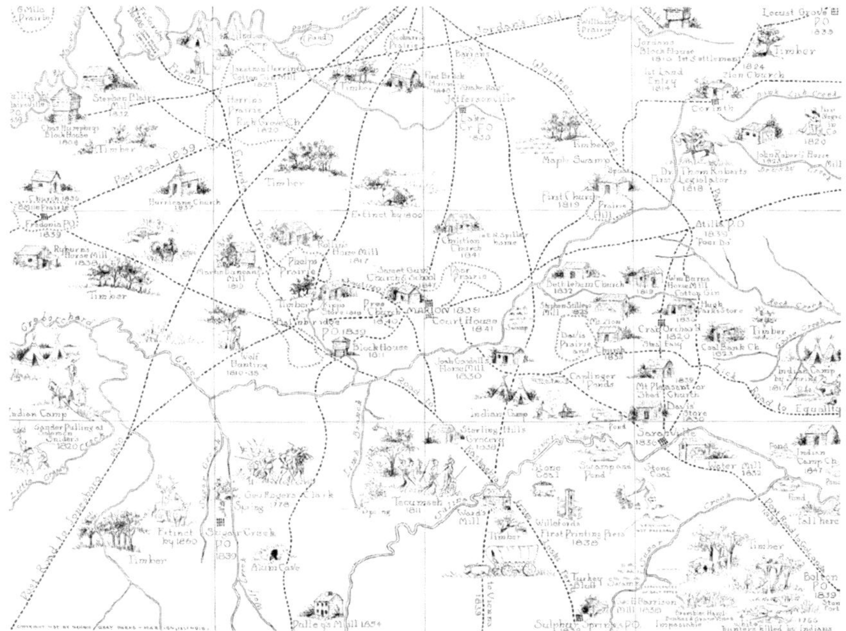

Map of Williamson County trails and settlement, drawn for the 1939 centennial by Nannie Gray Parks, a librarian at the Marion Carnegie Library. *Courtesy Williamson County Historical Society.*

of descendants, streets, buildings, banks and other businesses: the Herrins, Stotlars, Harrisons, Bruces, Dillards, Chittys, Coxes and Spillers. Durable names of the new wave of immigrants would enter the record decades later when the mines opened.

The "farming and trade" class didn't start with much. Erwin says that until 1830 there wasn't a man in the county worth $1,000—about $23,000 in today's economy.[55] In fact, most settlers moving to the area paid their last cash for a gun and ammunition, basic supplies and ferry fare across the Ohio River. As a result, much of the land was not owned. Their title to it was called "Tomahawk Rights" for the method of blazing trees with marks or names.[56]

Still, they had wild game and hogs, corn (for hominy and pone), pumpkins, beans and squash in patch gardens, and wild fruits and greens. Erwin says they "found herbs for medicine and beverage. There was savey and thyme for broth, sage for sausage, pink-root for worms, and wormwood for bruises, flowers for bouquets, and apples for friends."[57]

"The world has not exhibited an example of a more happy race than our early settlers," Erwin says. "Their houses were neat and tasty…in the yard a stump or box contained forest flowers; luxuriant branches of evergreens hung in the corners, and festoons of oak leaves and cypress vines covered the white-washed walls of the house; and panseys, ferns and pinks fringed the walks."[58]

"All history is local," historian Joseph Amato[59] says, and even Erwin doubts whether he can generalize his sometimes rosy take on settler life.

"I have asked our old ladies what hardships they had to encounter in the early settlement of this county," Erwin says, "but they gave so many and such varied accounts, that it was hard to generalize their troubles."

He goes on to give an example from his own experience that was "one of the hardest scenes that it is the allotment of men to meet": a handsome young widow who'd interrupted her plowing to nurse her infant.[60] I imagine the experience was a little harder on the young mother than on the men who had to witness her. I also bet this scene wasn't the worst of it.

It's not just that we've been left mixed views of settlers' lives, but it's as if versions are insulated from one another, unaware the others exist. On the one hand, we get the rough life and "barbarous" amusements of frontier people, as in this account of a celebration at Christmastime:

> *Plenty of whiskey was first provided, then a pony-purse was made up, or a premium offered. A gander was next taken and his neck thoroughly soaped, when he was tied by the legs to a springing pole, head downward, eight or nine feet from the ground; the riders then mounted and went at full speed; one man stood under the gander with a whip to keep the horses going. The first man who got hold of the gander generally turned the feathers the wrong way and made his neck sleeker than ever. The gander would flap his wings and squall for life, when an expert rider got hold of him, in such a manner as to make the blood grow cold. Sometimes a greedy fellow would hold on until his horse ran from under him, and then he would generally strike the ground with that portion of his body which, in a stooping posture, is the fairest mark for an assault.*[61]

On the other hand, we get this childhood memory of Christmas from Mary Logan, the wife of Union general John A. Logan. Mary grew up in Marion about this time:

> *If the* [Christmas] *tree was in a home, every member of the family, on Christmas Eve, brought to the home their gifts, all wrapped up and marked for the persons for whom they were intended. Early Christmas morning, every one interested, including the servants, assembled. The oldest man in the family was dressed up in cotton batting or furs, and, wearing a mask and a fur cap, played Santa Claus. When all were ready, some one played a Christmas carol. Then Santa Claus, scissors in hand, proceeded to cut off the presents*

> *from the tree, and distribute them as they were addressed. The exclamations of delight with which the recipients received each parcel rings in my ears as I recall those happy occasions. After every one had displayed all his gifts, a sumptuous breakfast was announced, and again all was merriment.*[62]

Both versions are probably true, but it's a bit hard to reconcile them when there were so few people in the county and the towns so rudimentary.

Other times it's not the general tone of life that's in question; it's the basic historical facts. It's agreed that Herrin began with a few log cabins built by pioneer names on what came to be known as Herrin's Prairie, a flat field, shaped like a bell, three miles north to south and two and a half miles west to east.

But Milo Erwin says that Isaac *Herrein* settled on Herrin's Prairie in 1817. A history of the county written in 1887[63] agrees on the year but spells his name *Herrin*. David Ruffin Harrison says that his great-grandfather Isaac *Herring* settled in 1819.[64] Ruth C. Herrin says that Herring made his land entry three years earlier in 1816.[65] Isaac Herring (indeed the first permanent settler) does have an 1816 land entry in state records, but it's under the name *Herrin*, while his son-in-law David Herrin is listed as David *Herring*.[66] In any case, Herring's Prairie became Herrin's Prairie, either because it was shorter or because of the tendency of the local speech to drop final consonants.

As I said, many of the first settlers had "tomahawk" or "squatters'" rights to their land. "Previous to 1804, no land was sold in the Northwest Territory west of the mouth of the Kentucky River," since land claims had to be straightened out with the Indians and the French. Surveys also had to be done so plats could be entered officially, and all this wasn't accomplished until 1814.[67] Many didn't buy after that in order to avoid taxes. Land entry in the area (starting with Frank Jordan's fort in Franklin County) "was slow and gradual…only about one-half of the public lands were entered prior to the year 1850."[68]

Those who bought land on or adjacent to Herrin's Prairie (Township 8 South, Range 2 East) before Williamson County split from Franklin in 1839 include:

> *1816, Isaac Herrin* [sic]*; 1818, Samuel K. Perkins; 1819, William R. Hines; 1829, David Herrin and Emanuel Hunter; 1831, Dudley W. Duncan and Benjamin Chitty; 1832, Josiah Dillard; 1833, William P. Duncan, Benjamin Spiller, James Duncan, Joseph Duncan, Roderick Reed, and Alexander and Jacob Arnett; 1836, Joseph K. Dillard, Robert Lipsey, Hardy W. Perry, Benjamin W. Thompson, Simeon Spiller, John W. Hoffman and Andrew Moak* [sic]*; 1837, William Harvell, George Cox, Joel Childress, Fred F. Duncan and Andrew Sanders.*[69]

Military land grant for a plot just south of Herrin's Prairie. Vanderbilt, a veteran of the War of 1812, probably sold it without taking possession. *Courtesy Herrin City Library.*

In 1820, the settlers built (with logs) the first church on Herrin's Prairie, called Rich Grove Church. Its first preacher, a Baptist, was Isaac Herring. A one-horse grain mill was built on the prairie in 1823 by John Lamb, and in 1825 Isaac's son Johnathan built a cotton gin. When it was successful, he built another horse-powered grain mill (a two-horse mill this time, though it still took two hours to grind a bushel of corn). As roads like the Frankfort–Brownsville (Jackson County) post road were built through Herrin's Prairie, men were expected to contribute five days' labor per year or an equivalent in cash for their upkeep.

George H. Harrison, who had a mill five miles south of Marion on the Saline, married David Herrin's daughter, Delila, and moved to Herrin's Prairie, where he opened a store and became a justice of the peace. When George died in 1848 of complications of malaria contracted during army service, Delila moved with her children, David Ruffin and Louisa, to a log cabin where Harrison House, in the northwest part of Herrin, stands now.[70]

The first schoolhouse in town, also made of logs, was built in 1844 on the site where the amusement park White City would be located eighty years later. After Samuel Stotlar moved to the prairie in 1856 from Ohio, he donated land he bought from David Herrin for a new school. The small frame building sat where South Side School is now and was called Stotlar School.[71]

In the more than four decades from the founding of the community to the start of the Civil War, Herrin's had been a frontier lifestyle. People hunted, kept free-range hogs, tanned their own leather, raised

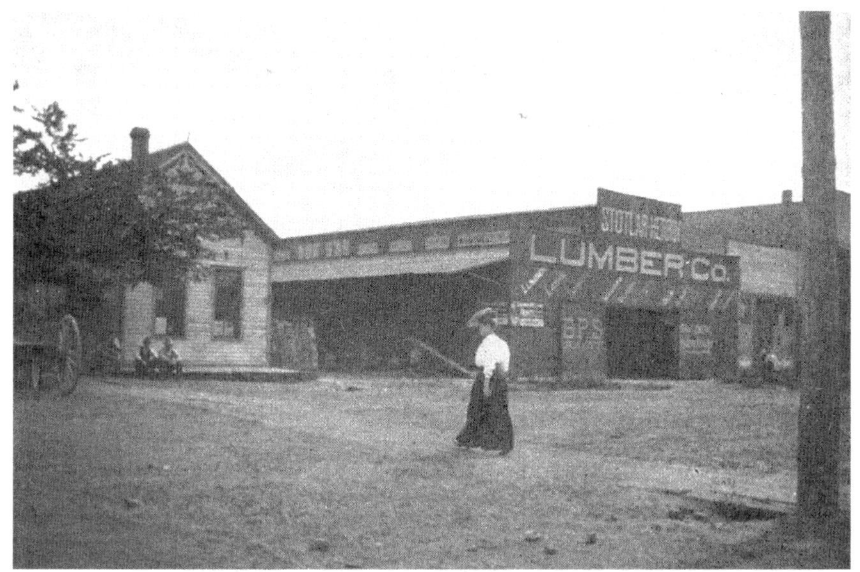

The founding families often got together. Stotlar-Herrin Lumber Co., circa 1905.

subsistence crops, bartered, traded, came together for mutual aid and stayed at a distance when they felt like it. It wasn't until 1830 that crops were even grown for market. But Southern Illinois, along with the rest of America, was changing rapidly. Population and towns grew, their needs increased and became more complex and businesses came and went. Cotton became the main crop in the region for the decade of the 1830s, followed by tobacco.[72]

Nannie Gray Parks, a Marion librarian, wrote in 1939 that Williamson County land was "as fertile as any in North America and produced wheat, hemp, rye, Indian corn, peas, beans, flax, tobacco, hops, grapes [both to cause trouble later], apples, pears, peaches, dyeing roots, and medicinal plants."[73]

But periodic drought was always a problem, as was that clay hardpan left by the glaciers. A conductor for the Illinois Central in the early twentieth century, Billy Bryan, used to call "Buckhorn!" when his train pulled into the Herrin station, "an old nickname for the land around Herrin, given in derision for its lack of fertility," where grows only a "low, branching weed that not even sheep will eat." It came to Herrin in clover seed for the farmers' first pastures, and "no lower estimate could be made of soil's value than to say that buckhorn was its best crop." Dynamite was even used to try to break up the soil and aerate it. Hubbs describes old-timers as saying, "The ground is so poor around Herrin you couldn't raise a fuss on it."[74]

In 1854, the Gradation Act, called the "Bit Act," was passed, and it reduced public lands in Illinois from $1.25 per acre to $0.12, or about one bit, per

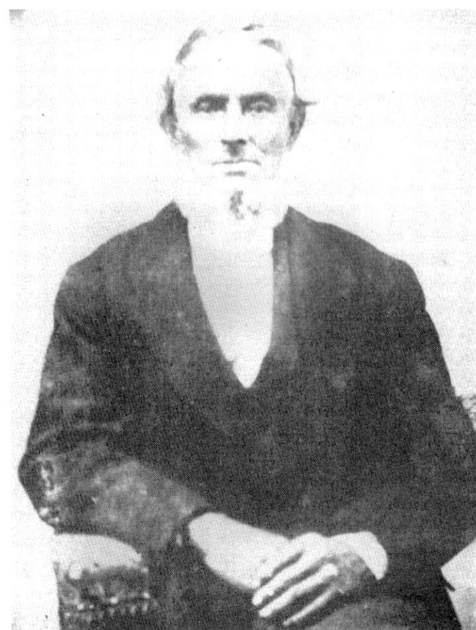

Left: Samuel Stotlar (1813–1876) believed in education.

Below: Williamson County sawmill, 1885. *Courtesy Williamson County Historical Society.*

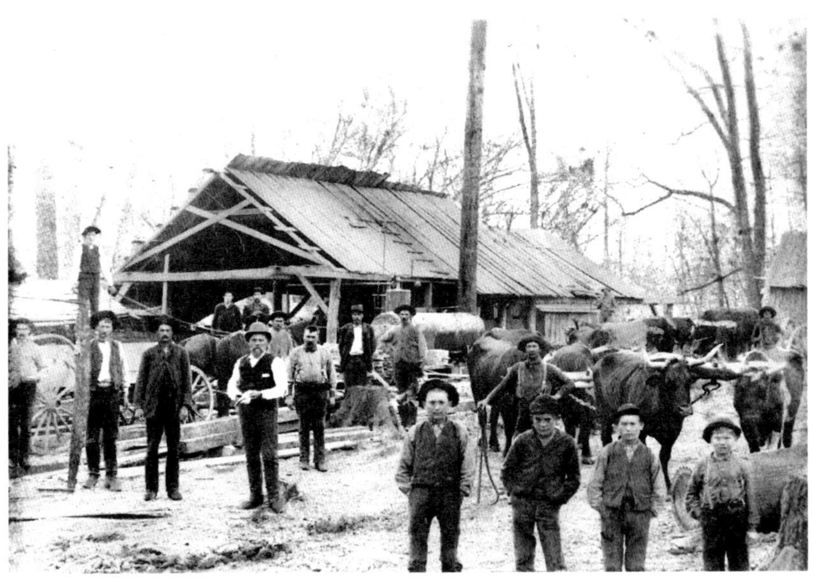

acre. In October of that year, the Shawneetown land office was flooded with entries by people buying up "all the lands they could possibly pay for. In a few years…most of the best lands subject to entry were taken up."[75]

The settlers thought their future lay in the land, and they were right. But it wasn't the topsoil that would transform the place; it was the unseen coal deep below the prairie, and that wouldn't be mined on a large scale for another forty years, in part because it was thought coal was only in the hills to the south.[76]

The Civil War marked the end of the 150-year frontier era in Southern Illinois. The unnamed prairie island that would become Herrin had been ruled by France (1682–1763) and Great Britain (1763–1783); governed by Virginia (1778–1783); and was ceded to the new federal government, becoming part of the Northwest Territory (1787) and then part of the Indiana Territory (1800) and Illinois Territory (1809). In 1818, Illinois became a state. Williamson County was still part of Franklin County, and "Herring's prairie road district" was designated in 1838 by the Franklin County commissioners' court.[77] In 1839, Williamson was formed from the southern half of Franklin.

The state of Illinois had filled from the bottom, like a well, with the seat of government shifting to reflect changes in population and power. The state capital moved northward from Kaskaskia to Vandalia in 1820, "brought about by land speculators, including some of the State's most prominent men, who felt that they could profit by instigating land booms in the unsettled areas." In 1836, Abraham Lincoln, who was a state representative—and from Sangamon County—introduced a bill to move the capital to Springfield, where it began operating in 1839.[78] This shift northward continued and remains, with Southern Illinois representing an older way, central Illinois representing the industrial age with its agri-business farming and Chicago a postmodern city perching on top.

Egypt thrived originally because it was easily accessible by settlers coming down the Tennessee, Cumberland and Ohio Rivers. Now it began to be marginalized, writes Southern Illinois historian John W. Allen. The National or Cumberland Road project, the first improved highway across the United States, ended at Vandalia in 1839, not farther south. New technologies such as the steamboat—which made easier headway against the current on the Mississippi—and a network of railroads made travel easier. Those who might once have ended their journey at Shawneetown or Kaskaskia or somewhere between the two now began to move on to unsettled lands farther north and west. Allen says this left Egypt in a "historical eddy," with a "static or slowly changing culture [that] remained relatively little changed until modern highways were built."[79]

As it turns out, that culture has endured to this day, side by side with other vibrant ones. But in the 150 years since the start of the Civil War, Herrin has experienced other changes that none of its residents at the time could have foreseen.

CHAPTER 4

CIVIL WAR AND THE RIPPLES OF VIOLENCE

By the start of the Civil War, Herrin's Prairie was slowly growing as a community of farmers and merchants, as well as their families. (Town populations in Williamson County were not recorded for the 1860 census, but there were 12,205 people in Williamson County then. For comparison, Cook County, where Chicago is, had more than 144,000.[80] Herrin still had only 779 people in the 1880 census.[81])

Despite the war, life went on, and farm prices were high. In 1858, David Ruffin Harrison, great-grandson of Isaac Herring, had become a shopkeeper with his uncle, Oliver Herrin, in the store that his father, George H. Harrison, had opened when Ruffin was a boy. On May 26, 1864, David Ruffin Harrison opened a fourth-class post office named Herrin's Prairie and became its first postmaster. He often had to pay the mail carrier himself, "for the sale of stamps on Herrin's prairie was small." A flouring mill, a cotton gin, Christian and Baptist churches and a Masonic lodge (after the war, in 1872) were built or organized.[82]

Many men served in the Civil War (235 dead are listed for the county[83]), including Ephraim Herrin, who would become the first president of the trustees when Herrin was incorporated as a village in 1898. He enlisted as a private in 1862 at the age of nineteen, fought at Resaca with General Sherman, was on Sherman's infamous march to the sea and paraded in the Grand Review in Washington.[84] Thomas Stotlar, who would organize the Stotlar-Herrin Lumber Company in 1903 and become president of Herrin's State and Savings Bank in 1904, served in the Ninth Illinois and had "his left arm shot in two" at Shiloh.[85]

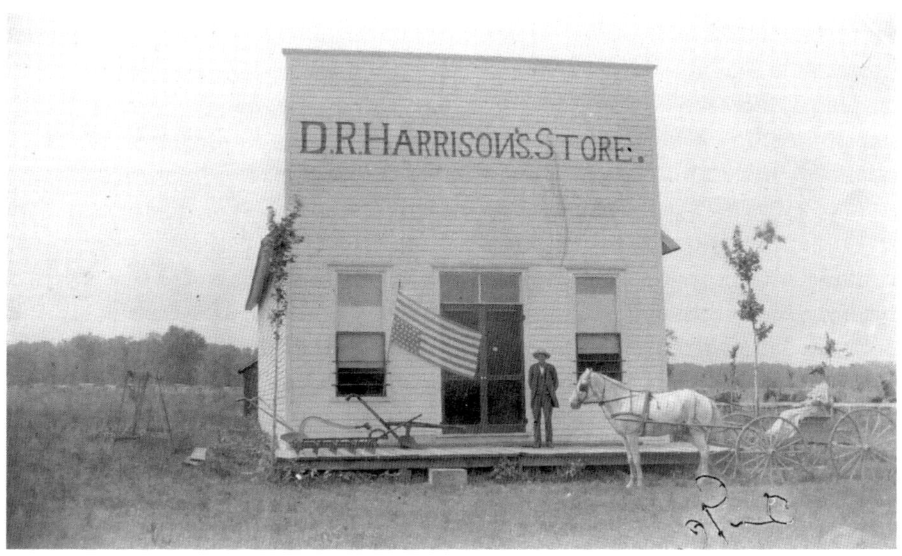

David Ruffin Harrison's store. The upside-down flag (usually a sign of distress) is a mystery, but with hints from Hubbs one wonders if it's for the death of Lincoln. *Courtesy Herrin City Library*.

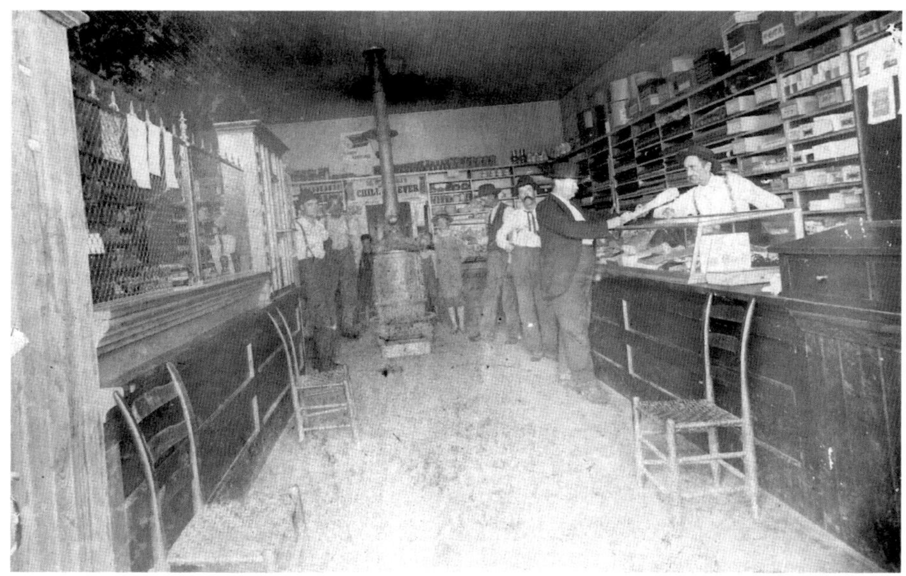

Upstairs in one of D.R. Harrison's stores—probably the one built in 1874, where the Masonic Lodge also met. *Courtesy Williamson County Historical Society.*

Yet sympathies in the area were mixed, and even after the war, men killed one another over what we might think of now, simplistically, as North-South conflict.

There's no denying the southern character of Egypt. Herrin lies almost exactly at the latitude of Richmond, capital of the Confederacy, and it's always looked more to St. Louis or even Memphis (one hundred miles closer) than to Chicago for regional urban identification.

While Chicago's identity comes in part from Great Lakes trade, Egypt is made more southern by its two great, south-flowing rivers. The original settlers came from the Carolinas, Virginia, Tennessee and Kentucky, and most of them up to the end of the Civil War were northern Democrats (not the party of Lincoln); some were Copperheads (Confederate sympathizers). My dad, who grew up in Southern Illinois, remembered anvil shoots when he was a kid to celebrate the anniversary of Lincoln's murder. (One wishes more had not dodged the anvil on its way back down.)

This clash of cultures continues. As I write, a group called "Southern Illinois Now!" has organized on the social networking site Facebook. Part of its mission statement reads, "Our goal is to secede from a state in which our voice is not heard and our rights are being suppressed."[86]

Illinois has been thought of as a "northern dagger into the heart of the south" since its boundaries were set. The shape of the state was determined in part to counter slave state additions to the union, such as Mississippi (1817) and Alabama (1819). The eastern border of Illinois was determined by Indiana and Kentucky, while the western border was, logically and traditionally, the Mississippi River. The Northwest Ordinance called for Illinois to have a northern border at the same parallel as Ohio and Indiana, at the south tip of Lake Michigan.

However, due to a mistake in the mapping of the extent of the lake, Illinois would actually not have reached it, leaving Chicago in Wisconsin and Illinois with no Great Lakes port. In the end, Nathaniel Pope, the delegate to Congress from the Illinois Territory, managed to get an even farther northern boundary for Illinois than Indiana or Ohio, "connecting the new state with the northern interests of New York and New England…swinging Illinois into the political orbit of the northern states, [and] 'affording additional security to the perpetuity of the Union.'"

Fourteen counties and eight thousand square miles were added to Illinois in this somewhat shaky political maneuver, but it "also set up the internal dynamics of state politics," and "much of the political conflict in Illinois since the 1850s can be interpreted in terms of this tension."[87] A federal report just before World War II states: "As far as social patterns are concerned, Chicago and even St. Louis (only 100 miles away) are in another world."[88]

In the campaign of 1856 "the Democrats were very noisy, and the Republicans were silent. [The election] was attended by many rough-and-tumble fights," Erwin says, "and whiskey was issued out by the bucket full. Men were generally allowed to vote as they pleased, but abolitionists were looked upon with contempt."[89] The Republican presidential candidate, John Fremont, received only ten votes in the entire county.[90]

In 1861, a group in Marion actually worked up the juice to draft and adopt a resolution to secede from the Union:

> *Resolved that we, the citizens of Williamson County, firmly believing, from the distracted condition of our country—the same being brought about by the elevation to power of a strictly sectional party, the coercive policy of which toward the seceded states will drive all the border slave states from the Federal Union, and cause them to join the Southern Confederacy.*
>
> *Resolved that in that event, the interest of the citizens of Southern Illinois imperatively demands at their hands a division of the state. We hereby pledge ourselves to use all means in our power to effect the same, and attach ourselves to the Southern Confederacy.*
>
> *Resolves, that, in our opinion, it is the duty of the present administration to withdraw all the troops of the federal government that may be stationed in Southern forts, and acknowledge the independence of the Southern Confederacy, believing that such a course would be calculated to restore peace and harmony to our districted country.*
>
> *Resolved, that in view of the fact that it is probable that the present governor of the state of Illinois will call upon citizens of the state to take up arms for the purpose of subjugating the people of the South, we hereby enter our protest against such a course, and as loyal* [!] *citizens, will refuse, frown down and forever oppose the same.*[91]

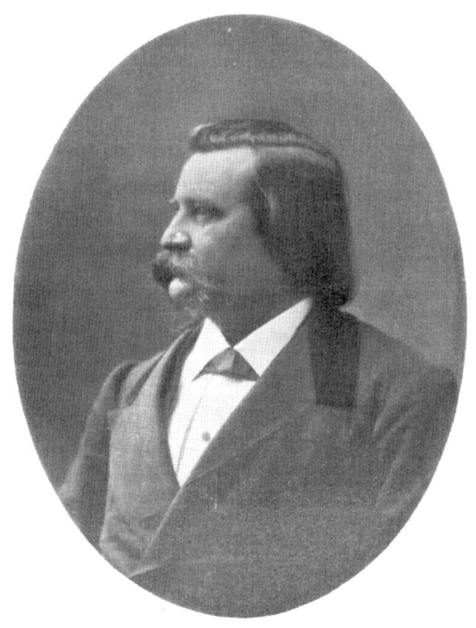

John Alexander Logan (1826–1886): lawyer, state representative, Union major general and U.S. senator.

The resolution was repealed the next day by fellow townspeople, and four months later John A. Logan, also from Egypt and also with ambivalent sympathies (his young brother-in-law ran away to join the Confederate army) but a future Union major general, delivered an impassioned speech, standing on a wagon in the Marion public square, that no doubt changed many minds. His wife later wrote:

> [A]*fter waving a salutation to the throng who surrounded him, he began to speak in a voice so clear and so full of volume that every person...could hear him distinctly* [and] *the most turbulent spirit in the crowd was as quiet as the dead.* [H]*e led them on for nearly two hours...Toward the close, he said:*
>
> *"The time has come when a man must be for or against his country, not for or against his state. How long could one state stand up against another, or two or three or four states stand against others? The Union once dissolved, we should have numerous confederacies and rebellions. I, for one, shall stand or fall for this Union, and shall this day enroll for the war. I want as many of you as will to come with me."*

"The effect upon his hearers was magical," Mrs. Logan writes, and to the sound of fife and drum, Logan marched around the square with more than 110 men who joined him in signing up.[92]

Yet a 1994 article in the *Illinois Historical Journal*, "Aiding and Abetting Disloyalty Prosecutions in the Federal Civil Courts of Southern Illinois, 1861–1866," says:

> *While southern Illinois reportedly contributed more than its share in filling enlistment quotas, federal court records reveal that it also had its share of difficulties in executing the draft. Enrollment officers were assaulted, shot, and threatened, and some were forced at gunpoint to relinquish their enrollment lists. Martial law was declared in Williamson County in order to complete the enrollment. At least fifty-six individuals in eleven cases were indicted for resisting, obstructing, or opposing the draft, including John Birge and Joseph Kern, who allegedly advised men to avoid the draft by maiming themselves and using noxious drugs.*[93]

It was also thought that "a band of armed men left for Kentucky to join the army of the Confederacy." A newspaper editor was run out of Williamson County by an anti-Union mob, and the Knights of the Golden Circle, a pro-Confederate secret society, had perhaps eight hundred members in 1862.[94]

In the end, Williamson County provided "two thousand soldiers [to the Union], a larger per cent than any other county in the state," Erwin says, and it went Republican after the soldiers came home, which made the "whole Democratic party [go] on a drunk."[95]

But the factional violence of the war was like a genie that, once released from its bottle, refused to be put away.[96] Erwin recites a litany of murders at this point in the county's history, and though some were committed for other reasons, many are associated with the war and its politics. Just a few, in or close to Herrin, will serve to illustrate:

In 1865, Christopher Howard, "a rebel sympathizer, was killed near Herrin's Prairie by some unknown party,"[97] "supposed to be on account of politics. He [oddly] was a Republican."[98]

"In 1870, Thomas Pinckney White, a prominent citizen of Herrin's Prairie, was seen crossing his field in his shirt sleeves. He was never seen again…He was an outspoken Republican, and his conduct in this line made him some enemies."[99]

Milton Stewart Colp (who owned the Laban Carter farm that later became the town of Carterville, and the father of John Colp, whose mine Colp was named for) was "assassinated" in 1874, "doubtless because of his strong adherence to the Union which he defended as a soldier in Company H, 31st Illinois infantry."[100]

Historian Paul Angle doesn't attribute Williamson County's "Bloody Vendetta" of 1868–76 to political factions but rather to the "peculiar characteristics of mountain folk" that immigrants from the Appalachians "were slow to lose." For Angle, these qualities included not only positive attributes such as hardiness, bravery and independence but also negative ones such as hot-bloodedness, pride, obstinacy, jealousy of family honor and a quickness to take offense at insults.[101] Similarly, Milo Erwin says that the feud was due to the "the knock-down style of the West, coming in contact with the code of the South."[102]

Erwin, however, who was writing just after the hanging of Marshall Crain, which marked the end of the Vendetta, makes it a point to say that the "leading" families involved in the decade-long feud were Democrats on one side (Bulliner, Hinchcliff, Crain) and Republicans on the other (Henderson, Sisney, Russell), though members of both sides had served the Union.[103]

The Bloody Vendetta came along in time for the burgeoning media to pick up on it, and it is the origin of the "Bloody" in "Bloody Williamson." Much more so than the mine violence that came fifty years later, the Vendetta seems to lack any meaningful cause and effect, which added to the prurience. But as with the Herrin Massacre and the subsequent bootlegging wars, local law enforcement and the courts seemed unable to stop or punish the violators.

"As far as the officers of the law are concerned as to making arrests and prosecuting criminals, Williamson County might as well be without them," wrote a reporter for the *St. Louis Democrat*.[104]

The Bloody Vendetta started on the Fourth of July 1868, when several men of the Bulliner family were playing cards with Felix "Field" Henderson in a tavern near Carbondale. In an argument over a hand, Henderson called one of them "a damn lying son-of-a-bitch" and got himself beaten severely.

Separately and one year later, a Bulliner neighbor, George W. Sisney, won a lawsuit over a crop of oats against a Bulliner. Months after that, a fight broke out between them, and then the Bulliners attacked Sisney with guns in his home. Though wounded, he defended himself. Each person involved was fined $100 in court.

Two years later, "a series of brawls" brought the big Crain family into the Vendetta on the side of the Bulliners. Crains fought Sisneys now, too.

Other parties joined in on one side or the other, and murder followed murder—resulting only in acquittals and dropped prosecutions, a bad precedent in the county—until "the name of Williamson County had become 'a hiss and a by-word.' Strangers were shunning the region, property was dropping in value, and there was no prospect of exploiting the veins of coal that were known to underlie the topsoil."[105] Though media throughout the state and region called angrily for the "pusillanimous" governor to intervene, it was money that finally ended the thing, when cash rewards for the chief suspects brought out witnesses willing to testify. Marshall Crain was hanged in Marion for the murder of William Spence, and six others went to prison.

Though Herrin played no real role in the Vendetta—much of it happened five miles away in Crainville, and even in Jackson County—Williamson County had attracted unwanted notice by outsiders and been tagged with the epithet "Bloody."

"[J]ustice was the universal desire of our people…[but] the newspapers were holding a regular matinee over us, and sending a devastating storm of shot at our blood-stained county," Erwin says. "The abuse from without aggravated the evil influence within, which caused the banks of crime to overflow, and spread ruin and woe over the fairest lands of 'Egypt.'"[106] That particular plague would revisit the county—and Herrin—more than once.

CHAPTER 5

COAL

The first recorded discovery of coal in the area that is now the United States was on the Illinois River near Starved Rock, by Marquette and Joliet in 1673. It was first mined as a commodity in Illinois on the Big Muddy River, near Murphysboro, in 1810. There William Boone and an African American "assistant" took coal they gathered from an outcrop to market in New Orleans six times in two years. Others began to do the same. Until 1823, Jackson was the only county in Illinois mining coal, and production was low—maybe one hundred tons each of the first five years.[107]

But as America's industrial revolution began to build steam, those railroad engines, factory boilers, power plants and homes needed fuel. In ten years, from 1850 to 1860, Illinois' number of rail miles increased from about one hundred to three thousand. Correspondingly, in 1840 the state produced only 17,000 tons of coal, but in 1850, 300,000 tons; in 1860, nearly 730,000 tons; and by 1890, the decade in which Herrin started its commodity mining, Illinois dug more than 15,000,000 tons of coal.[108]

David Ruffin Harrison says that coal was found in Williamson County in 1845 near the surface in Spillertown (between Marion and Johnston City) and on land near Hurricane Creek (west of Herrin), where it was gathered and used by blacksmiths. "Soon after," he says, it was found on the Walker farm three miles south of Herrin.

There's some confusion about the mines in that area attributed to Laban Carter—whose name was given to Carterville—but it appears he found coal as early as 1864 while farming a one-hundred-acre plot he owned. He leased

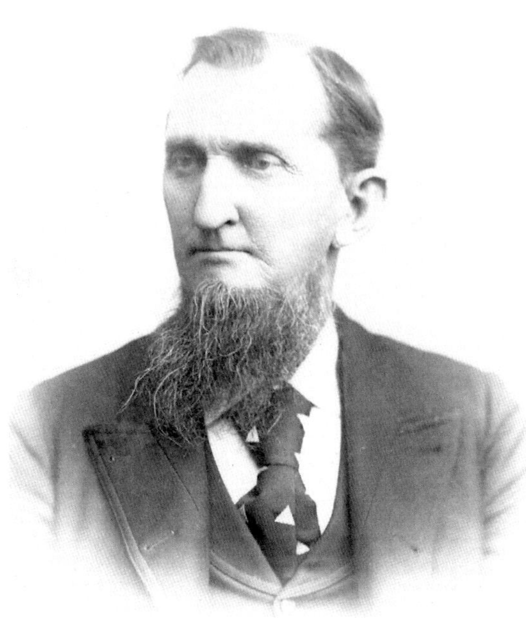

David Ruffin Harrison (1834–1911), great-grandson of Isaac Herring, was a merchant, the first postmaster of Herrin's Prairie and a partner in the first coal exploration in town. *Courtesy the* Southern Illinoisan.

land to an A.C. Briden, who opened a slope mine there, shipped Williamson County's first coal about 1869 and later managed the Carterville Coal and Coke Company. A Carbondale Coal and Coke Company worked the local Dodd shaft and Laflin slope mines. In 1881, John Adam Young opened a mine around Carterville that "furnished the larger portion of coal for local use." Barr Shaft opened in 1888 on a farm one mile northeast of Carterville, and others north of the city followed. The seam they were working averaged nine feet thick and was often located less than sixty feet underground.[109]

Despite this, Angle says, "Williamson County lagged behind other sections of the state." By 1890, production in the county was more than 200,000 tons per year, but it placed twentieth of the forty-eight coal counties in Illinois.[110]

Part of the reason for this is that they didn't yet know what they had. Milo Erwin says in 1876, "There are ten separate and distinct veins of bituminous coal in this county, which spreads out and underlies three-fourths of its surface, and in dozens of places crops out where it can be cheaply and easily mined; and the veins average nine feet in thickness."[111]

While there are several seams of coal at various depths under the state, what he thought were "distinct veins" was, in reality, the Herrin (No. 6) Coal seam, which runs continuously under most of the Illinois Basin—not just Illinois but also western Indiana, western Kentucky and a portion of northern Tennessee.

The name of a coal seam is "usually taken from where it is first scientifically described or most 'typical,'" writes Illinois State Geological Survey scientist Scott Elrick. "As I understand it, at one point the Herrin Coal seam was known as the 'Energy seam' (from Energy, Illinois) and a few other [names]. Not until later did we discover it was one and the same coal seam."[112]

As David Ruffin Harrison said, people in the area had thought "coal was only on the hill portion" of Southern Illinois' countryside,[113] probably because outcrops could be found closer to the surface there. But in 1892, Harrison, his sister, Louisa M. Williams, and his cousin, Ephraim Herrin (all great-grandchildren of Isaac Herring, Herrin's first settler), had reason to believe they should drill a prospect hole on the southwest corner of Williams's farm, where their properties touched. (Harrison himself says it was 1890.) The men fronted the money and Mrs. Williams boarded the workmen, and at 184 feet they struck an 8-foot vein of coal. Another hole was sunk on George Harrison's land, south of town, and coal was discovered at 146 feet.

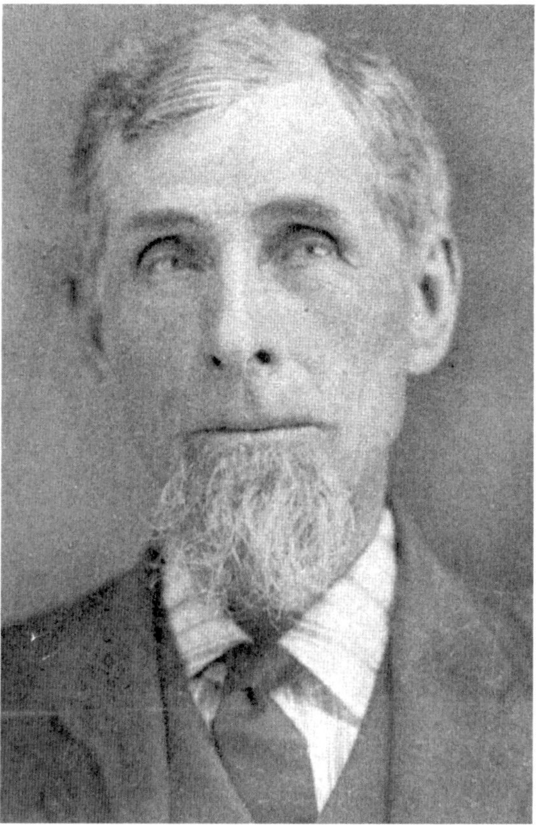

Ephraim Snyder Herrin (1843–1918), also a great-grandson of Isaac Herring, was a soldier in Sherman's army, partner in coal exploration and first president of the village trustees in 1898. *Courtesy Williamson County Historical Society.*

In 1895, Ephraim Herrin persuaded the engineers of the Chicago and Carbondale Railroad Company to route their line—effectively the Illinois Central within two years—through Herrin's Prairie, and the first station was built that year.

On May 8, 1896, D.R. Harrison's post office was officially renamed Herrin. On December 4 of that year Harrison and Herrin had the town platted on twenty acres each of their land.[114] It was incorporated as a village on April 26, 1898, and as a city May 16, 1900.[115]

Charles Ingraham began to publish the *Herrin News* in 1899 and was behind the effort for electrification. In March 1899, "Ten arc lights turned night into day along Herrin's business district."[116]

All of this growth in the county attracted attention. Investors from Chicago, Boston, Cincinnati, Indianapolis, St. Louis and elsewhere had

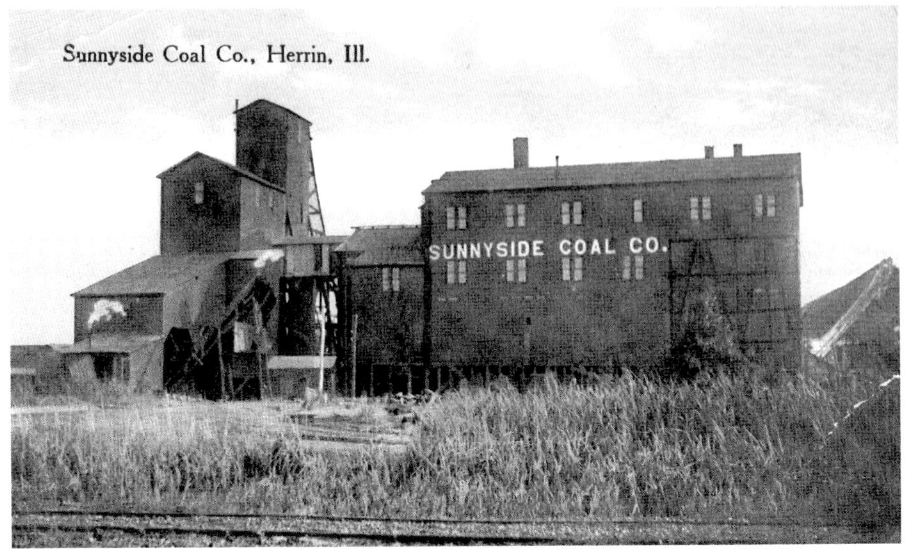

Sunnyside Mine, west of town, was the second in the Herrin field. It opened in September 1899. Big Muddy Coal & Iron Mine #7, east of town, was the first, in 1896. *Courtesy Williamson County Historical Society.*

capital and were eager to corner the developing market. In 1900, four groups sent drill crews who "quietly prospected" around the county and found coal everywhere they looked.

The investors were delighted to find that farmland in Williamson, Franklin and Saline Counties produced less than half the corn of counties in the farm belt of central Illinois and had been subdivided into plots of eighty acres or less, making even subsistence difficult. Land dealers bought and consolidated parcels on behalf of wildcatters such as Joseph Leiter from Chicago, who bought 7,500 acres by 1903 in what he'd call Zeigler, and companies such as the Illinois Central Railroad and the Illinois Steel Company. The land, with rights both on and below the surface, went for as little as ten dollars per acre, since few of the farmers knew what they had.

Success in the first mines led to more interest, and soon thousands more acres at a time were bought by other railroads, wildcatters and steel companies. By 1907, most mineral rights were accounted for and held—with the exception of some of the original pre-boom mines and small "gopher hole" workings that employed one to six men—by a dozen companies backed by outside money.[117]

A federal report notes that local businessmen were unprepared to invest in mines on the scale of urban investors:

> *Only a few local entrepreneurs were able to gather enough capital for speculating in coal-land options, let alone for extensive development of*

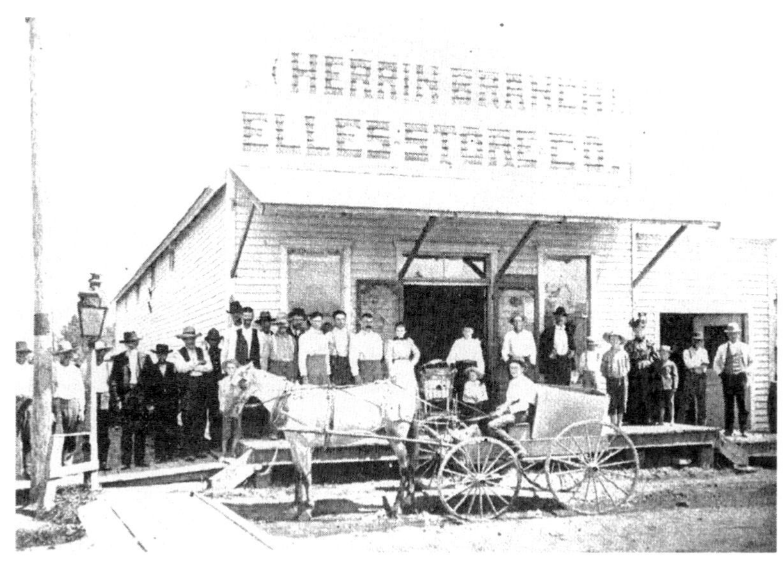

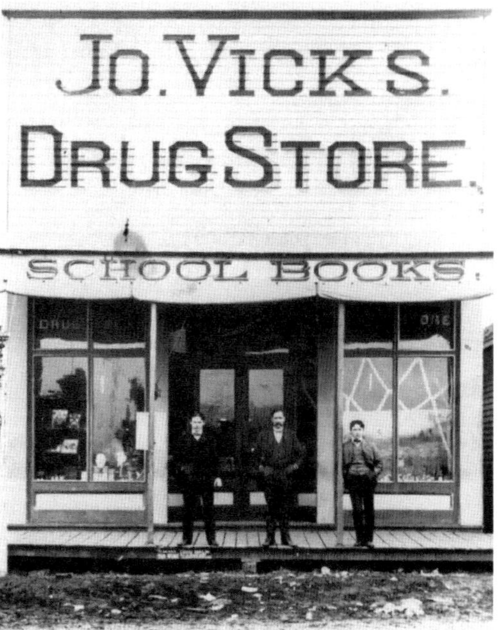

Above: The fifth branch of the Elles family stores in the region, 1899. Herrin Supply would follow.

Left: Jo Vick (middle) at his pharmacy, the first store in Herrin to have a lighted outdoor sign. It ran by gas, as did the interior lighting, and made a sputtering *phut-phut* noise when lit. *Courtesy Herrin City Library.*

producing mines. From the first the absentee investors controlled the greater part of the output of the southern Illinois mines, and not many years passed before they had almost complete ownership...In 1900 bank deposits in [Williamson, Franklin and Saline] *counties totaled $523,403, scarcely enough to develop a single good-sized coal property.*[118]

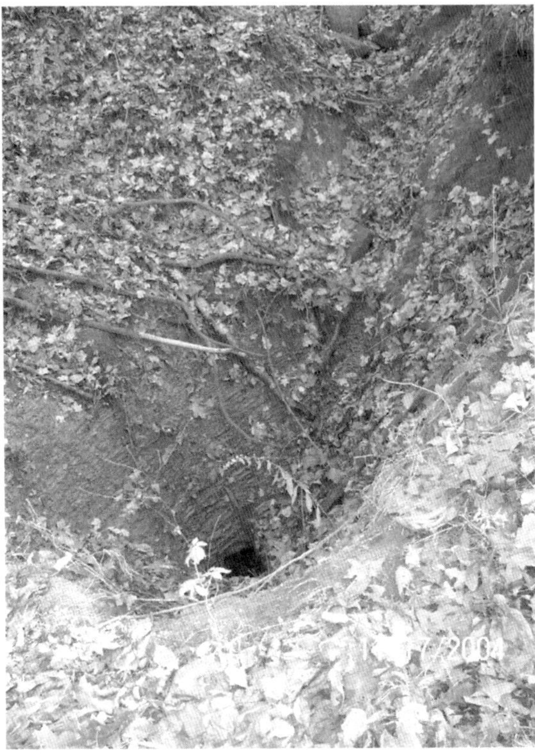

A "gopher hole," near Carbondale, a small-scale coal mine worked by a few men on private property. *Courtesy Joe Pelc, Abandoned Mined Lands Division, Illinois Department of Natural Resources.*

The First National Bank of Herrin, "the pioneer bank of the city," had been a private bank from 1895 to 1899, run by D.R. Harrison. In 1900, it incorporated with $25,000 capital stock, which had increased to $50,000 by 1905.[119] That $50,000 would be equivalent to about $1.2 million today. "In normal times, a bank should be able to lend several times the amount of the value of its capital stock," says an economist at the University of Illinois. "There were probably enough funds for a few mines, but bankers want to be diversified. A bank would not want to have all of its funds tied up in one mine." In addition, they might have issued stocks or bonds to raise money, too.[120] But none of that could compare with the likes of someone who received $1 million (then) from his father upon graduating from Harvard (read on).[121]

In the end, money that might have gone back into the community, if locals had owned the mines, was taken out instead. Appropriately enough, this is called "extractive wealth," and the city of Herrin was literally built by undermining the ground below it. In a sense, America's great cities owe part of their existence to Southern Illinois' labor and resources.

Still, the town was transformed for a time by the rock that burns. What had been a small farming community for decades suddenly exploded with growth as men came to work the mines, start businesses and raise families. At the time of the 1900 census, there were still only about 1,550 people in Herrin. The population more than quadrupled in ten years, to 6,864,[122] and by 1917, Herrin was a city of 10,402,[123] at which it has hovered ever since. By 1925, Herrin had the third-largest birthrate in Illinois.[124] The increase in numbers, however, came almost exclusively from immigration.

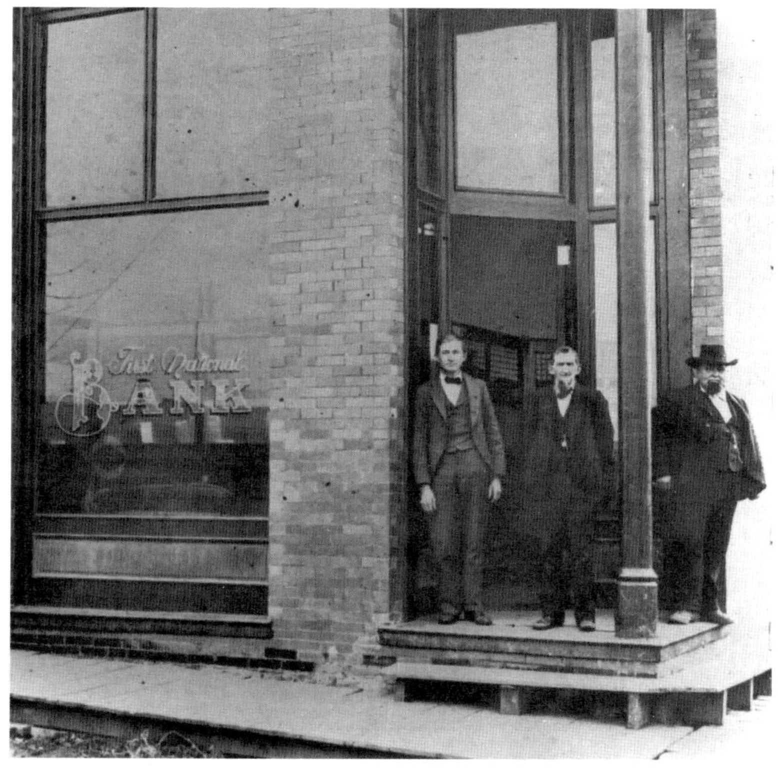

First National Bank, 1910. David Ruffin Harrison (center) started it as the Exchange Bank in 1895. *Courtesy the* Southern Illinoisan.

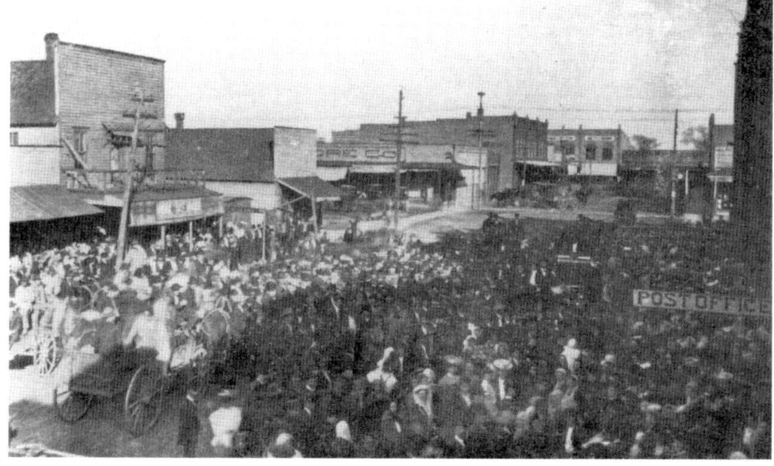

Busy day in Herrin, looking east on Cherry Street. Note the buckboard wagon. *Courtesy French Studio, Ltd.*

Bart and Caesar Colombo were the first Italian settlers in the county; they came, as so many did later, from Lombardy in early 1884. They lived first in Fredonia (now Cambria), and so many followed that the name of the post office was "Dago" for a while. When the small mine there closed, they moved to Herrin, where coal had been discovered. They organized the Lombard Society in 1898 as a mutual aid society and opened the Lombard Society Store in 1901.[125] Italians opened the Herrin Opera House, the Hippodrome Theatre and the European Hotel.

Businessmen in Herrin at the end of World War I included (with birthplace and business): Pete Cardani (Buenos Aires, moved to Italy and then to the United States: architect), the Lockos brothers (Batras, Greece: O.K. Shining Parlor and hat repair works); Jerry Palladino (Campagne—perhaps Campagna, Salerno—Italy: cleaning, pressing, tailoring); Lee Wah (Chinese, by way of Chicago: laundry); Frank Taveggia (Cuggiono, Italy: confectioner and tobacconer); John Maurizio (Torino, Italy: ice cream and confectioner); Joseph Helleny (Hini, Syria: "linens and notions"); and M.P. Zwick (Russia: dry goods and clothing). These names were now added to "native" ones such as Herrin, Harrison, Stotlar and J.V. Walker (born Williamson County, 1858).[126]

There were tensions in this sudden growth. One evidence of it is the creation of separate communities, mutual aid societies and businesses that made it possible, for instance, for an immigrant never to have to learn English. Along with Bart and Caesar Colombo's Lombard Society, the Rome Club opened in 1899,[127] and in 1901, the Lombard Society Store and Meat Market was a small cooperative partnership. In 1917, the store incorporated and by 1919 had four hundred members, doing "next to the largest business of any store in this end of the county" in dry goods, shoes, domestic and imported groceries, hardware and miners' supplies. But not just Italians, northern or otherwise, shopped there,[128] and with plenty of work available, ethnic tensions were kept to a minimum.

The city felt only hope, ambition and civic pride. A high school was constructed in 1903; the opera house was built by Louis Dell'Era and Joseph Berra in 1904. The Coal Belt Electric Railroad ran up Park Avenue.[129] Under C.E. "Mage" Anderson's two-term tenure as mayor of Herrin from 1911 to 1915, waterworks were built in the town (a $150,000 project in their dollars), as well as a sewer system ($60,000–$78,000), two paving districts ($110,000), "granitoid" sidewalks ($66,00–$75,000) and a city hall ($22,00–$30,000).[130] Teddy Roosevelt made a visit to the county and went down in the Squirrel Ridge Mine in Herrin in 1914.[131] Our Lady of Mount Carmel Catholic Church, or St. Mary's, was built in 1925 to replace the original thirty- by seventy-foot building from 1901, the new one reputed to be an exact copy of a medieval cathedral in Lombardy.[132]

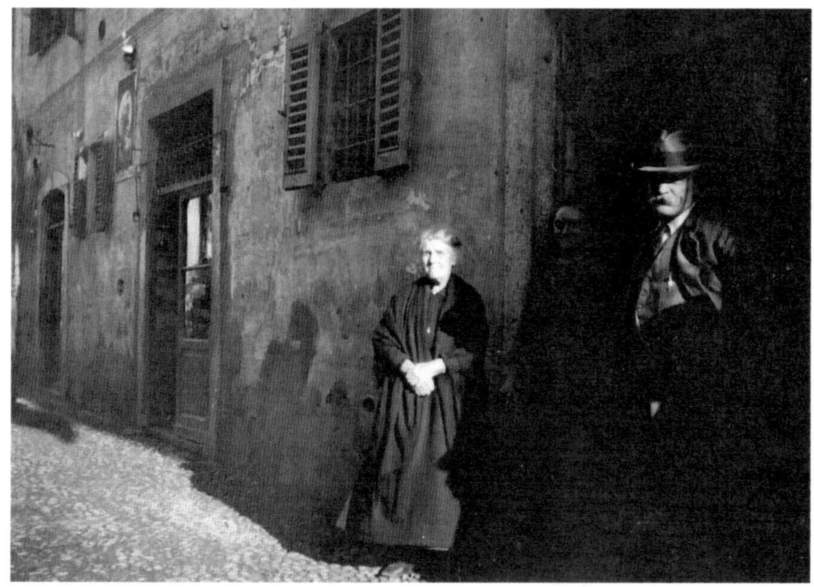

Photo taken by Hal Trovillion on a trip abroad. On the back he possibly wrote, "Joe De Elera's ["Dell'Era"?] grandmother, Cuggiono, Italy, Oct. 1929." Many Italians came to Herrin from this town. *Courtesy Hal Trovillion Photograph Collection, Special Collections Research Center, Southern Illinois University Carbondale.*

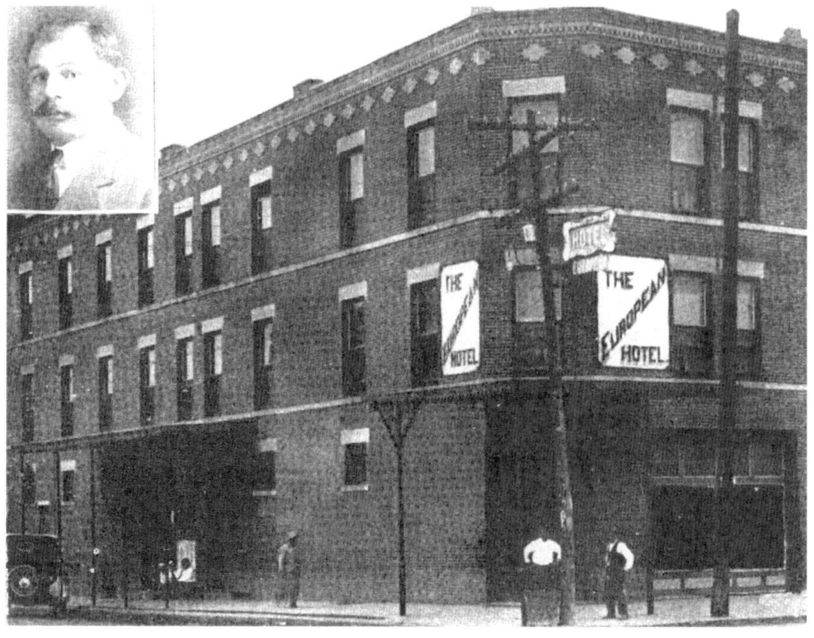

Louis Dell'Era (born Cuggiono, Italy, 1866), who built the European Hotel and the Herrin Opera House with partner Joseph Berra.

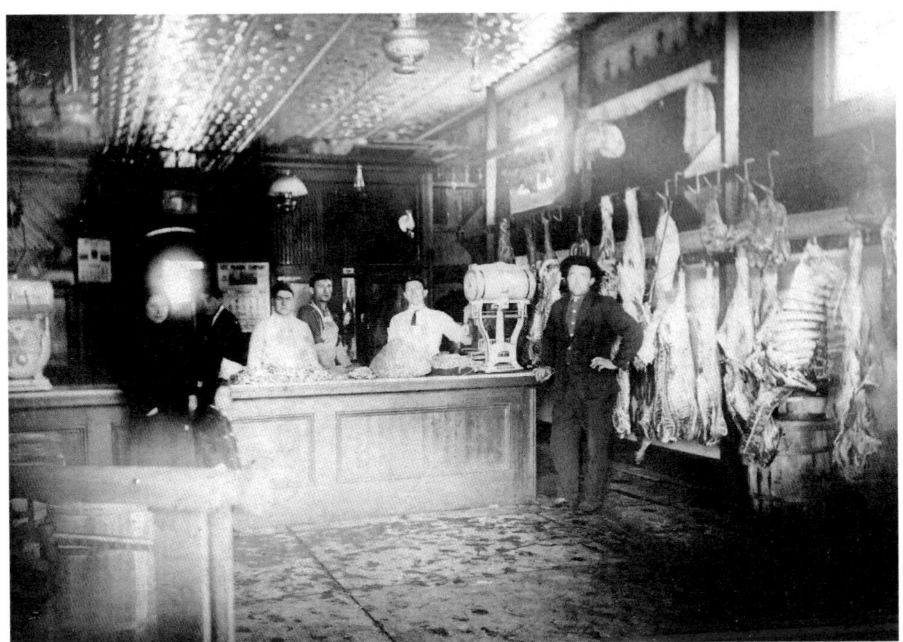

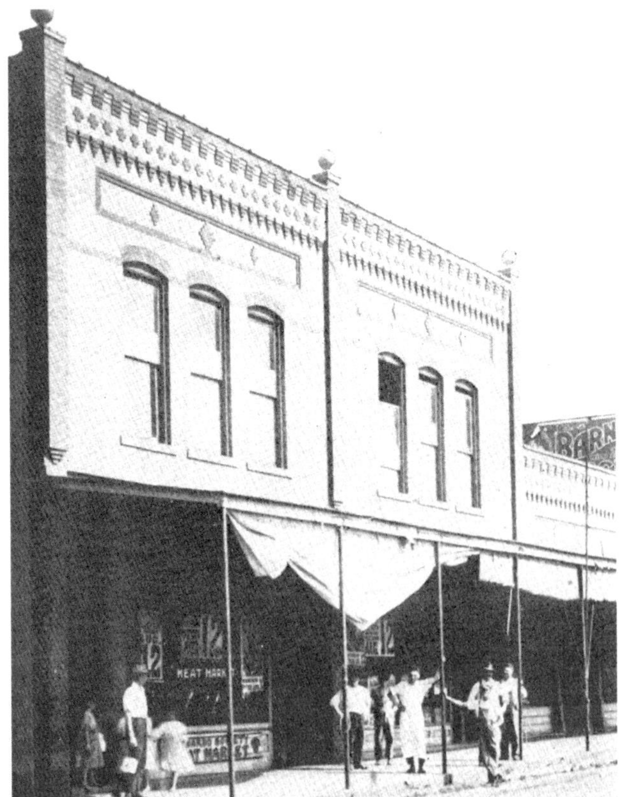

Above: Lombard Society Store. *Courtesy Herrin City Library.*

Left: Lombard Society Store and Meat Market, circa 1919.

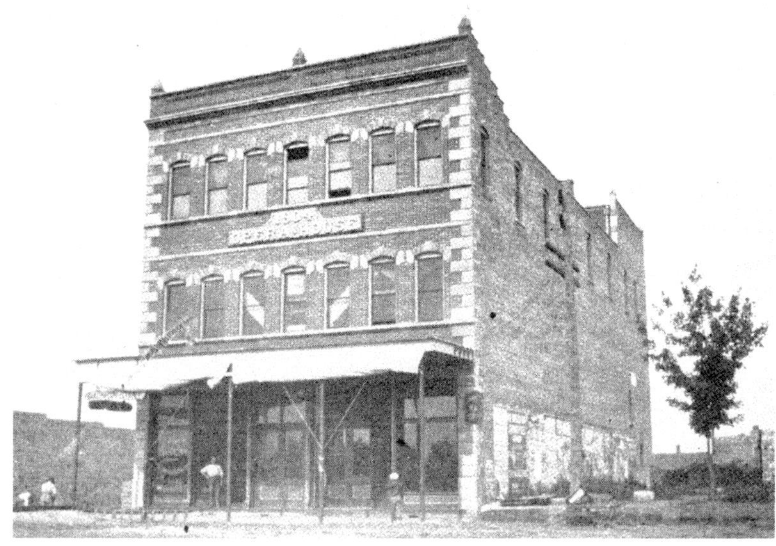

The Dell'Era/Berra Opera House, within one year of being built in 1904.

Electric Line Connecting Marion, Herrin and Carterville, Ill.

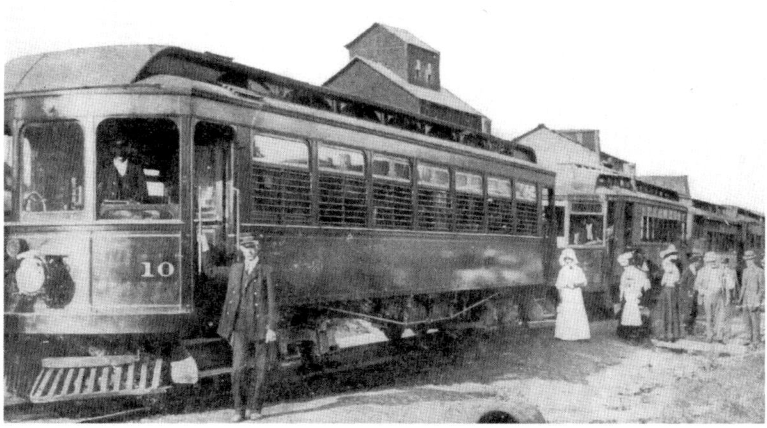

The Coal Belt Electric Railroad, the "Interurban," served Herrin, Marion and Carterville. It started running in 1901 and stopped in 1926. *Courtesy Herrin City Library.*

A federal report notes:

> *Every single year for a quarter of a century, from the discovery of coal on Herrin's Prairie in 1896* [sic] *until the post-war depression in 1921, there was always some advance and never a backward step.* [A]*verage net increase in employment* [in the mines] *each year between 1900 and*

1923 was 1,400 men. The average growth of coal output during the same period was 1 million tons, roughly equal to the total output of the field during the year 1900.[133]

"The working miners enjoyed a satisfying degree of economic independence. If a miner disliked his boss, or if he objected to lax safety practices, or if he found his earnings falling because of poor coal, he could always quit his job, knowing that in a week or so he could find another one," the report says.[134]

Part of this confidence came from the fact that Herrin was never a "company town," as in "I owe my soul to the company store." (Zeigler, just to the north, was one of only two nonunion ventures in the area, discussed in the next chapter.)

Civic pride extended to the national level. During World War I, not only did Williamson County do its duty by sending men to the front, but it also heeded the president's call for "more coal!" for the war effort. Mines in the county increased production from 7,904,528 tons in 1916 to 11,685,101 tons in 1918. This wasn't accomplished just by hiring more workers. Each man employed in the mines increased his output, on average, from 930 tons to 1,043 tons in those years.[135]

It wasn't always easy to choose whether to serve on the Western Front or on the homefront:

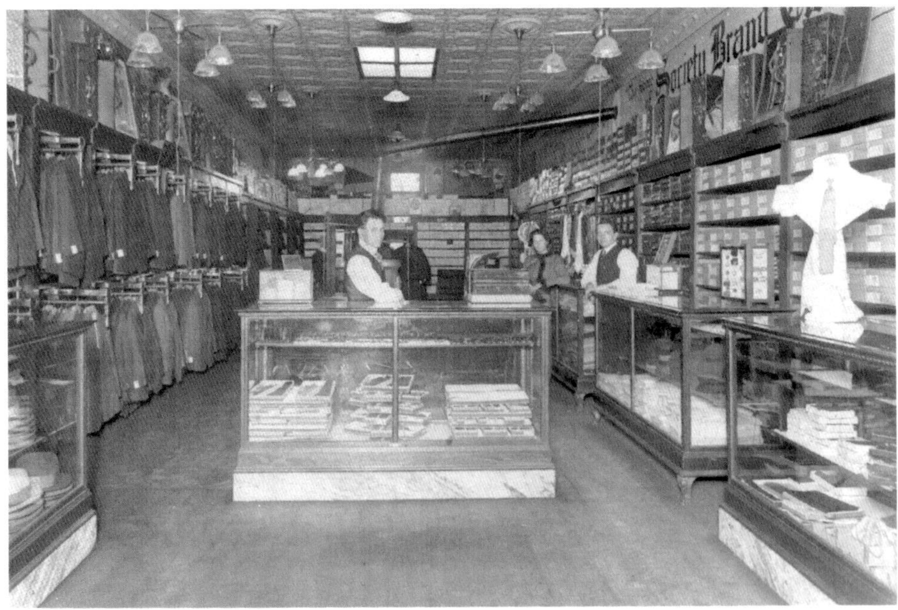

Sohn's men's store, 1916. *Courtesy the* Southern Illinoisan.

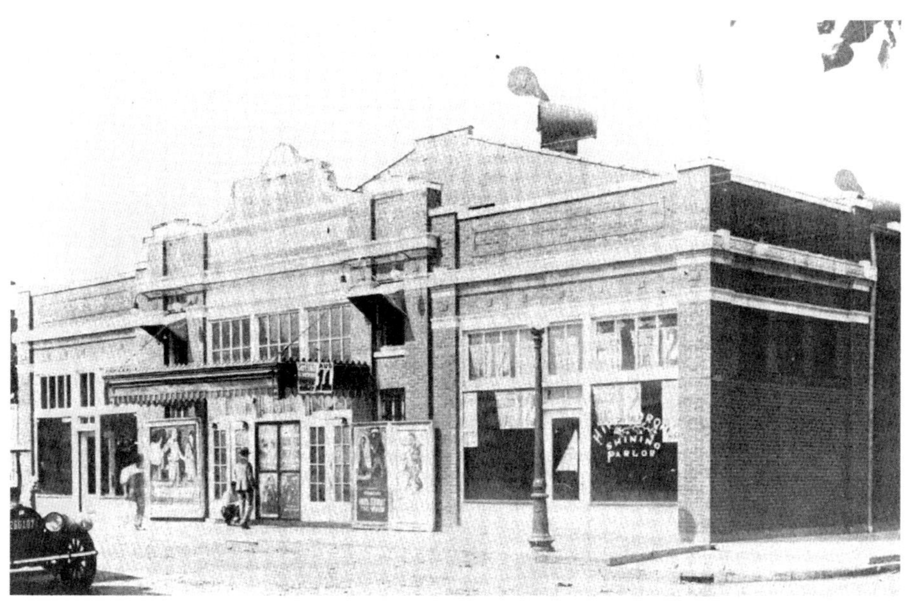

Hippodrome Theatre, built in 1917 by John Marlow at a cost of $65,000. It seated 1,500 and was billed as the largest ground-floor theatre of its kind in Illinois. It burned down in 1938.

> *The mines, railroads and all other commercial institutions in the county were going at top speed and had been for months preceding our declaration of war against Germany. Never before had this county experienced such high wages, nor had labor been as scarce...It was therefore a matter of...repeated urging before the spirit of national loyalty took hold of the community at large and especially the young men. There were few volunteer enlistments in the army in the industrial centers of the county until the war got into the second year.*[136]

By the end of the war, Herrin called itself the "largest soft coal mining city in the United States" and the "[b]est wage city in the Mississippi Valley [with a] greater number of working days the year around and a higher wage for the working man than any other city in the state and probably the Middle West." Supposedly one could "stand on the roof of the city hall and see smoke from 16 mines every day,"[137] while the whistles from thirty-five big shipping mines could be heard around town.[138]

Building and loan associations, banks and stores all grew. The Herrin Ice and Cold Storage Co. kept the town from "ice famines" that other towns suffered: it could make seventy-five tons of ice per day and store six hundred tons more, along with twenty tons of produce for wholesale fruit and grocery companies, and it could make one thousand gallons per day of "Jersey" ice cream. It employed fifteen and ran five trucks.[139]

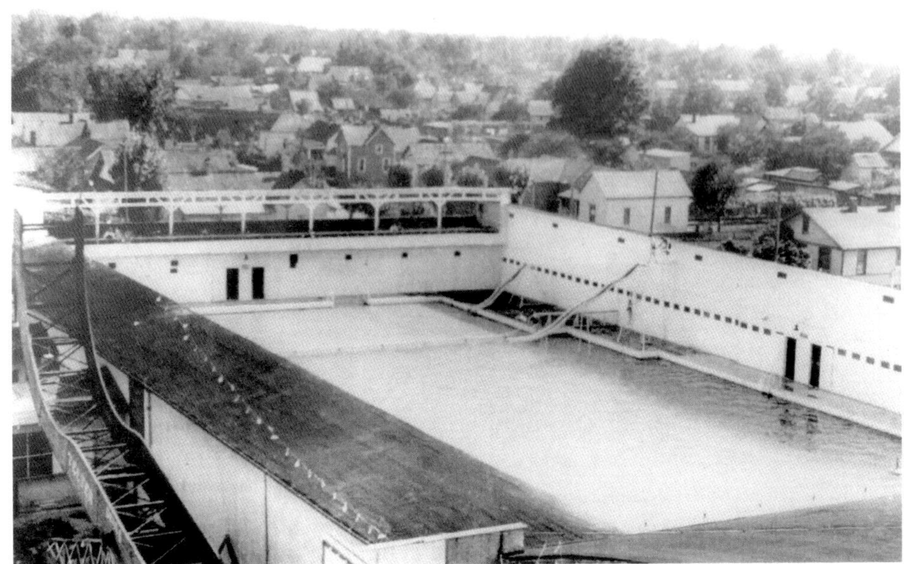

The 1.5-million-gallon saltwater pool at White City. *Courtesy City Herrin Library.*

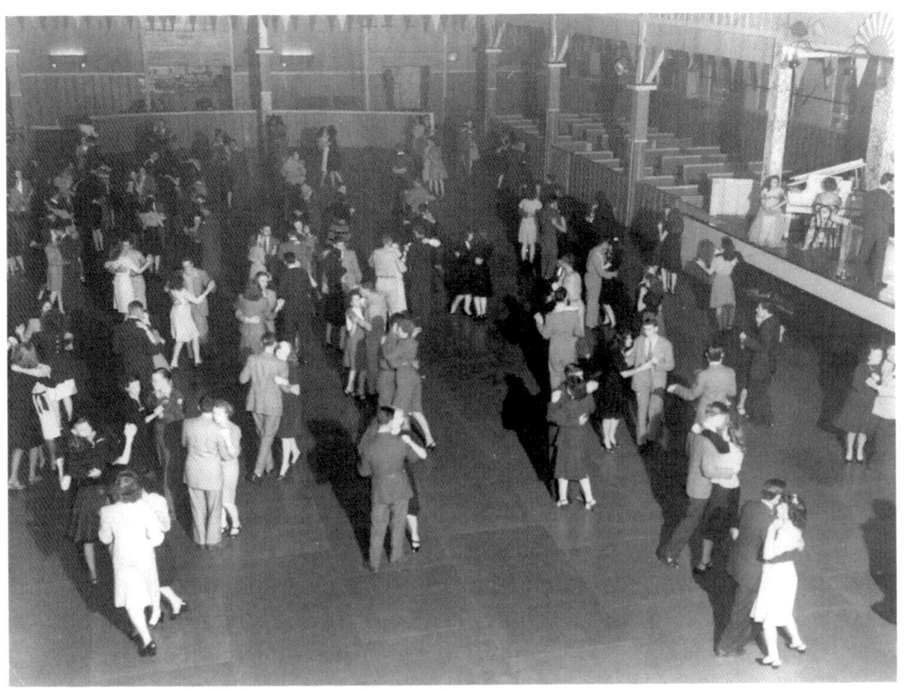

Dancers at White City, the amusement park owned by John, James and George Marlow and Paul Colombo. It opened on May 30, 1924. *Courtesy City Herrin Library.*

A page from the 1923 Herrin phonebook lists "25 boosting points" for the city, including having the "largest and most modern Hotel south of Chicago," "more miles of concrete side walks than any other city of its size in Illinois" and the fact that "more automobiles are owned in Herrin than in any other city of its size in America—If you don't believe this try crossing Park avenue some busy Saturday night about eight o-clock."[140] (In 1924, there was 1 car for every nine people, about 1,400 cars.)[141]

White City Park, a kind of Herrinite Coney Island, opened on May 30, 1924, and had a 1.5-million-gallon saltwater pool and a hall in which five hundred couples could dance to the biggest bands of the day.

The true boom years of bituminous mining in Williamson County lasted twenty-three years, in which one hundred mines shipped millions of tons of coal, first to Chicago and other midwestern markets and then to the rest of the country and even internationally. Later, these would be called the "silk-shirt days," an implied criticism of workers who possessed and spent money.

But they never earned overmuch for their dangerous, filthy work, and mostly they were buying homes, raising families, starting businesses and building their town: all-American activities, not to exclude a few benders. When the work and money began to dwindle, that way of life would change, and violence crept back.

CHAPTER 6

MASSACRE

As we settle into watching a movie at home, my two young sons always want me to tell them who the bad guys are. The better the movie, as with history, the harder that is to answer. I've also been interviewed recently by radio hosts who want me to give listeners the short version of what happened in the Herrin Massacre. That's complicated, too, and I've stumbled trying to get it right.

The short version is that in June 1922 a mine owner named William J. Lester shipped coal from his small strip mine southeast of Herrin. He did this during a national coal strike and in violation of an agreement he'd made with the local UMWA, which was willing to let him strip the overburden of dirt but not to load or ship the coal.

This was not illegal, just ill-advised, and hundreds (thousands, by some accounts) of union supporters from all over the region—certainly not just from Herrin and probably not just from Southern Illinois—surrounded the mine and its fifty nonunion men. Gunfire was exchanged, and when morning came on the second day, the nonunion men surrendered.

Under pretense of being shipped from the county, they were led on a death march that perhaps coincidentally ended in Herrin. Their fates varied, but the march led to humiliation, torture and murder—some were shot, hanged or beaten to death; and some had their throats cut and were urinated on as they lay dying. White and black, "native" and immigrant-ethnic and even women and children participated in some of it. The corpses were displayed publicly in a makeshift morgue in Herrin's Dillard building, where they were cursed, shouted at and spit upon. Twenty nonunion men died, along with three union miners.

Within one day, the national media, chambers of commerce and politicians across the United States began declaring their outrage, but while there were a coroner's jury, a grand jury, two criminal trials (in Marion) and an Illinois House of Representatives investigation, not a single person was convicted of any crime, mostly because of false testimonies that gave the indicted alibis.

When justice was not done, the media seized on the miscarriage, too. Herrin was called "an unconquered province of lawlessness" and "a stench in the nostrils of humanity," "about to complete its secession from the United States of America."[142]

That so completely misses the description of the town in which I grew up, the people I knew and the stories I'd heard about better days that my attempts to reconcile this have led to some of my deepest understandings about human nature.

It's not possible to defend, condone or apologize for these murders, and I have no desire to try. The union had won already, in a sense, forcing Lester to shut down the mine. They were able and in the process of evicting the "scabs" from the county but instead took pleasurable revenge on unarmed men. Even one of the legal defenses in the case, self-defense, sounds like a mockery of justice. In addition, you keep seeing some of the same hooligans' names over time; men indicted in the Massacre show up again in histories of the Prohibition war to come.

But that was in the past, and those people are gone now, except for a few of the elderly who remember being taken as children to see the victims' bodies. Even some of those doubt themselves and wonder if they were really taken there or if they're remembering others' stories.

What happened was incredibly violent, grotesque and regrettable, to say the least, but to give only the easily digested version is to fall victim to facile stories. Worse, though, is silence. Without understanding the context of the Massacre, it can't be processed properly, and the town will feel itself unforgiven—perhaps most importantly by itself—and will seem to others defensive and even unrepentant.

The slightly longer version isn't adequate either, but here goes.

First, it was not the city of Herrin that did those crimes; it was a mob of individuals. (Mayor A.T. Pace protested rather weakly at the time that Herrin's name was on the reporters' bylines simply because it had the telegraph office, but that's untrue, too.) Many no doubt came from Herrin, but there were also many others from surrounding counties and maybe even some from outside the region. Others in Herrin condemned the actions but put up bonds for the indicted; others stayed silent from fear; others sympathized but would never have taken part; others *would* have taken part but had to work that day or their wives kept them home and so on. In a town of eleven thousand, there will be many opinions.

Second, anger on that scale doesn't come from nowhere. Mining always has been bloody, dangerous work, let alone the hard physical labor (especially when there was only hand-digging and hand-loading) and the psychological effect of working underground, often in freezing water or poorly ventilated rooms. Look at the large-scale fatalities in Illinois alone, in the years before the Massacre:

> *Wilmington Coal Mining & Manufacturing Company, Diamond Mine, Braidwood, February 16, 1883. Sixty miners drowned when mine flooded.*
>
> *Zeigler Coal Company, April 3, 1905. Forty-seven miners killed in explosion, three more asphyxiated while trying to rescue them.*
>
> *Cherry Mine Disaster, St. Paul Coal Company, Mine #2, November 13, 1909. Two hundred fifty-nine died in mine fire.*
>
> *Franklin Coal & Coke Mine #1, October 27, 1914. Fifty-two died in gas explosion.*[143]

These don't even account for individual and familial disasters every year. The state's Annual Coal Report lists these deaths in Herrin for 1902 alone:

> *Jan. 14, 1902, William Butcher, driver, age 27 years, married, was killed by being caught between a loaded pit-car and the side of the entry in the mine of the Chicago and Carterville Coal Co., at Herrin, Williamson county. Deceased was hauling a loaded pit-car through a cross cut from the* [?] *west entry to the first west entry on the north side. In attempting to get on the front end of the car he slipped and was caught between the car and the side of the entry. He died a few minutes after the accident. He leaves a widow and one child.*
>
> *Feb. 24, 1902, Aleck Calcatarra, miner, age 41 years, married, leaves a widow and three children, was severely injured about the body by a fall of slate in the Big Muddy Coal & Iron Co.'s shaft No. 7, Herrin, Williamson county. Deceased was cautioned by the mine examiner to be careful of some loose slate at the face of his working place; in reply he said that he could take care of himself. He was mining off some coal that had been loosened by a blast the previous day, when the slate fell which caused his death five hours later.*

May 7, 1902, Robert Oliver, driver, age 20, single, was severely injured by a collision of a pit car and mule in the Chicago & Carterville Coal Co.'s shaft, located at Herrin, Williamson county. He died two hours after the accident.[144]

In all, a startling 42,898 coal miners were killed in mine accidents in the United States from 1884 to 1912, a mere twenty-eight years.[145]

Along with these dangers and discomforts went low pay, no benefits and no rights in employment.

The coal industry had long had problems, and Illinois, especially Southern Illinois, had long been at the heart of American unionism meant to redress those ills. The American Miners' Association, organized in Belleville, Illinois, was the first miners' union to extend beyond a single state (but went inactive after 1868).

Famous labor leaders with Illinois connections included John Mitchell (born in Braidwood), John Hunter Walker (moved to Braidwood from Scotland), John L. Lewis (lived in Panama, Illinois, and Springfield), "General" Alexander Bradley (Collinsville and later Mount Olive), Mother Jones (lived in Chicago, buried in Mount Olive), Alexander Howat (Braidwood, briefly) and Adolph Germer (Staunton)—and several had worked the mines as children.

The UMWA, formed in 1890, came into existence at the same time as the era of coal in Herrin, and there was little doubt that it helped miners, their families and their communities. "By 1919, [District 12: Illinois] had become the largest and most powerful, as well as the most radical, district union in the United Mine Workers as a whole," writes the labor scholar John Laslett.[146]

A federal report notes:

In 1898, just at the opening of the first mine on Herrin's Prairie, the [UMWA] *won their first considerable victory in the State* [of Illinois] *and successfully negotiated contracts with most of the Illinois operators. Nearly all of the few small mines that had already started operation in Williamson and Saline Counties signed contracts in 1898, and the transition to collective bargaining at each new mine developed after 1898 came for the most part without great strain or friction.*[147]

"Investigators for the United States Coal Commission, probing the causes of the Herrin Massacre a year after it happened," Paul Angle writes, "contrasted conditions in Williamson County before and after unionization. [Their report reads in part:] 'When mining began…it was upon a ruinously competitive basis. Profit was the sole objective; the life and health of the employees was of no moment.'"

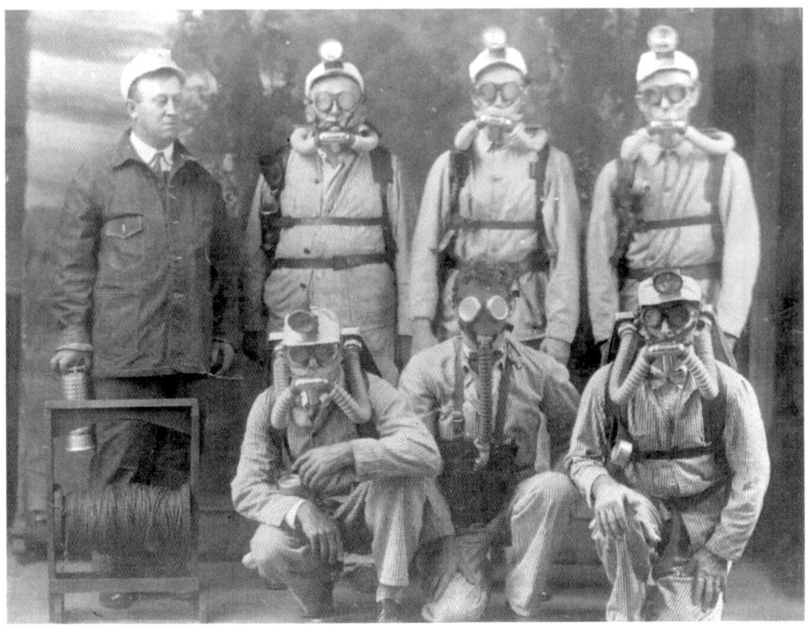

Collective bargaining led to improved working conditions. Mine rescue team, 1913. Madison Coal Corporation, No. 9 mine, Williamson County. *Courtesy Illinois State Geological Survey.*

Into this Gilded Age jungle came the union, and "the Workmen's Compensation Law was enacted. Earnings [that had been as low or lower than $1.25 per day] advanced to $7.00 and even $15.00 a day; improvement in the working conditions was reflected in the appearance of the workmen, their families, their manner of life and their growing cities [such as Herrin] and public improvements."[148]

Congress passed the first federal statute ("relatively modest legislation," admits the U.S. Department of Labor) governing mine safety in 1891, which required mine ventilation and banned children as workers under the age of twelve.[149] These small advances combined with bargaining that made mine owners responsible for other things, on a contract-by-contract basis:

> *The company shall keep the mine in as dry condition as practicable by keeping the water off the road and out of the working places. When a miner has to leave his working place on account of water, through the neglect of the company, they shall employ said miner doing company work when practicable and provided that said miner is competent to do such work; or he will be given another working place until such water is taken out of his place.*

Clearly, though, much in agreements still favored employers:

> *In the event of an instantaneous death by accident in the mine, the miners and underground employees shall have the privilege* [!] *of discontinuing work for the remainder of that day: but work, at the option of the operator, shall be resumed the day following, and continue thereafter. In case the operator elects to operate the mine on the day of the funeral of the deceased, as above, or where death has resulted from an accident in the mine, individual miners and underground employees may, at their option, absent themselves from work for the purpose of attending such funeral, but not otherwise. And whether attending such funeral or not, each member of the U.M.W. of A., employed at the mine at which the deceased member was employed shall contribute 50 cents and the operator $25 for the benefit of the family of the deceased, or his legal representatives, to be collected through the office of the company. In the event that the mines are thrown idle on account of the miners or other employees failure to report for work in the time intervening between the time of the accident and the funeral, or on the day of the funeral, then the company shall not be called upon for the payment of the $25 above referred to.*[150]

In effect there was a class war being fought in the United States at the turn of the twentieth century, which found vent in race, ethnicity, religion… and employment. There'd already been a number of skirmishes and all-out battles in the coal fields, both close to Herrin and elsewhere in the country, and it was serious business for both sides. "[T]he struggle for a mere existence is constant and intense," wrote the secretary of the Illinois Bureau of Labor Statistics in 1896. "The opportunity to earn the bare necessities of life, even at the hardest and most hazardous employment, is a prize to be fought for."[151]

After an 1897 strike by the UMWA, miners won eight-hour workdays and a 60 percent increase in pay, to forty cents per ton produced. But four coal operators in central and Southern Illinois, complaining that they couldn't compete in the Chicago market, decided to work without the union and brought in African American strikebreakers from Alabama to work for twenty-five cents per ton. At Pana on August 24, 1898, a gunfight broke out between nonunion black miners on one side and the police and union miners on the other, but no one was seriously injured. The National Guard was sent to occupy the area.[152]

On October 12, 1898, the owners of the Chicago-Virden Coal Company mine brought more black workers in on a train to break a strike and to "drive a wedge between white and black." This was the final provocation at the

Virden, Illinois mine, which already had a stockade around it and was guarded by "ex-police from Chicago and private detectives from St. Louis [with] brand new Winchester rifles." Local union miners opened fire on the train when it arrived. A mine guard said that "the Battle of Virden [was] hotter than San Juan Hill." Eight union miners and four mine guards died, and at least forty-five more men were wounded, including one black strikebreaker.[153]

Closer to Herrin, Samuel T. Brush, from Carbondale, had found backing from St. Louis and Cincinnati and formed the St. Louis and Big Muddy Coal Company in 1890. His mine located one mile north of Carterville became the largest-producing mine in Illinois in 1897. But overproduction and "fierce competition" made the price of coal drop, which meant that operators looked to cut wages to reduce costs, while the union fought hard to keep people working at a fair wage. Brush rode out two union strikes, but in the third he imported African American miners from Tennessee to replace local men who'd walked out.

While Brush was a mildly progressive industrialist, instituting his own eight-hour workday and paying slightly more than union wages, he refused to even talk to the union. Tensions were high, and some of his black miners walked out, too. Brush tried to replace them with black miners from the Pana mine, and the train carrying them was attacked at Lauder (now Cambria) by union men in a field of wheat next to the station. The wife of one of the Pana miners was killed. Brush's black miners retaliated by shooting into and burning down a "hamlet" where the black union miners lived.

The National Guard came in for two and a half months to pacify the "500 or more union and non-union men at war in Carterville." But six days after they left, a race riot broke out; five black men were shot dead, and the two state militia companies, bolstered by a third, returned. Nine were indicted for the shooting of the miner's wife and another twelve were indicted for the murder of the five men, but in a repeat of the Bloody Vendetta defenses, alibis were concocted for many of the defendants, and all went free. Brush sold the mine to the Madison Coal Company in 1906, and it became Madison No. 8—a union mine.

Joseph Leiter, who by 1903 had bought up 7,500 acres eight miles north of Herrin, opened a mine and his own company town called Zeigler, after his father's middle name. (Dad gave Joseph $1 million after the boy graduated from Harvard, so it was probably the right thing to do.) The mine was more modern than "anything of its kind in the country" and "approached complete mechanization as closely as was then possible." The company town had wide streets, good workers' houses at "reasonable rates," a schoolhouse, a "well-equipped" hospital, thirty ethnic stores, a newspaper, a potato chip factory, three theatres, a public swimming pool and twenty miles of sidewalks.[154]

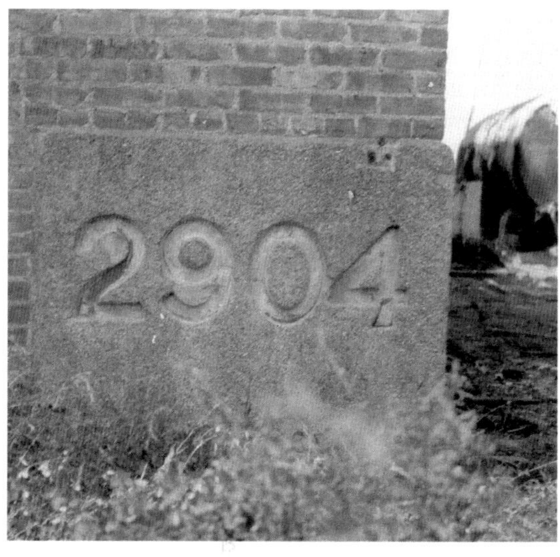

The cornerstone of Joseph Leiter's 1904 powerhouse in Zeigler was mixed with champagne, not water. It was dated 2904 because Leiter joked that the mine was one thousand years ahead of its time. *Courtesy Chicago History Museum.*

On July 7, 1904, right after the first coal had been hoisted, the union went on strike for recognition and bargained wages. Leiter said he actually preferred to hire union men, because "a well-paid, intelligent employee is preferable to a non-union man," but he intended only to be labor's "friend" and to run an open shop the way he wanted to run it. He especially couldn't agree with the union's complaint that, mechanized or not, he should pay the fifty-six cents per ton that was scale in the district at the time.

All strikers were evicted from their homes in his town, and forty-two Pinkerton guards patrolled Leiter's property. He built an enclosure around the mine works, a high fence around that, two two-story log blockhouses armed with machine guns, two smaller blockhouses (including one at the Big Muddy pumping station that supplied water) and a big searchlight on the top of the mine tipple, which towered 125 feet over the surrounding countryside.

For six months, Leiter brought nonunion miners and other workers in, and the union men tried to dissuade or frighten them from working. Despite there being "shooting in town practically every night, or the blowing of dynamite here and there," only one man, an Austrian strikebreaker, was killed, in November 1904. Just after that, two of Leiter's mine officials were ambushed but got away, and the National Guard was sent for. Despite their presence (a company of seventy), along with that of forty deputy U.S. marshals, various members of a private army and the "blinding" company searchlight searching its surrounds, the mine came under fire every night.

The mine exploded on April 3, 1905, killing up to fifty-one men, and Leiter accused the strikers of sabotage. But three separate investigations attributed the disaster to marsh gas buildup from poor ventilation, which when it exploded touched off forty-one kegs of blasting powder stored illegally in the mine. Leiter continued to work the mine, but there was another fire, another explosion that killed twenty-six and yet another that killed three. Leiter was finally disheartened. His mother told him, "If [he] didn't make an arrangement to get somebody else to run the property she was going to foreclose on it and sell it out to somebody else." Bell and Zoller Mining Company then ran the Zeigler No. 1 mine for another thirty-eight years—with union men.[155]

The Colorado Coal Field War ended on April 20, 1914, when the Colorado National Guard and private guards from the infamous Baldwin-Felts Detective Agency, hired by John D. Rockefeller, attacked a two-hundred-tent colony at Ludlow, Colorado, that held twelve hundred striking miners and their families. Machine gun and rifle fire, burning and looting by the militia followed. Twenty-five died, including eleven children, two women, a passerby and three militiamen, in what came to be known as the Ludlow Massacre. The women and ten of the children suffocated in a "death pit" under a burning tent, where they'd hidden for refuge.[156]

For one week in 1921, the year before the Herrin Massacre, the Battle of Blair Mountain raged. Ten to fifteen thousand coal miners—reacting generally to years of tension between capital and labor and specifically to the murder of the mayor of Matewan, West Virginia, by Baldwin-Felts men—fought a private army hired by the coal companies in what's been called the "largest organized armed uprising in American labor history." The U.S. Army sent bombers from Maryland to disperse miners with gas and explosive bombs, and federal troops were called in, at which point the miners hid their weapons and dispersed to their homes. Up to thirty coal operators' guards and fifty to one hundred miners were killed.[157]

Later some tried to dismiss the significance of the event by saying that the miners were just "gun-totin', moonshining, and feuding" mountain people anyway. Whatever else they were, they were also a grass-roots army, with paramilitary training and noticeable discipline, doctors, nurses and tent-colony bivouacs. A scholar writes:

> *A sizable proportion of these marchers were from out of state, approximately 2,000 of them were World War I veterans, and all of them were from industrialized backgrounds. Indeed, the older patriarchs of the clans in the hills had no identity and little sympathy for labor unions and industrial protest…That this particular explanation about the armed march has been allowed to persist may be due to historians' unwillingness to take class violence in the United States seriously.*[158]

The brutality across the country on the part of mine guards, deputy sheriffs, private armies of "Pinks"[159] and state military forces earned them a hatred beyond compare. In addition to policing mine properties, private guards discouraged union organization, collected rents in company towns, spied for the coal operators and often cursed, bullied, beat, maimed and killed anyone they perceived as crossing them. Miners in West Virginia even claimed that "guards had kicked the fetus out of a miner's pregnant wife and had cut the breasts off of another woman." Whether this was true or not, the rhetoric had effect. Just before the Herrin Massacre, a miner said in a speech, "We must show the world this ain't West Virginia."[160]

Herrin was as close to 100 percent unionized at it was possible to be. Angle says, "Unionism had permeated every craft and industry, so that the miners had the active sympathy of the entire laboring population." If it wasn't the UMWA, it was other trade and craft unions, and the sympathies of families, friends and business owners who depended on miners' income for their own lives. Williamson and Franklin County held half of the state's sixty thousand miners,[161] who felt they were fighting for their very lives, literally and culturally, as well as for dignity and self-realization.

On April 1, 1922, the UMWA announced what would become "the most massive [coal miners' strike] in American history," in which 600,000 miners in both union and nonunion mines in every coal-producing state eventually stopped work. Even more than a show of union solidarity, it showed the miners' anxiety about the "deteriorating position of the coal industry, its union, and the men who mined the mineral."[162] In many ways, they were already doomed but didn't know or believe it.

Add to this unholy stew of history an undeniable wildness in the culture that had persisted from its frontier days. Due to the population explosion, the tendency might have actually increased. Just as there are wildly different accounts of the pioneer Christmas, it was true that families,

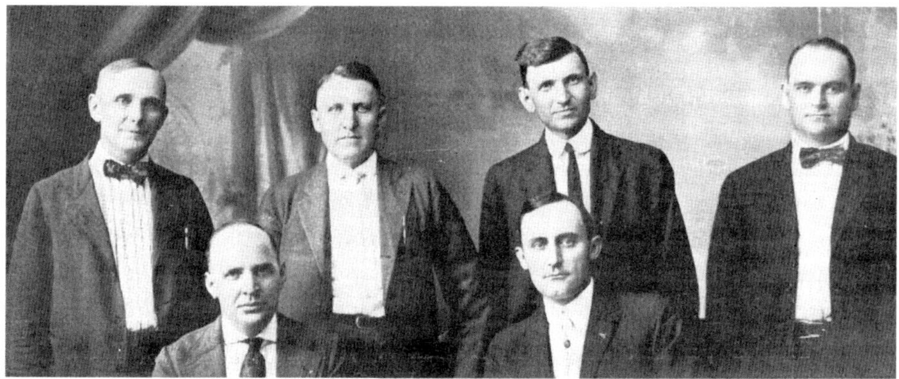

UMWA officials in Herrin, 1919. *Top, left to right*: A.T. Pace, traveling auditor, District 12; Hugh Willis, board member, District 12; William G. Davis, secretary-treasurer, Sub-district 10; Fox C. Hughes, vice-president, Sub-district 10. *Bottom, left to right*: George F. Cooper, investigator, Sub-districts 9 and 10; William J. Sneed, president, Sub-district 10.

churches, businesses and other forms of civic life were thriving right next to what was called the "wide-open" aspect of life in Southern Illinois. This wildness—including liquor, prostitution, murder and theft—was well known in many communities, including Herrin:

> [T]*he city was full of dives of various sorts. Liquor was dispensed openly over the bars* [despite Prohibition] *at post-war prices, bawdy houses flaunted their shame on important thoroughfares, gambling was unmolested and gamblers battened on the earnings of hardworking miners and others.*[163]

There was also the seemingly ubiquitous presence of guns, as in this portrayal of Zeigler:

> *Everybody had guns and they would shoot at anything that moved. They killed all the birds and they killed anything that ran or walked. I think this was part of the recklessness around here…I can remember the first night that I was here. It was about ten o'clock and the guns were shooting all around and the people were screaming and the landlady was running up and down. Well, I didn't know what to do so I lit out through the park and I went over to get my brother, who was here at the time, and he said, "Oh, don't worry about the shooting. This goes on all the time."*[164]

Combine all that with the southern Appalachian culture's belief in what Milo Erwin calls "the law of the bush," as well as recent immigrants' sympathy in some cases for political radicalism, and you get a culture of what a friend of mine calls, admiringly, hard bastards—hard cases, with hard rows to hoe—so we can perhaps begin to understand what happened at the Lester mine that day in June 1922.

William J. Lester, who owned the Southern Illinois Coal Company, opened his mine southeast of Herrin in early September 1921. The mine was a few hundred yards east of what is now North Skyline Drive, a mile and three-tenths north of Old Route 13, on property currently owned by Primex. On the Illinois State Geological Survey map for the Johnston City Quadrangle, it's mine index number 6747, in T9S-R2E, Section 3, but it was later operated by the Caloric Coal Company (1922–23) and Mammoth Coal Company (1923–27), and the pit was enlarged by the Energy Mine (index 882, 1947–72), so it's hard to discern on the map.[165]

Lester employed about fifty UMWA men and shipped his first coal a few months after opening. When the strike came four months after that, on April 1, 1922, he got permission from "local union officials" to do repairs on his two big steam shovels and then to uncover coal but not load or ship it. By early June, he had a big pile of temptation in his yard: sixty thousand tons or more, ready to ship to market, which represented a profit of $250,000, or some $3 million in today's money, at a time when most of his competition across the country was stalled. Lester was "heavily in debt," and though his peers told him that to go against the union in this part of the country would be suicide—not to him literally, of course, as he lived in Cleveland and was often in Chicago for business—he said, "It's legal, and I need the money. Why shouldn't I?"

He fired the union men on June 13 and two days later brought in about twenty-five other workers for the steam shovels, locomotive and commissary. He also brought in twenty-five or so private mine guards. All of them came from Chicago employment agencies, and that, too, was not insignificant. On June 16, he told the Burlington Railroad to come pick up sixteen loaded coal hoppers, and though the first crew refused, a second did as asked.

The mine guards bullied, cursed, robbed (of small change) and even pistol-whipped local residents, while Lester and his mine superintendent, C.K. McDowell, made blustering threats probably designed to subdue the miners and their sympathizers.

"We came down here to work this mine, union or no union," McDowell said. "We will work it with blood if necessary, and you tell all the Goddamned union men to stay away if they don't want trouble."[166]

Despite more warnings by everyone from Colonel Samuel N. Hunter, the ranking officer of the adjutant general's office, to Major Robert W. Davis of the National Guard, State's Attorney Delos Duty and Sheriff Melvin Thaxton, Lester went ahead.

On the morning of June 20, hundreds of union miners held a meeting at the Sunnyside Mine in Herrin. That afternoon, two telegrams were printed in the local papers. The first was from my grandfather, William J. Sneed, who was a state senator and the president of UMWA Sub-district 10. He'd asked UMWA president John L. Lewis if the American Federation of Labor had given the men at the Lester mine permission to strip and load coal. Lewis had replied in part, "Representatives of our organization are justified in treating this crowd as an outlaw organization and in viewing its members in the same light as they do any other common strikebreakers."

On the morning of the twenty-first, a truck carrying more strikebreakers to Lester's mine was ambushed on its way from Carbondale, and three nonunion men were injured. That afternoon, an "indignation meeting" of several hundred miners was held in the Herrin cemetery, and mobs began looting hardware stores for guns and bullets. By 3:30 p.m. McDowell had called to say that his mine was surrounded and hundreds of shots had been fired.

Accounts vary wildly over who fired the first shot, but the first casualties may have been union men: one killed and two more fatally wounded. Lester was found

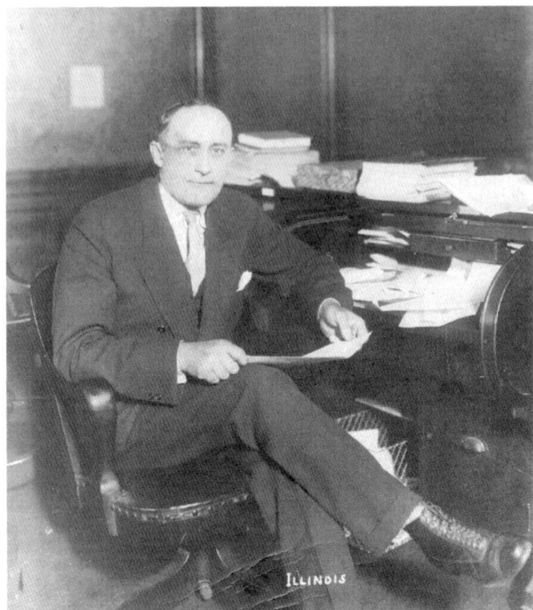

Left: William J. Sneed (1883–1949), my maternal grandfather. *Courtesy of the author*.

Below: John L. Lewis (1880–1969), *right*, UMWA president, with the chairman of the Labor Committee of the House of Representatives, two months before the Lester mine incident. *Courtesy Library of Congress Prints and Photographs Division*.

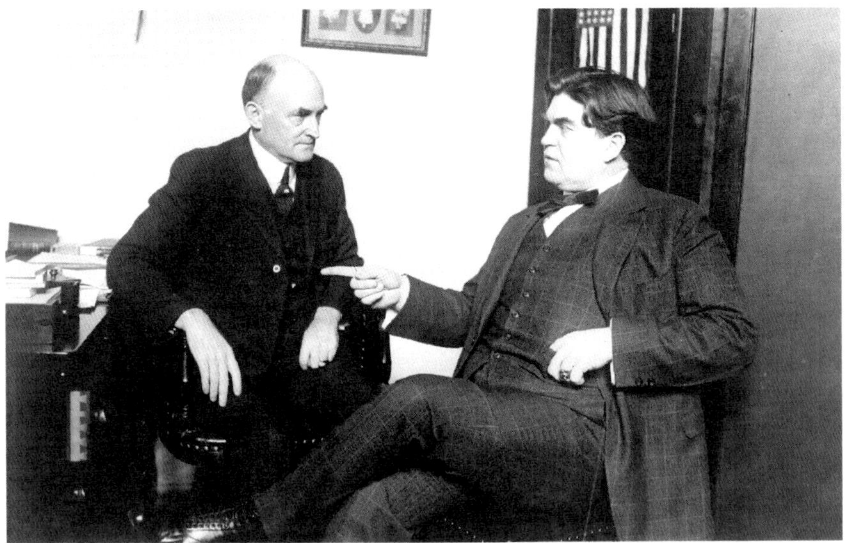

at the Great Northern Hotel in Chicago and agreed to shut down the mine. A truce was arranged, but despite several people involved in its implementation, it never did go off as planned. No one seemed willing or able to stop what came next, and current scholarship is inadequate to explain who was most at fault.[167]

By that evening of the twenty-first "men and boys…packed the streets [of Herrin and Marion]. Policemen had great difficulty in keeping traffic moving. Cars loaded with armed men made their way at high speed in the direction of the Lester mine."[168] They and many others laid siege to the mine, shooting, blowing things up with dynamite and trying to make incursions into the camp.

At dawn, the men in the mine surrendered, evidently to the promise that they'd be sent out of the county. They were lined up and marched along the rail spur from the mine, in a northwesterly direction, and the mob instantly began to grow out of control, punching, cursing and threatening them. At Crenshaw Crossing, a cluster of houses a half-mile from the mine, direct threats were made about killing them all. A half-mile more at Moake Crossing, on the Crenshaw Road heading west, C.K. McDowell attracted attention by being unable to keep up; he had a wooden leg. He was taken down a road and shot.[169] Another mile west on Crenshaw Road at the intersection with Bandyville Road[170] was the powerhouse for the Coal Belt Electric Railroad. Here there appears to have been a change in the leadership of the mob. Those who perhaps intended to send the strikebreakers out of the county were deposed in favor of those willing to kill.

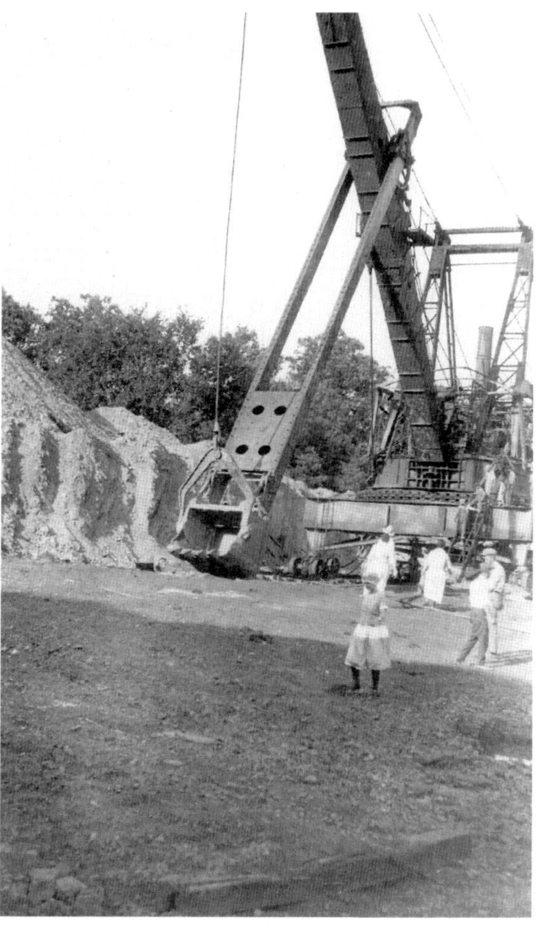

Big shovel wrecked in the Lester mine riot, June 21–22, 1922. *Courtesy Williamson County Historical Society.*

Hugh Willis, a state board member of the UMWA, pulled up to the procession in his car and told the mob something to the effect of, "Take them over in the woods and give it to them. Kill all you can."[171]

Three hundred feet north of the powerhouse, at a barbed wire fence in the woods, the strikebreakers were told to run.

"Here's where you run the gauntlet," a bearded man in coveralls said. "Now, damn you, let's see how fast you can run between here and Chicago, you damned gutter-bums!"[172]

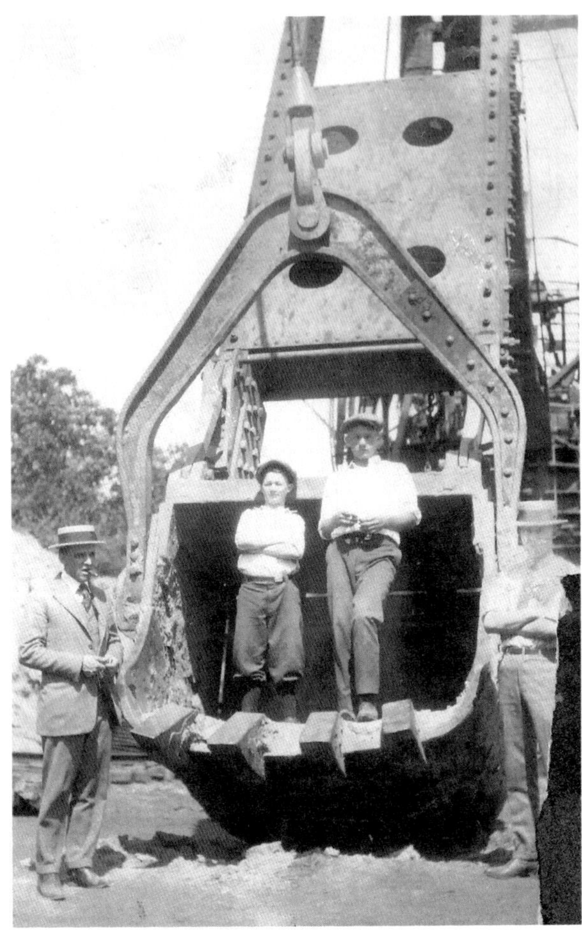

This and next two pages: In the days after the Herrin Massacre, crowds toured the Lester strip mine to witness (or re-visit?) the destruction—two wrecked steam shovels, trashed and still-burning rail cars and looted buildings. These photos give a good idea of how small the mine was, for the size of the trouble it produced. *Courtesy Williamson County Historical Society.*

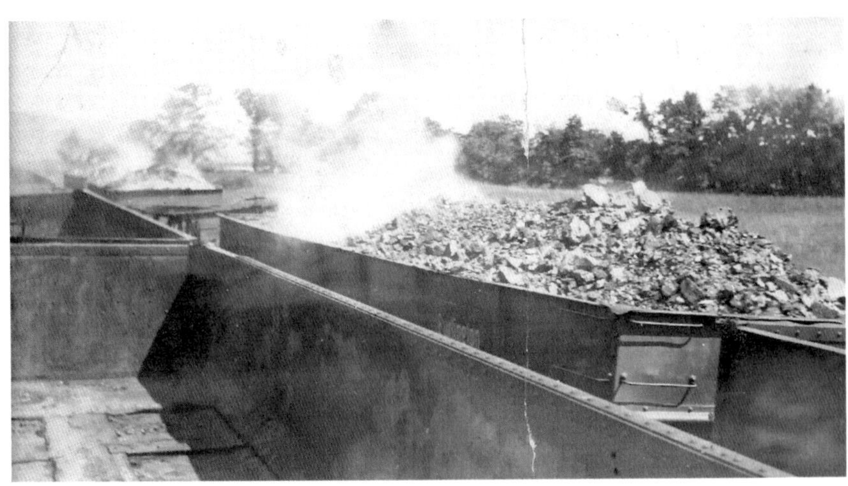

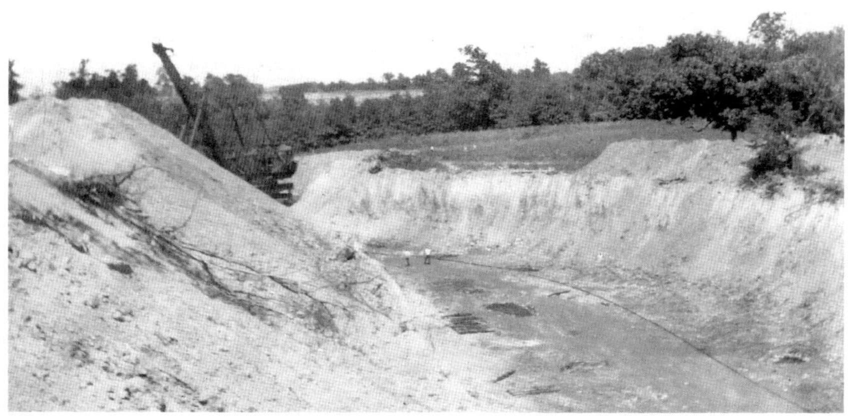

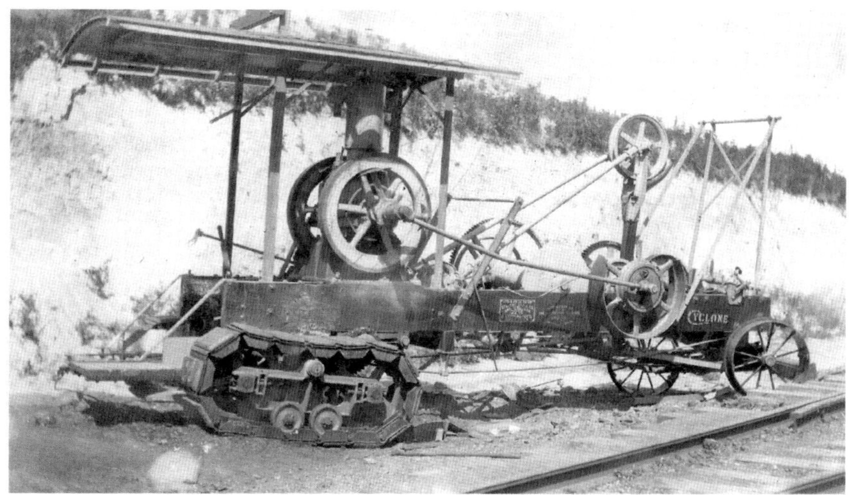
CYCLONE

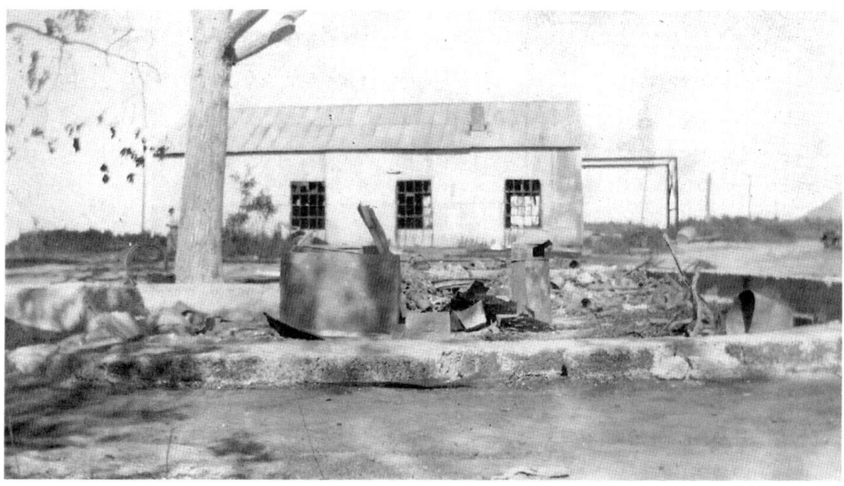

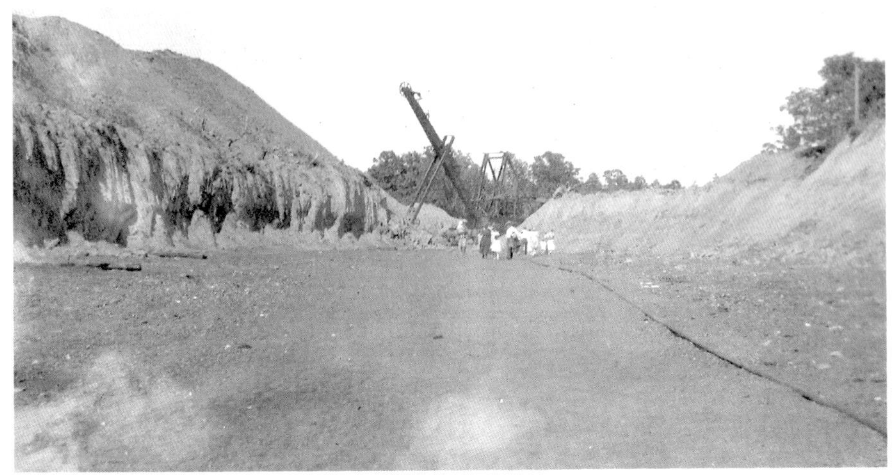

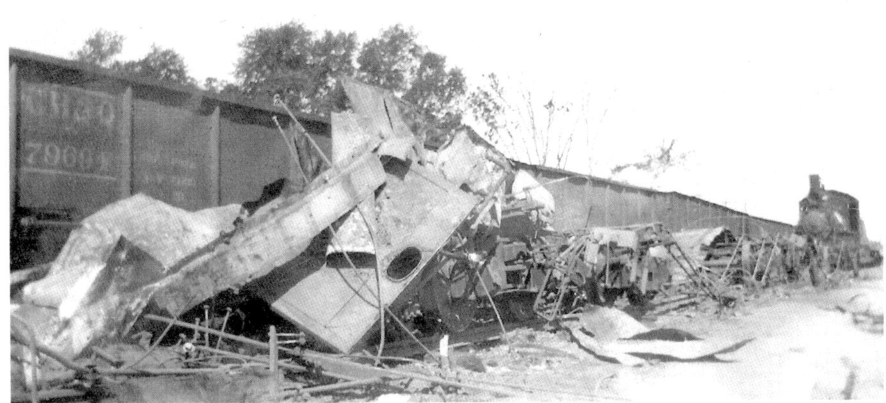

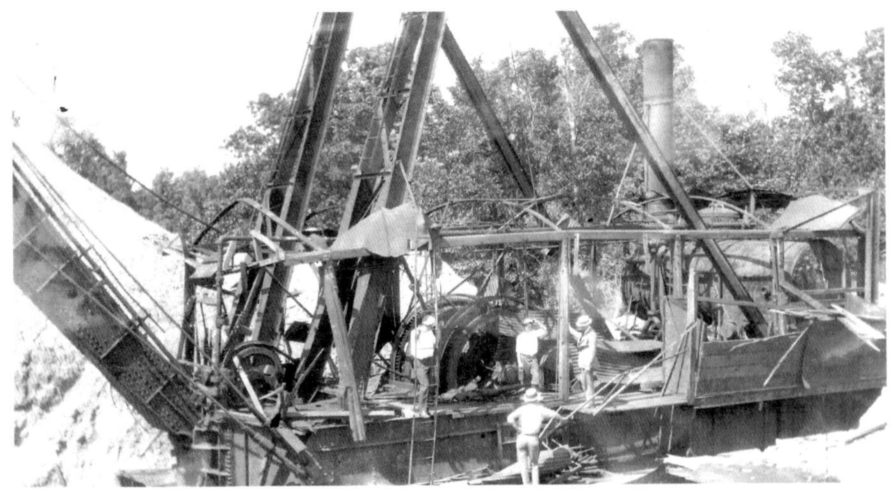

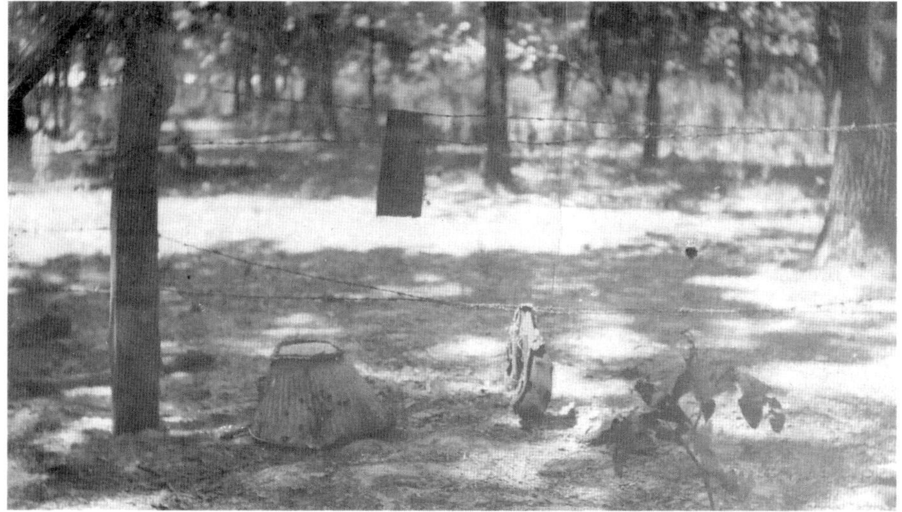

The infamous barbed wire fence, where nonunion men were forced to run the gauntlet; many died. Bits of clothing still hang from it. *Courtesy Williamson County Historical Society.*

The nonunion men ran up against the fence, jumped over it or crawled under it; several were shot. The wounded and recaptured were beaten and shot, and some were hanged. Those who escaped ran northwest through what's shown on old plat maps as "Harrison's Outlots," known even then as Harrison's Woods. (There's still a small patch of these woods left, just to the southeast of Herrin's current First Baptist Church.[173]) At various places in those outlots several more were captured or shot. The mob members became separated in their pursuit, but some came together again in the schoolyard at South Side with a total of six captives.

A crowd of two hundred marched those six men east on Stotlar Street toward the Herrin Cemetery. They kicked and beat them, yelling "scab" and other curses, and children threw stones. At the cemetery, the men were tied together by the neck, shot several times and had their throats cut. When one still living begged for water, a young woman holding a baby either kicked or put her foot on the man and said she'd see him in hell. One man pissed in the victims' faces.

By midmorning, Williamson County sheriff Thaxton, who'd been conspicuously absent through most of the events, had the wounded survivors taken to Herrin Hospital and the dead to the empty Dillard building. People from all over came to file through the makeshift morgue and make comments. The body of C.K. McDowell went to a morgue in Marion.[174]

The nonunion men whose bodies were not claimed were buried quietly in a potter's grave in the Herrin Cemetery.[175] Meanwhile, the funerals for the union miners killed were the largest in local history to that point.

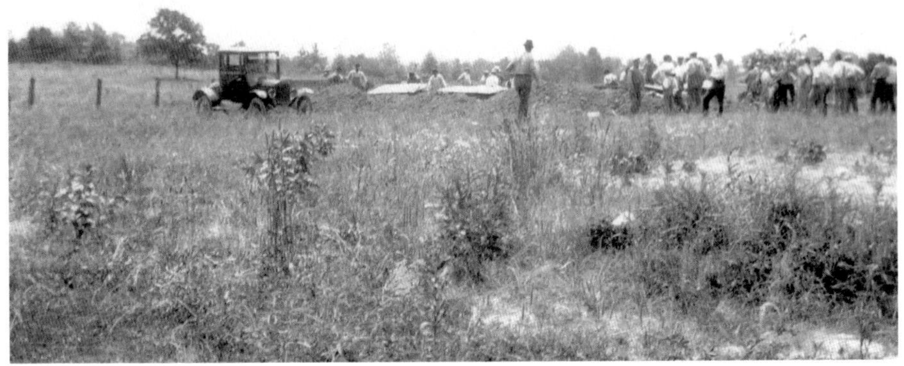

Union men burying nonunion workers in a potter's grave in the Herrin Cemetery, after the Herrin Massacre. *Courtesy Herrin City Library.*

As I said, the media, chambers of commerce and some politicians began declaring their outrage immediately, which only intensified when legal proceedings failed to find any individual guilty of any crime—despite 262 indictments.[176] The word "massacre" appears immediately. We're inured to it now, since sports teams "massacre" one another daily, but then it had a specific connotation: the surprise attack and murder of an unarmed group by those with more power, and that it certainly was.

In fact, arguments for the defense included a "self-defense" theme—"that the guards and gunmen were aggressors, and that they brought the fatal attack upon themselves."[177] After the first trial, the defense issued a statement that read, "If this trial has taught the lesson well that hereafter the weapons of the employers' private army shall not be directed against human breasts, then the trial with all its sacrifices has not been in vain."[178]

This interesting reverse tactic may have been part of what some reacted so strongly to, along with the community's closed solidarity against outside condemnation. Alibis were provided. Bond money was given so freely by both native-pioneer and newly ethnic names that Circuit Judge Hartwell said it was "like taking the census." Mayor A.T. Pace, a traveling auditor for the UMWA, led the bail drive and verbally defended miners, saying he had no apologies to make.[179]

All this made reaction to the situation worse, because it was seen from the outside as a collusion of loyalties that amplified the urban-rural, labor-capital, cosmopolitan-industrial and north-south splits in the country in an age already fearful of "Reds" and other perceived dangers.[180] (Those indicted in the Battle of Blair Mountain coal war were accused of "treason against the state.") The stories presented in testimony and in the press of women and children taking part may have been a factor, too, as if the bigger culture needed to believe that those groups were too demure or innocent to participate in violence. Even the cooperation of races and ethnicities in the mob seemed to heighten reaction.

One scholar seems to suggest that it was the *Chicago Tribune* that resurrected the "Bloody" epithet from the Vendetta days.[181] The paper had no problem making blanket statements. "Herrin is a murderous community," it said. "[C]ivilized opinion of the entire United States convicts them of wholesale murder and perversion of justice, and will punish them by contempt and ostracism from the society of decent people."[182]

(Not all their reporters had a simple view of things. One wrote: "The law abiding element in the county, which probably is in the great majority, appears to be absolutely cowed by a turbulent, reckless, lawless, gun toting minority. Good citizens walk in fear and trembling."[183])

A friend and writer from the American Bottom said to me over lunch recently, "I know it's not what I'm supposed to think or say, but there's been lots worse happen than the Herrin Massacre. How many died? Twenty-three? Look at any aspect of American history and you'll find worse violence than that."

Yet, undeniably, the reaction was not only big but sustained. My mother told the story of how, twenty years after the Massacre, she tried to check into a nice hotel in St. Louis. When the manager saw her address, he said she was from that damned "Bloody Williamson" and that he didn't want her type there. She called her dad, the former Senator Sneed, who talked to the man and set him straight.

In fact, feelings about the event still persist—though not outside the region, for the most part. Having lived in several parts of the country and served in the U.S. Army here and abroad, I can tell you that no one I met had ever heard of Herrin—except one man, a snack truck driver on an army post abroad, who lovingly recounted the entire season of Herrin's 1957 State Championship basketball team. No, the feelings are mostly within the town or at best the region, kept alive by treating history as something that must be whispered. My friend had gone on to say, "It's almost as if pride overlays the supposed shame, as if keeping things secret makes them more important." Can Herrin forgive itself for what happened? Does it want to?

Some have said that the Herrin Massacre is to blame not only for Herrin's decline but also for the union's and even for the coal industry's worsening problems soon to come. But decline was inherent in the system from mechanization, overproduction and a changing market, and it seems now, looking back, that there was no good escape from the issues of 1922. As in classical tragedy, the seeds of the players' destruction were there all along, though their struggles could be impressive and sometimes admirable.

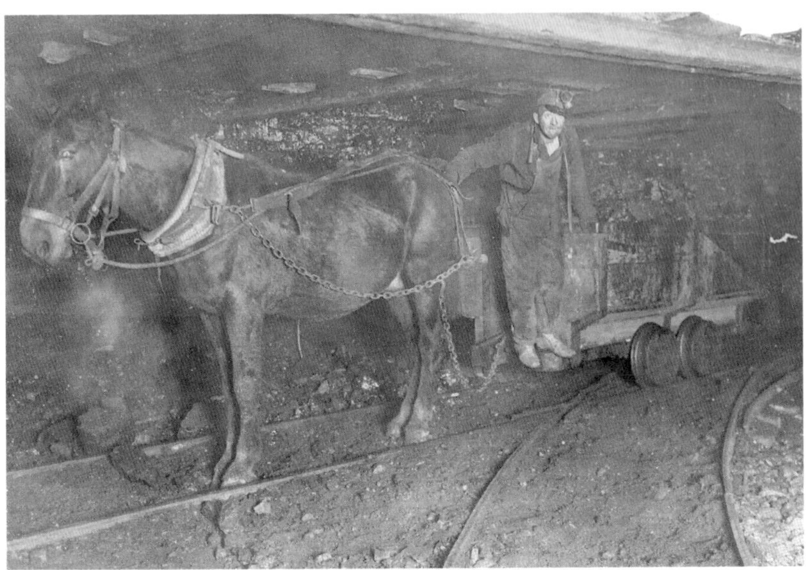

Old school: a mule pulling a coal car, unknown local mine. *Courtesy Williamson County Historical Society.*

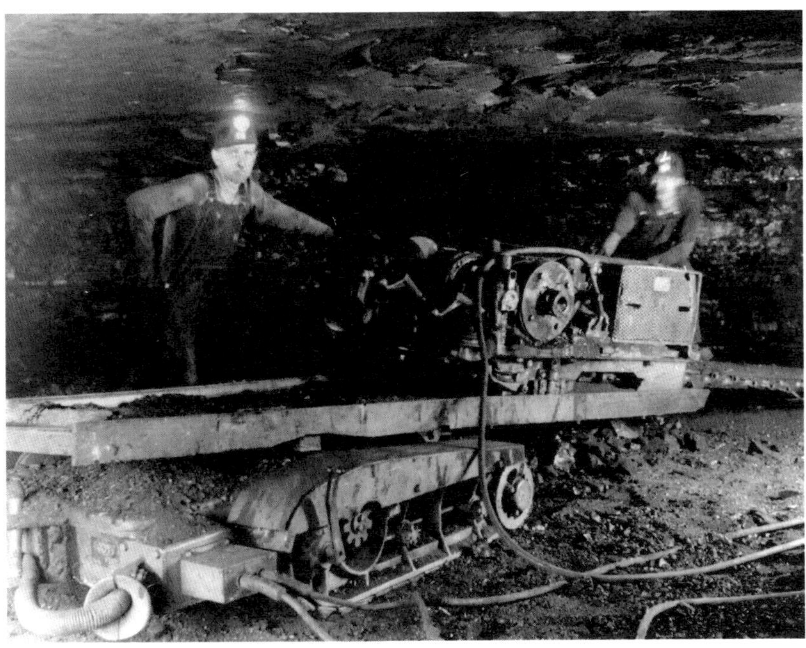

Bell & Zoller Coal Company, No. 1 Mine, Zeigler, 1915. The coming of machines, such as this Joy undercutter, changed employment in the mines forever. *Courtesy Illinois State Geological Survey.*

How aware were they of this, and what did they hope to achieve in their struggles? *The WPA Guide to Illinois* quotes William Allen White, who won the 1923 Pulitzer Prize for writing about labor, on evidence of a "new doctrine" in what had happened in Herrin:

> *Labor is beginning to feel that skill has the same status as property. The right to apply their skill in the place where it will produce value, labor seems to regard as an essential human right. This is astonishing. But we can not ignore it—this belief of the laborer in his right to what he calls his job. He feels that so long as the place where he works is a "going concern" his right to work is exactly upon the same footing as the owner's right to profit.*[184]

It's astonishing to think it wouldn't be so.

I told an acquaintance once that I thought some Southern Illinois miners believed they were working for a kind of British socialism—at least those who became part of the Progressive Miners of America, which split from the UMWA in 1932. The PMA was organized in downstate Illinois, and its differences in ideology with the UMWA helped pull apart the union.[185] My acquaintance scoffed and said there was no comparison.

But as the labor scholar John Laslett has pointed out in a direct comparison between Scottish mines and Illinois District 12 mines, "[T]he commitment which the Lanarkshire miners finally made to the Labour Party in the years between 1918 and 1922 helped materially to transform that party from a minor irritant on the left flank of the Liberals, into the majority party of the British working class. If the UMW had followed a similar course, the political history of the U.S. labor movement might also have been different."

In fact, "the more militant socialists in District 12" did try to propose "financial support for the nascent Illinois Farmer-Labor Party, which seemed then to have a chance of capturing several offices in the state."[186] It was voted down, and more moderate forces took control.

In the long view, it seems that all actions, constructive or malevolent, were futile. Even the British colliers suffered from devastating unemployment and other hardships, from which they never recovered. In the United States, John Lewis went on to "develop…a network of organizers on the International payroll who were assigned to keep track of local and district opposition and to collect potentially damaging information on his opponents." Later there would be more Red scares and baiting and internal blame for Communists "pushing the issue of nationalization of the mines and for pressing for a strike in 1922 in an effort to bankrupt the union."[187]

In the next years after the Massacre, under economic pressure and censure, Herrin's discord spread until it seemed as if all fought all.

CHAPTER 7

WET/DRY WAR

What happened in the years that followed the Massacre can only be described as a brief war of impossibly, ridiculously complicated alliances, one that ended in widespread exhaustion, just as had happened with World War I.

Again, here's the short version: bootlegging, rumrunning gangsters, emboldened by the lack of a single conviction in the Massacre trials and the presence of an already "wide-open" culture, moved in and set up shop on a large scale in Herrin and the surrounding area, which helped the already burgeoning Ku Klux Klan gain a foothold in the county, since they presented themselves as the only law-and-order group willing to enforce Prohibition. When enough Klan and gangsters had killed one another, and the Klan had used up all its financial, legal and political resources, the gangsters were left to slug it out, which they happily did until they, too, took too many losses, and the end of the era came symbolically with the death of one of their leaders who, despite being smart, charismatic and a wily sociopath, became the next-to-last person in the state of Illinois to be hanged.[188]

As one example of the tangled webs of loyalty in town, my grandfather was about this time "of the Baptist faith, a thirty-second degree Mason-Royal Arch and Shriner, [and] a member of the Odd Fellows, K[nights] of P[ythias] and Red Men."[189] More than one of those could have led to Klan membership, but the national Klan often had an anti-union stance (it saw unions as "un-American"), and Sneed had been a miner since he was fourteen and had served most posts in the union available to him, including that of an officer in District 12, whose constitution prohibited Klan membership.

Yet "the men employed at the coal mines constituted probably the largest occupational group in the Williamson County Klan,"[190] and Herrin's Klan newspaper was pro-union.

The Masons were often anti-Catholic, and the Klan claimed that 60 percent of Masons were members, but Masonic leaders denounced the Klan, while the Klan denounced Catholics.[191]

S. Glenn Young's perverse Klan funeral was held in the Baptist church at which Sneed and his family were members (and where I went to vacation Bible school as a boy), but my mom always said that he despised Young and his type as American fascists.

Protestant men often leaned toward wet; their wives leaned dry. Yet Sneed clearly believed in family, civic duty and community-building (a Klan platform). But he was not, I think, a "dry."

In short, as I was reading up on the Klan in Williamson County in this period, I waited on each new page to see my grandfather's name. When I found it, I learned that he was one of six Herrin citizens appointed by a representative of Governor Small to a "Citizens Committee" of "the best citizens of Williamson County who had not been involved in the factional war" to "take leadership in the reconstruction of the county" after the wet-dry war had in effect collapsed the government.[192] But who could have predicted it?

All of which is to say that by 1923 Herrin was ripe for factional strife between people of different religions, ethnicities, cultural traditions, political ideologies, club memberships, loyalties to unionism or family and other factors.

Arthur T. Pace, Herrin mayor in the early 1920s, said of miners in the World War, "Notwithstanding the great number of so-called foreigners, the miners were one hundred per cent Americans [and did their duty]."[193] The mayor doth protest too much. Certainly, when you look at the roster of names who served, it's obvious that families of recent immigrants had done their share. But if there was no issue about how "American" they were, why bring up this "foreigners" business at all?

In truth, the area was sharply subdivided by ethnicity, and fewer than half of foreign-born whites in Herrin in 1920 had become naturalized.[194] There had been a lynching of an Italian miner in Johnston City in 1915 and an anti-Italian riot in Franklin County in 1921. Even within Herrin's Italian community, people knew who was from southern Italy—areas such as Sicily—as opposed to those from northern Italy's Lombardy, especially the town of Cuggiono, west of Milan, where many Herrin Italians were from. And both of those groups had cultures distinct from the Piedmontese—also from northern Italy—whom Herrin native Bill Tonso has called "the other-other Italians."[195]

Many immigrant families had been sharing wine at table for generations if not millennia. Ernest Hemingway says of this time, "In Europe then we thought of wine as something as healthy and normal as food and also as a great giver of happiness and well-being and delight…it was as natural as eating and to me as necessary, and I would not have thought of eating a meal without drinking either wine or cider or beer."[196]

Among the "nativist" stock there were those who drank (some of them heavily; call them sons of the frontier) and those who didn't (often due to fundamentalist Protestantism). And there were people of all creeds who were indifferent to the drinking of alcohol but cared deeply about crime and its effects on business and home values. Others hated more to see vigilantism used as an excuse to abuse ethnic and religious groups.

Many were also eager to correct the rest of America's perceptions of Williamson County, whose people had been portrayed as everything from "Reds" to "fiends whose hands dripped blood."[197] At a mass meeting in Marion in August 1923, "practically every" Protestant minister in the county and many of their parishioners, two thousand strong, gathered in the courthouse yard to demand that officials clean up the liquor, gambling and prostitution.

"It's time to show that we're one hundred per cent American!" shouted Reverend P.H. Glotfelty of the Methodist Church of Herrin.

The Reverend L.M. Lyerle of Carterville shouted, "Mr. Sheriff, Mr. State's Attorney, Mr. Judge, you'd better do your duty. If you don't, something is going to happen, and that little mine trouble out here will be but a drop in the bucket compared to it!"[198]

Sheriff Galligan was famously wet, of course, and from Herrin.[199] Others who were wet (or at least anti-Klan) at the start of the crusade included the state's attorney, the city judge of Herrin, the mayor of Herrin, most of the city police and half of Herrin's city council. Dries included the Williamson County Board of Supervisors and many constables and justices of the peace.[200] Governmental units were pitted against one another in the fight.

A recent doctoral candidate in history at the University of Illinois, Masatomo Ayabe, claims in his dissertation that the Ku Klux Klan in Williamson County in the 1920s was different from the Klans in America after the Civil War and during the civil rights era. Ayabe finds no real ethnic, racial or religious motives in the Williamson County Klan's activities, and he quotes the *St. Louis Post-Dispatch*, which, despite being anti-Klan, said at the time, "The fight…has not been a religious or racial affair. It has been a campaign to 'clean up' Herrin by stopping the open sale of liquor."[201]

"[N]ot a single foreigner or son of foreigners [was] among the casualties of the three-year conflict," Ayabe says.[202]

However, Paul Angle says that "the Italian community in Herrin provided an easy, unresisting target. [T]wenty per cent of Herrin's population…

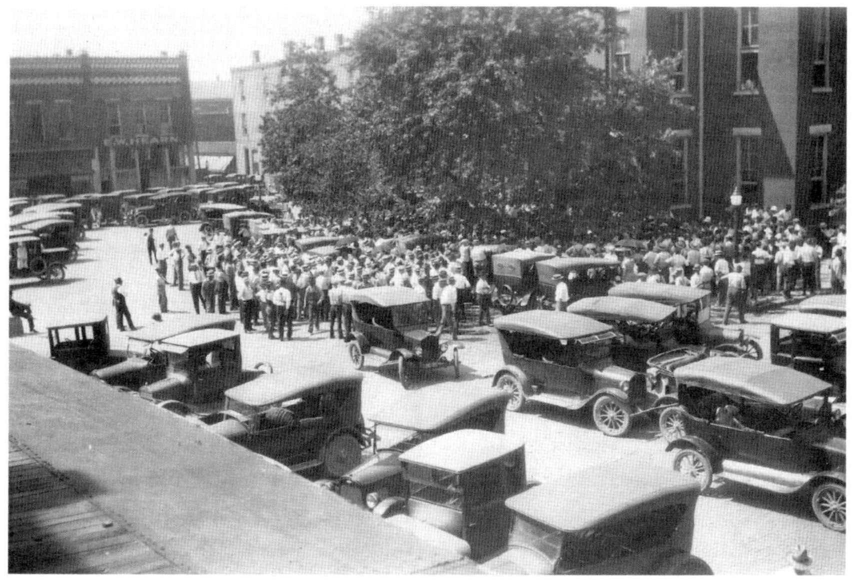

Two thousand dries gather outside wet Sheriff Galligan's office at the Marion Courthouse, August 1923. *Courtesy Williamson County Historical Society.*

[t]hey had prospered from the beginning, and had been accepted by the 'Americans,' yet they were Catholic, 'foreign,' and fond of wine. Some, moreover, had taken to bootlegging after the county went dry [as did a cross section of America, such as the Russian-Jewish Charlie Birger and the native-born Protestant Shelton brothers]. A whipping-boy is a handy fellow to have around, and the Italians of Herrin admirably fitted the part."[203]

Angle also says that "ugly stories of rough treatment, robbery, [and] planted evidence" were so prevalent that the French and Italian consuls protested to the U.S. State Department.[204] And a Williamson County grand jury said in 1924, "We further find that during the so-called raids by the Ku Klux Klan…numerous people were robbed, beaten, abused and in many instances imprisoned secretly without any legal process and wholly without justifiable cause."[205] Several recent acquaintances in Williamson County also say that Ayabe seriously underplays things.[206]

Suffice it to say that during boom times ethnic and religious tensions in Herrin were suppressed, though the town was a "patchwork of native and immigrant blocs" (which did not include African Americans, by the way).[207] Groups had their own neighborhoods, churches, fraternal organizations and even cemeteries, all a kind of semivoluntary segregation that "lessened the potentiality of social disruption."[208]

Drinking was a watershed issue long before the Volstead Act of 1919. "A history of political parties of Williamson County would be incomplete without a reference to the prohibition party, the oldest of all the three parties," says a 1905 publication on Williamson County. Though the dries' national ticket was not organized until 1869, a temperance movement came to the area as early as 1845, "when a traveling temperance lecturer waked the county up as it had never been waked before." A "reformed drunkard named Knowles of Greenville" lectured sometime later; "Knowles wound up by getting $15 and a suit of clothes and then getting gloriously drunk." "The party now counts its followers by the hundred," says the publication.[209]

Even before Prohibition, Herrin and the other towns in the county alternately went wet and dry when one or the other party won an election. Herrin changed its stance four times between 1900 and 1916, a year in which Herrin supposedly had one saloon for every one hundred people.[210]

"Law and Order Leagues" and "Law Enforcement Leagues" had been formed in the early years of the century by "prominent citizens" to eradicate bootlegging and other vice. Herrin's Law and Order League was formed in 1909, Marion's in 1923. The Ku Klux Klan used these groups for its organizational base when it came into the area.[211]

The Klan was already well established in the Midwest on a platform of racism, anti-immigration, anti-Catholicism, anti-Semitism and "nativism," and modeled itself on fraternal organizations that were all the rage—Woodmen, Redmen, Elks, Masons and so on. Millions would join nationwide, and Illinois would become the fifth-biggest Klan membership state, with 83 of its 102 counties having at least one Klan chapter in the 1920s. The Klan made its first public showing in Chicago in 1921, and by the time of the Herrin Massacre, Chicago had 200,000 Klan members. The Klan wouldn't be active in Williamson County until late 1922 and 1923.[212]

Illinois Supreme Court justice W.W. Duncan said, "After 1922 the gunmen and thugs of East St. Louis, St. Louis, Chicago, and elsewhere came to Williamson County believing that this county was a haven for criminals and thieves. These thugs opened up road houses along the roads in our county and sold illicit liquor." Even a non-dry (but later Klansman) said things were "so bad that a woman couldn't go on the streets without being insulted" by drunks lying in the street.[213]

Ayabe believes that "revisionist" histories of the Klan written since the 1980s—his is one of this movement—show that:

> *American right-wing movements…had real, legitimate grievances rather than simply expressing their irrational anger and fear…Focusing on specific local communities, using Klan membership rosters, and sometimes mobilizing statistical techniques,* [scholars] *have shown that Klansmen were ordinary Americans, not different from non-Klansmen in socioeconomic*

> *status. Far from outsiders, Klansmen were often the people who were most interested in local civic affairs.*[214]

In that statement may be the most direct tie from the shame of the Massacre to the violence that came afterward. "Service" to the community, as some defined it, "an expressed willingness to work for civic betterment," was on all lips, especially in the fraternal organizations.[215] Those who wanted to clean things up joined organizations such as the Citizen's Party, the Williamson Anti-Saloon League and the Williamson County Law Enforcement League, which "shared membership with the secret order."[216] "The issue [that superseded other problems] was liquor law enforcement, over which members of the miners' unions [and even political parties] had disagreed among themselves for a long time."[217]

The small war that resulted lasted two years. It wasn't just between actual bootleggers and the "extra-legal vigilantes" of the Klan; it also pulled in amateur winemakers, saloon owners, innocent bystanders, the pious—everyone—and when it was over nineteen people had been killed. The National Guard came to the county five times, and a kind of "anarchy" reigned. The attempt to remove the "blot" from the good name of the county after the Massacre made it a "more lawless and nationally notorious community."[218]

S. Glenn Young first came to Williamson County as a federal Prohibition officer, from the East St. Louis division, in August 1920.[219] In the first big action in the county since the start of Prohibition, he raided the European Hotel in Herrin and confiscated 450 gallons of whiskey, 150 gallons of brandy, 100 gallons of port wine and more, valued at $40,000 (now close to $500,000). Manager Joe Dell'Era was arrested and fined $1,000; this was considered part of the cost of doing business. Smaller bootleggers and "soft-drink parlor" operators would be fined $50 or $100, and life went on as before.[220] Young left.

City police and the sheriff's office conducted several raids (including the first done in conjunction with the Klan in June 1923), but Williamson County "remained a wet paradise."[221] A big federal raid—also assisted by the Klan—on September 7, 1923, netted 1,200 cases of beer. That night fires broke out in a home and in the grocery of two Herrin Klan leaders—the first violence in the "war."[222]

Young was back about November 1, 1923.[223] How he got there is a bit of a mystery, and he deliberately clouded his background, in part because he had no authority for much of what he did: by that time he was not a federal agent but a "freelance detective."[224] After a series of visits to various "parlors" and roadhouses to collect evidence, Young and the Klan looked for authority from anyone willing to offer it—finally getting it, in a visit to Washington, from

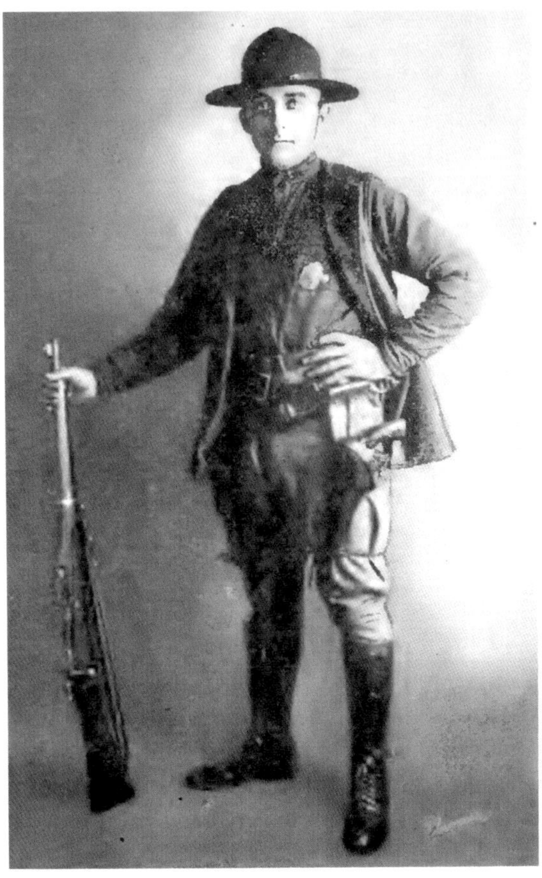

Seth Glenn Young (1886–1925), federal raider turned moral crusader and then dictator.

Prohibition Commissioner Roy Haynes, who agreed to send a federal agent along to make things legal.[225] Their first big raid was on December 22, 1923. Two more followed within two weeks, and they made 256 arrests, including Otis Clark (a primary defendant in the Herrin Massacre trials), Ora Thomas, Joe Dell'Era (again), the brother of labor leader Hugh Willis and bootlegger Charlie Birger.[226]

Whatever this war was, it wasn't a quiet in-house cleaning. It was theatre from the start and could often look like farce.[227] When a deputy from the sheriff's office (wet) arrested State Representative Wallace Bandy (dry and a Klansman) in his Marion home for having a bottle of "white mule"—moonshine—S. Glenn Young stepped in to claim that he'd confiscated the booze earlier and left it with Mrs. Bandy for safekeeping. Then Young got in an argument over it with a Marion restaurateur, and the man was beaten. When Young showed up in court to defend himself for this battery, he and his men were heavily armed, including with a "portable machine gun they used on raids." Despite Young's lying under oath that he was working directly for Prohibition Commissioner Roy Haynes,[228] the jury returned "almost immediately" with an acquittal, and the crowd clapped and cheered.[229]

Young had the support of what he said were seven thousand Klan members in Williamson and Franklin Counties. He continued to raid with deputized legions (including the likes of State Representative Bandy) sworn in by federal agents only nominally in charge.[230]

Even Sheriff Galligan couldn't ignore him, especially when Adjutant General Black came to town with National Guard troops, eager to make up for what many had said was the Guard's failure to act during the Herrin

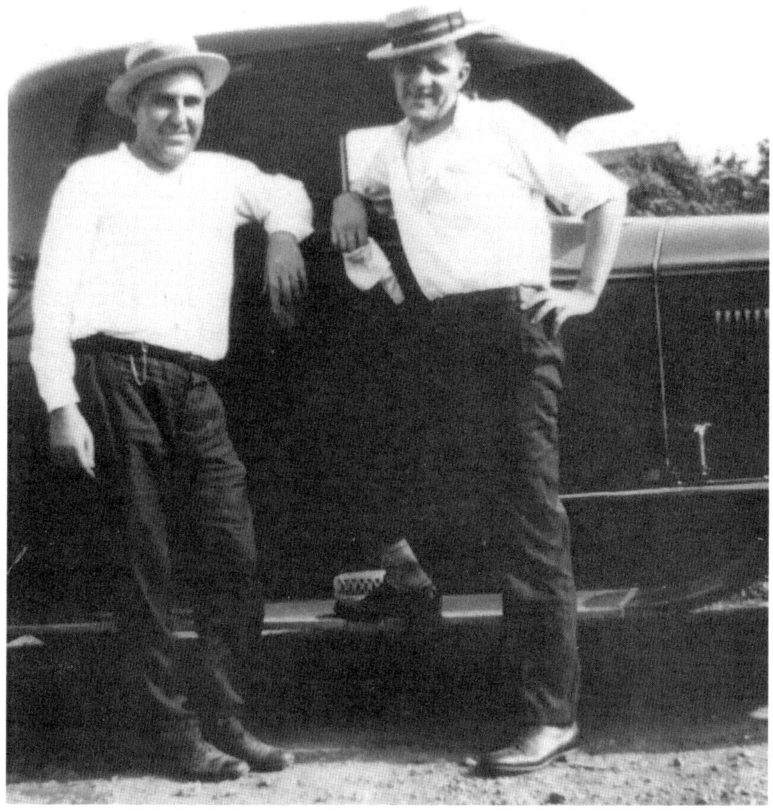

Two of the Shelton brothers: Big Earl, *left*, and Carl. *Courtesy Taylor Pensoneau.*

Massacre. Galligan had his chief deputy call together eighty-three of the area's saloonkeepers and bootleggers at the Rome Club in Herrin. The deputy told the men to find some other line of work, since Young and the Klan were applying for injunctions in federal court to have them shut down. Three agreed.[231]

In and around all this, real gangsters were rising in power and visibility. Carl, Earl and Bernie Shelton had already made the move from Wayne County, Illinois, by way of East St. Louis, and just after Young returned to Williamson County as a freelancer, Charlie Birger was wounded in a shootout in his Halfway saloon. Ora Thomas—a Herrin bootlegger and sometime deputy who also headed the Knights of the Flaming Circle, a secret order dedicated to keeping vice rolling (and similar in name to the Knights of the Golden Circle, the pro-South Civil War society)—had brought one member of the St. Louis gang Egan's Rats to Birger's joint, and Birger killed him.[232]

Young had his own problems. He was disavowed by the Prohibition commissioner, the county was told to stop all "citizens' raids," the feds said there would be no more assistance in the county and Young was named in five criminal warrants that included assault and robbery on alleged bootleggers and members of the Flaming Circle.[233] The Klan that supported him found itself increasingly in a position of defying elected officials, such as Sheriff Galligan, and supporting what amounted to a vigilante with no authority.

Despite this, by 1924 Young claimed that Williamson County was "the cleanest in the United States" and that he still held influence: the Herrin police, for instance, "from the chief…on down" was under Klan control. He vowed to get the place "100% perfect" before he left, and he lied (again) by implication that he was still a government officer. The Herrin police raided nearly every day and brought in not only liquor violators but also others they thought were morally corrupt, such as "men and women in night clothes" arrested at "petting parties at the Aberdeen Hotel."[234]

The biggest raids were on February 1–2, 1924. Police Magistrate Abe Hicks of Herrin and Justice of the Peace John Arms of Johnston City issued state warrants executed by 1,200 to 1,500 deputized citizens. They raided fifty-one sites, most in Johnston City, Colp and Dewmaine, and arrested about 130. The prisoners were taken to Benton on a train paid for by the Klan and were marched at gunpoint through the streets to be humiliated, but some of them were laughing. Only after the fact were federal warrants issued

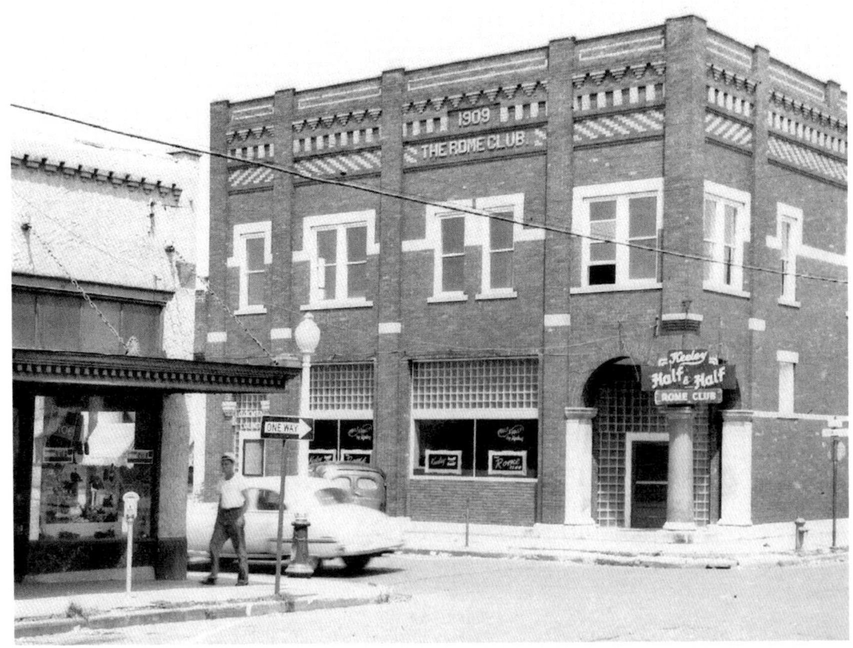

Rome Club, about 1950. Photo was taken by Paul Angle while researching his book *Bloody Williamson*. *Courtesy Chicago History Museum.*

and the prisoners arrested on them. In the days that followed, complaints were filed by victims of the raiders' illegal entry, abuse and looting.[235] Yet there were more raids.

Violent retaliation, "the civil war so many had feared," finally followed. According to Angle, it started when Sheriff Galligan learned of a meeting of anti-Klansmen at the Rome Club on Friday night, February 8. He walked in on it with his deputy, John Layman, and told the men that they must remain peaceful. Someone else burst in and said the Klan was coming, and everybody pulled guns. It turned out to be Herrin police chief John Ford and policeman Harold Crain, both pro-Klan. They were disarmed and held at gunpoint.

The "anti-Klan" group was in fact pro-bootlegger and included Carl and Earl Shelton, Ora Thomas and others. Layman, Galligan's deputy, grabbed Ford, the police chief, by the hair and shouted, "You damn dirty Ku Klux son-of-a-bitch, we've got you where we want you!"

In the scuffle that followed, someone shot Layman in the chest. Galligan grabbed the two Klan policemen and took them to Murphysboro—partly an arrest and partly for their own safety from a lynch mob. Layman was taken to Herrin Hospital.[236]

What really happened in that Rome Club stairwell, as with so many incidents in Herrin history, is hard to determine, given factional points of view and alibis produced. Angle was informed in his writing by Herrin editor Hal Trovillion, who was hugely anti-Klan. Ayabe, on the other hand, is sympathetic to the law enforcement origins of the Williamson County Klan[237] but portrays their corruption over time. In any case, Ayabe's version is also understanding of Galligan, but for different reasons, as follows.

Policeman Albert Jones was leaving a meeting of his union local at the Rome Club when an armed group came in. They said, "Galligan sent us and we're going to have a little party." Albert Jones, a Klansman, called Thomas Thornton, another Klansman, who called Police Chief John Ford.

When Ford and Harold Crain got to the Rome Club, they were set upon by the eighty to ninety men Galligan had called together to deputize. Galligan did this on the suggestion of the governor, who had told him it was his duty to maintain order. Unfortunately, Galligan had by then lost all public support except from those in the Flaming Circle, so it was them he called for help.

When Harold Crain was thrown downstairs, he was caught by Deputy Layman, and when someone jumped toward Crain to knife him, Layman pushed Crain aside and caught the bullet intended for Crain.[238]

About this time, Constable Caesar Cagle, who'd switched sides in the war from bootlegger to Klansman, was at a social at the Masonic Temple across from Herrin Hospital. His eleven-year-old son was walking home from the Hippodrome Theatre and was stopped by a man outside the Rome Club, who said to go get his father. When the boy told his father, Caesar Cagle started for the Rome Club, but near the Jefferson Hotel, twenty or more men met him, butt-stroked him, fractured his skull and then shot him three times. He, too, was taken to the Herrin Hospital, where anti-Klan Layman also lay wounded.[239]

The Klan swarmed to Herrin. Young arrived within thirty minutes from Marion and put Klan patrols on the streets and roadblocks at entry points to the city, ostensibly to look for Cagle's murderers, whom the Klan said were Sheriff Galligan, Herrin mayor "Mage" Anderson, Ora Thomas and others.

Meanwhile several of the men they were looking for had barricaded themselves in the Herrin Hospital, run by Dr. J.T. Black, who let bootleggers hang out there so often that the hospital had been called "a veritable barracks" of the Knights of the Flaming Circle. When Young and several hundred Klansmen demanded to come in to serve warrants, Black refused. Again, as with the Herrin Massacre, accounts vary as to who fired the first shot. Angle and Ayabe both say that the Klan shot first, while the self-serving *Life and Exploits of S. Glenn Young* notes that it was those inside the hospital. Hundreds of shots broke the windows facing the street, and patients dove off beds to the floor. The National Guard showed up at 3:00 a.m., one hour after the shooting started. No one was killed, but a boy who had an appendectomy that afternoon died the next day, "undoubtedly from the shock of the night's events."[240]

Though twenty National Guard troops were now in town, Young, with no legal authority (and who wasn't even *from* Herrin), took over city hall, calling himself the acting chief of police. In this he profited by the actions of his foe Sheriff Galligan, who'd taken the real police chief to jail in Murphysboro.

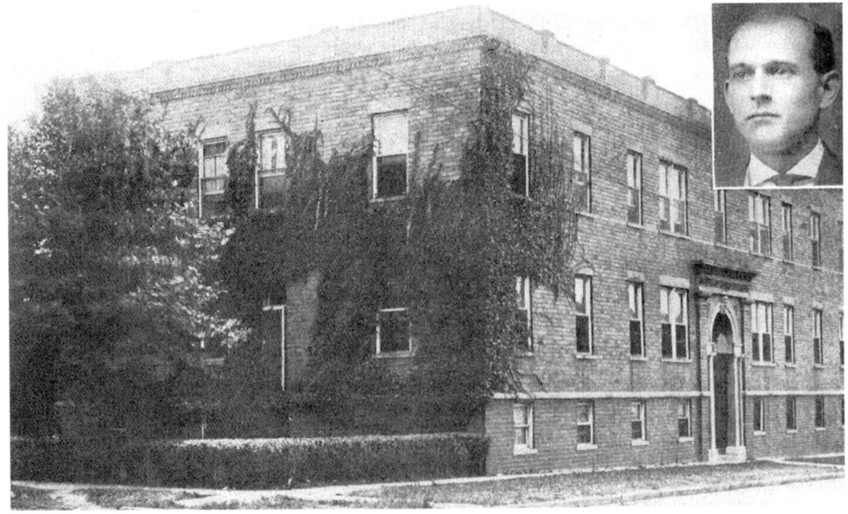

Herrin Hospital and the sopping-wet Dr. J.T. Black. S. Glenn Young and the Klan opened fire on Black's hospital on February 8, 1924.

Young had more than twenty anti-Klansmen arrested for the murder of Caesar Cagle, including Sheriff Galligan, Mayor Anderson, Hugh Willis and Special Deputy Ora Thomas. Young sat in the city judge's chair, wearing his Smokey-bear hat and pearl-handled pistols, and said (at least to the sheriff), "I find you guilty of the murder of Caesar Cagle." Prisoners were given no chance to make bail and were thrown in the basement of the Elks Club. Galligan was refused medicine for a recurring fever.[241]

The Klan held a funeral that Sunday for Caesar Cagle, perhaps the largest in the county's history to that point, at the First Baptist Church in Herrin. As many as five thousand people passed the flag-draped coffin with its blanket of white flowers and KKK letters in green flowers, next to a "fiery cross" of red roses. The funeral procession headed for Carterville, hometown of the Cagles, and Sheriff Galligan and four of his "special deputies" who'd been arrested were forced to join in. But the Klansmen driving those cars turned off and headed for Urbana instead, to put the five in jail there for "safekeeping." The prisoners were treated "roughly." Galligan, who believed he was about to be lynched, begged for one of their guns to kill himself. He fell out of the car; he said he'd resign and go to Cuba. (He was retrieved from Urbana two days later by Coroner McCown, Herrin's acting sheriff.)[242]

On the Monday after that weekend, Doc Black wrote the governor a quick note to beg for martial law, even though there were by that time nearly 1,400 Guardsmen in town (again) with fixed bayonets and machine guns

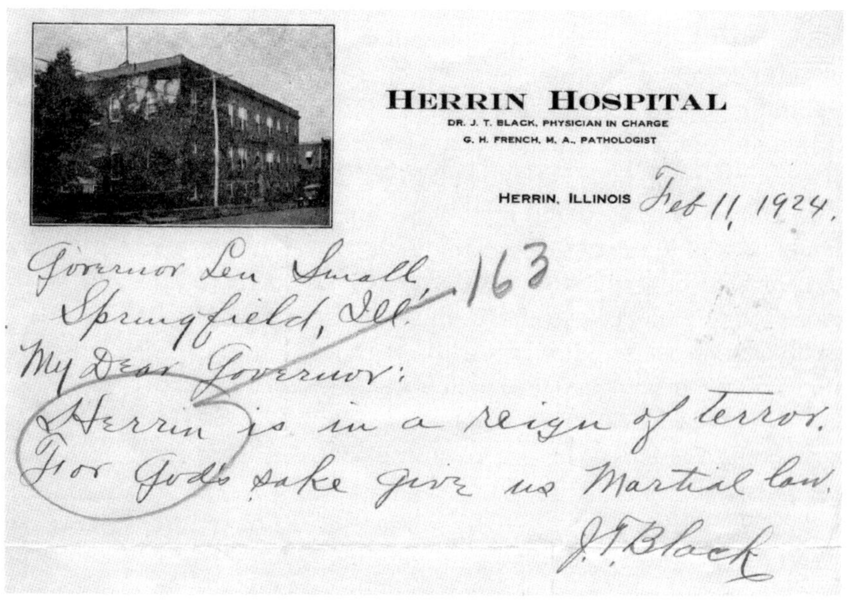

HERRIN HOSPITAL
DR. J. T. BLACK, PHYSICIAN IN CHARGE
G. H. FRENCH, M. A., PATHOLOGIST

HERRIN, ILLINOIS Feb 11 1924.

Governor Len Small, 163
Springfield, Ill.
My Dear Governor:
Herrin is in a reign of terror.
For God's sake give us Martial law.
J.T. Black

Doc Black's SOS note to the governor. Chances are he had a drink before he wrote it. *Courtesy Abraham Lincoln Presidential Library & Museum (ALPLM).*

mounted at strategic intersections.[243] (Martial law would be the assumption of government by the military, not just occupation by troops.) Newspapermen "flooded to Herrin" again, and the *Chicago Tribune* said that the county's "mob spirit…has merely broken in another form, and under other leaders."[244]

Within three days, all who had been arrested were released when a coroner's jury of leading citizens of Herrin placed the blame for Cagle's murder on "one Shelton, described as tall and slim, and one Shelton, described as heavy set and sleepy eyed." Carl and Earl Shelton were not among those in custody. Earl had a grudge against Cagle, who'd pistol-whipped him in a raid on Shelton's roadhouse at the start of that year.

Glenn Young left Herrin for a while after the coroner's jury and after the National Guard commander made it clear that Young had no power and must disarm. The "Citizens Committee" on which my grandfather served with thirty or forty others, including A.K. Elles, O.W. Lyerla and Charles Murrah, met to broker a deal between Klan and anti-Klan factions to return working government to the county.

A county grand jury returned forty-eight indictments in the events leading to Cagle's death, most against Klan raiders who had acted illegally. A grand jury of the Herrin City Court in a similar finding returned ninety-nine indictments, fifty-five counts against Young alone, including "parading with arms, false imprisonment, conspiracy, kidnapping, assault with attempt to murder, assault with deadly weapons, falsely assuming an office, robbery, larceny, riot, and malicious mischief."[245]

Young didn't help things when he acted arrogantly at the U.S. District Court in Danville, which met at the same time to try those arrested in the liquor raids. There Young taunted Charlie Birger, and the scene nearly ended in disaster. (Birger, among many convicted of the 178 brought to trial, got one year in jail and $2,500 in fines. Ora Thomas also went to jail.)[246]

Young was about to be cut loose from the local Klan payroll, but he still had his followers. One to three thousand Klan supporters rallied at the Christian Church in Herrin on March 18 and staged a "protest parade" after the grand jury released its findings. Many of Herrin's Italians "fled to Carbondale for safety." Afterward, Klan supporters cheerfully, laughingly, signed bonds for the indicted, which had been set at $2.5 million in an attempt to bankrupt their organization.

The Klan swept Herrin city, township, school and Williamson County elections in March and April 1924, and on April 8, a large cross was burned next to city hall. It was lit by Glenn Young, who said, "[W]ho says we can't burn a fiery cross in Herrin[?]"

It's a measure of Young's understanding of his own position, though, that he next took a job offered by the Illinois KKK as the kleagle, or head, of the East St. Louis district, which was having problems. He left

Williamson County at the end of April, declaring it "the cleanest in the entire state."

He couldn't stay away, though, and returned on May 1 for a big Klan barbecue and initiation rite in a field one mile south of Herrin, where two thousand cars were parked that day. He went on to Klan speaking gigs in Centralia, Oklahoma City, Equality, Marion and Belleville.[247]

On May 23, he and his wife left a Klan meeting in Harrisburg, stopped for lunch in Marion and may have stopped in Herrin, where Art Newman, a gangster, said that Young announced he was headed for East St. Louis to clean it up, to a crowd that included the Shelton brothers. As Young and his wife drove through the Okaw River bottoms in Clinton County, men in a Dodge touring sedan opened fire on Young's Lincoln, hitting Young in the knee and blinding his wife.[248]

Klansmen in Herrin again donned their tin stars and searched cars entering town throughout the night, looking for the shooters. Though I can't imagine why, the Dodge came roaring up about ten o'clock the next morning. Shots were exchanged, and the car was stopped. Jack Skelcher was killed and thrown from the car, and Charlie Briggs was hit in the leg and tried to run and fight. Both were associates of the Sheltons and had long criminal records.

When the usual coroner's jury convened, witnesses were uncooperative, and the usual verdict was returned: the dead man died "from gunshot wounds at the hands of parties unknown."[249]

The Sheltons turned themselves in on June 7—they were still indicted for the murder of Caesar Cagle—and at a preliminary hearing in Clinton County, where the Young shooting had occurred, S. Glenn Young identified them and Charlie Briggs as his assailants. Fifty deputies with shotguns kept order for the "biggest [and certainly most heavily armed] crowd in Carlyle's history."[250] Everyone walked on bond, and a "war of charges and counter charges and arrests and counter arrests, which sometimes reached the point of absurdity," ensued, making each side harden against the other.[251]

Young, in Marion shortly afterward to post bond for a concealed weapons charge filed by Ora Thomas, cursed the clerk and acted combatively. The next morning, Sheriff Galligan saw Young driving with his gang around the Marion square, leaned from his office and taunted him, "Hello, Young!" Young stopped the car and yelled back, "Come out here and say that, you dirty crook!"

Tensions heightened quickly. Klansmen sent 147 telegrams begging Governor Small to send the Guard or to do something about the sheriff and his bootlegging, ex-convict deputies. He refused. The Sheltons were set free at the Herrin City Court on their Cagle murder charges without trial when State's Attorney Duty said that the one witness had disappeared and after

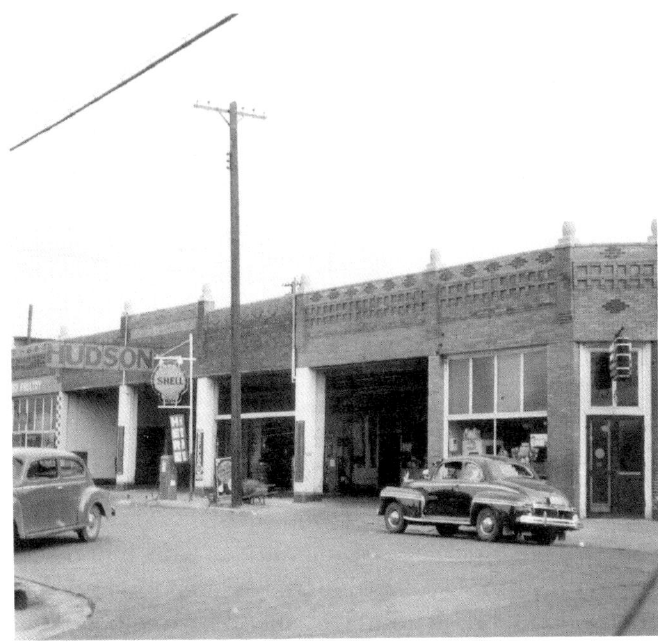

John Smith Garage in Herrin, about 1951. On August 30, 1924, a shootout here left six dead. Another wounded man died later. *Photo by Paul Angle. Courtesy Chicago History Museum.*

Tim Cagle, father of the murdered man, begged that the case be dropped. Tim admitted that he (Tim) had been involved in the Bloody Vendetta and wished that all fighting in the county would stop. "[W]e have all made mistakes on both sides, let us stop where we are, be men in a country, the greatest country on earth," he said.[252]

As court released, a man named Buck Skelcher came up to State's Attorney Duty. The car that had been used in the Young shooting, and in which his brother Jack Skelcher was killed by Klansmen at the roadblock, was being held at the John H. Smith Garage in Herrin. Buck wanted it. Duty told Sheriff Galligan to pick it up and take it to Marion first to check if it was stolen.

Galligan took his usual deputized cronies with him, including Ora Thomas and the Sheltons, to the pro-Klan garage, instead of official deputies the Klan had approved. When the garage workers didn't move fast enough for their liking, the sheriff and his deputies began to curse and beat them. A passerby, Chester Reid, waved his handkerchief and said, "Don't do that, boys." Three Klansmen drove up, too, and the sheriff's men disarmed them and put them against a wall. One of the Sheltons fractured the skull of Harry Herrin. Another four Klansmen drove up, and a gunfight broke out.

Later, of course, no one could say who started shooting first, but six died and five were wounded (one of those died later). The coroner's jury even had to puzzle out if State's Attorney Duty, Judge Bowen and Dr. Black were present. (One of the few witnesses was Mrs. Chester Reid, Black's sister, who watched her husband get killed.) Black's alibi was that he'd been having dinner with the Sheltons' lawyer in East St. Louis at the time, and the jury didn't include the others in the report. They recommended John Smith be held for Reid's murder, while two of the dead men had killed each other, and the other three—naturally—died "at the hands of parties unknown."[253]

The usual tit-for-tat resulted. Duty issued warrants on eleven Klansmen for murder, while the Herrin police magistrate issued twenty-one warrants against anti-Klansmen. For the third time in eight months, the Guard came to Herrin and averted disaster, but even they got swept into the argument. Ora Thomas paraded in a car past the Smith garage with his girl, which a military officer called "a silly performance" and told him to get out of town. State's Attorney Duty, who was anti-Klan, insisted Major Davis search two churches, the Masonic Temple and a grocery store for guns. Davis waited a day to do it, angering Duty. When Adjutant General Black subsequently said he planned to withdraw his troops, Duty publicly accused him and the governor of being Klansmen.[254]

Members of the local Klan became just as belligerent. Williamson County men began to raid in Jackson and Franklin Counties, which was resented deeply. Four sometime members were arrested: one for transporting a stolen car across a state line, the other three in a bank robbery in Pope County. S. Glenn Young, who'd been convalescing in Atlanta, made a threatening show of checking into the Ly-Mar Hotel in Herrin to give bond in Benton under federal indictments.

The next day, he was kicked out of the Klan by Illinois Grand Dragon Charles G. Palmer for his "inordinate craving for personal publicity… ostentatious displays of firearms and braggadocio [and a tendency to] shoot at the drop of a hat, and give utterance to the most incendiary thoughts." It was the beginning of a perception shift. People began to abandon the Klan, including new Herrin police chief A.M. Walker and his son Harry, the assistant chief.

Young came to Herrin again in October and beat up two men in two weeks, and for several months he and his supporters conducted raids in and around Herrin. (They were deputized by local constables, but the Herrin jail began refusing their prisoners, and Arlie Boswell, a state's attorney and former supporter, refused to prosecute.) In November, Klan leaders offered Young $1,000 to leave the county for good. Young agreed and planned to move to Florida and give up "law enforcement." But local Klansmen who felt bad about his wife's blindness continued to invite him to meetings and give him money, and Young decided to make Williamson County home.[255]

On October 11, 1924, Sheriff Galligan made Ora Thomas—Young's "archenemy"—his personal deputy. Young and Thomas hated each other even more than average, and Thomas reputedly said, on January 23, 1925, to some Cairo policemen, "It is just a question of time until I will have to kill Young, and when I do, I know they will kill me."[256]

The very next afternoon, Young and Thomas had an argument in Herrin. That night, Thomas finished serving as bailiff of the Herrin City Court and walked down Park Avenue with other officials. Someone shot toward them and hit a concrete pole, and they hid behind parked cars.

S. Glenn Young was nearby in a restaurant frequented by Klansmen and came out with others to see what had happened. He and his group went into the European Hotel, but it was an anti-Klan establishment, and they left quickly. Then Young went back in to the Canary Cigar Store adjacent to the hotel lobby to harangue a union miner and anti-Klansman he thought had been spreading rumors that Young had been one of the strikebreakers at the Lester mine.

When Ora Thomas came in to see what the angry argument was about, at least one other man was watching Young and his victim. Young turned around, saw Thomas with his hand in his pocket or his overcoat and said, "Don't pull that gun, Ora!"

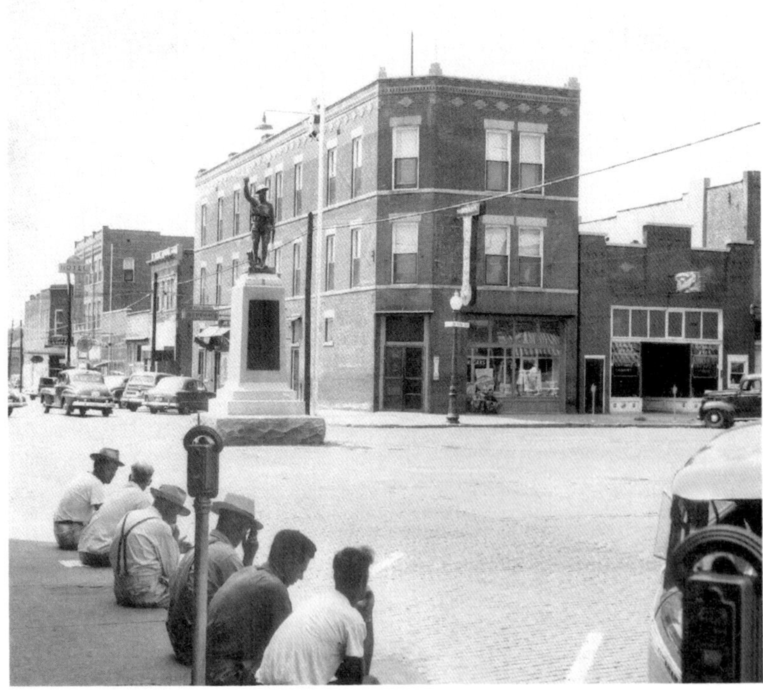

European Hotel, about 1951, where S. Glenn Young and Ora Thomas were killed on January 24, 1925. The *Doughboy* statue was dedicated on September 6, 1927. The hotel building burned down in 1998. *Photo by Paul Angle. Courtesy Chicago History Museum.*

The store erupted in gunfire. Ora Thomas managed to empty his gun; Young got off only two shots. Thomas was shot between the eyes. Young was shot twice in the chest, and one of those went through his heart. They both died in the store. One of Young's guards lay dead in the doorway, and another was dead on the sidewalk outside. The usual cacophony of voices in the aftermath made it impossible to tell if there were other shooters. The coroner's jury ruled that Young's two guards died by the hands of parties unknown.[257]

Inexplicably, neither the Herrin police nor the sheriff showed up that night. A *Chicago Tribune* reporter evidently tipped off the governor, who sent troops for the fourth time in one year. Five thousand people came to Ora Thomas's funeral at his home on January 27. Two days later, anywhere from ten to forty thousand people passed S. Glenn Young's casket before his funeral at the First Baptist Church.

He'd been dressed in the purple robe of a Klan kleagle—though he'd been fired from that job—and his blind wife sat stroking his face while at least four Protestant ministers eulogized him. Afterward, the funeral procession formed up with two hundred hooded Klansmen on foot and six more mounted on horses in Klan regalia. Five hundred cars followed. A cross was burned at his mausoleum in a Klan burial ritual. Armed men guarded the tomb in the Herrin cemetery for several nights.[258]

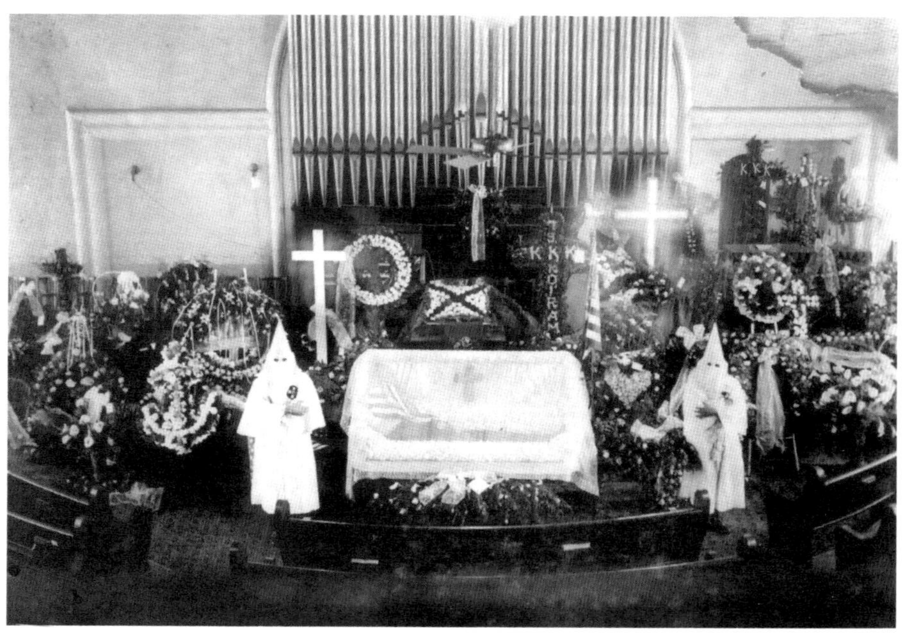

S. Glenn Young lying in state in the old First Baptist Church, 1925. He fought the law and the law won, sort of. *Courtesy Herrin City Library.*

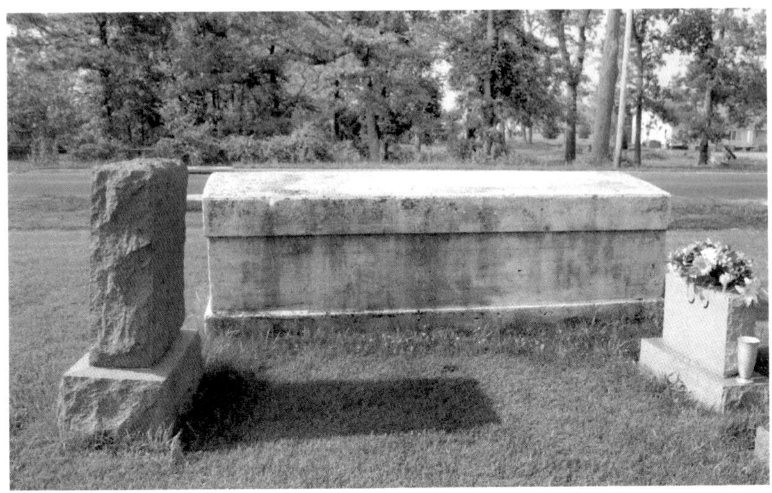

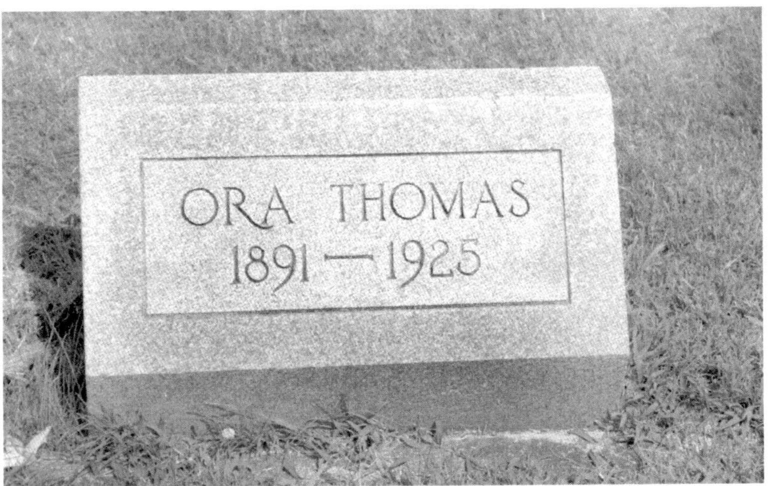

Insult to injury: the tomb of S. Glenn Young and the grave of Ora Thomas lie within a few hundred yards of each other at the Herrin Cemetery. *Photos by the author.*

The press eulogized Young in other ways. The *Belleville News-Democrat* called him "a subnormal personality, with an abnormal psychology under the psychosis of a moron."[259] He was under seventy-three indictments when he died. Ora Thomas was under thirteen.

Though Mayor Anderson tried to assert that this event meant the end of Herrin's "troubles," tensions ran high enough in the months after the gunfight that Hal Trovillion, working with Presbyterian minister Meeker of Herrin, brought in a Mississippi evangelist named Harold S. Williams to "bring God back to Herrin." The first revival meeting was held on May 24,

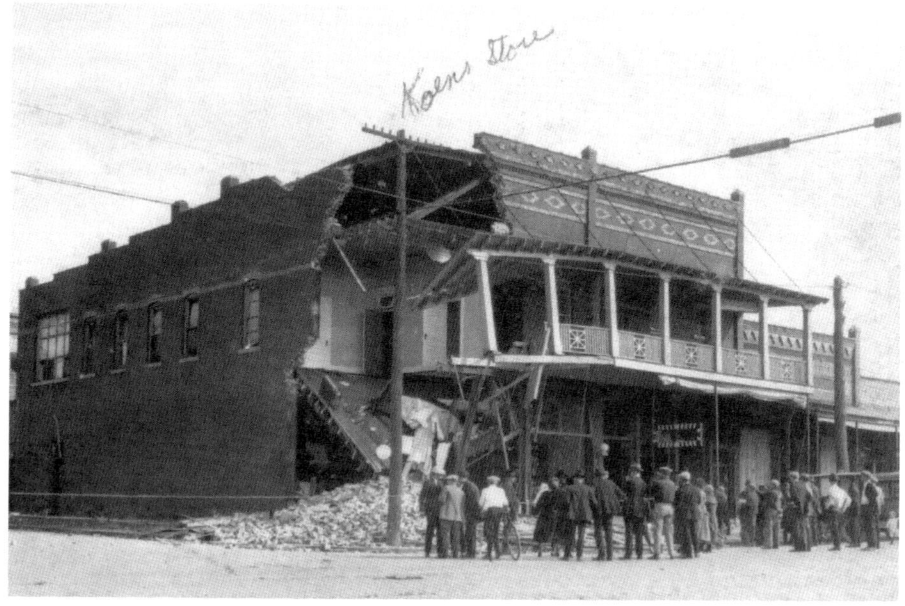

Fowler's Grocery Store stood where the post office is now. Anti-Klansmen bombed Harry Fowler and his wife out of their bed on March 9, 1926. *Courtesy French Studio, Ltd.*

1925, for thousands in the Herrin High gym. For six weeks, businesses closed daily for prayer meetings. Many vowed to change their wicked ways. During his "Officers of the Law Night" meeting, Williams asked the five thousand present to recognize Sheriff Galligan as "the symbol of law and order in Williamson County. The audience rose and cheered, and several hundred men, including some of [his] inveterate enemies, pressed forward to shake his hand."[260]

Williams's visit had a visible, calming effect on behavior in town. In addition, in the middle of the revival the *Herrin Semi-Weekly Herald*, a Klan newspaper, went bankrupt and closed. The Klan's reputation worsened when more members were arrested for armed robbery, bribery, assault, murder (of Otis Clark, the Massacre defendant), rape and more. The average citizen's taste for conflict was diminishing, and everyone, even its local leaders, thought the Klan was effectively dead.[261]

But someone kept the fight alive. On the night of March 9, 1926, an explosion destroyed the grocery store and home of Harry O. Fowler, an admitted Klansman. The blast blew the Fowlers out of bed, broke windows two blocks away and collapsed a floor of the building into the street. The Fowler's son, Glenn, had been a "lieutenant" of S. Glenn Young. The bombing seemed to shake up everyone on both sides, and another community push was made for peace.[262]

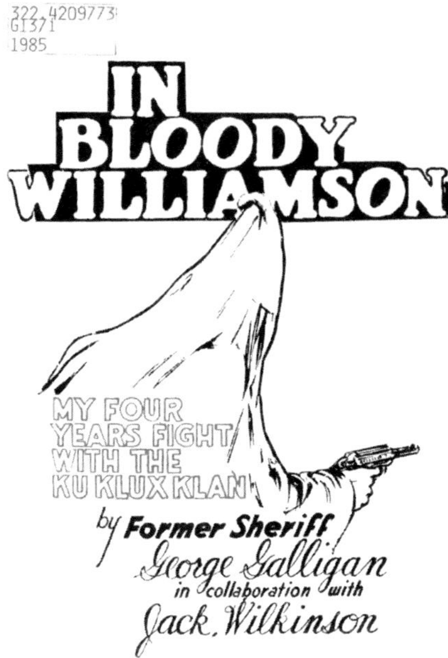

Left: Garish cover of George Galligan's book, co-written with his chief deputy.

Below: Masonic Temple, site of the "election-day riot" of April 13, 1926, in which three wets and three dries were killed by gunfire. *Courtesy the* Southern Illinoisan.

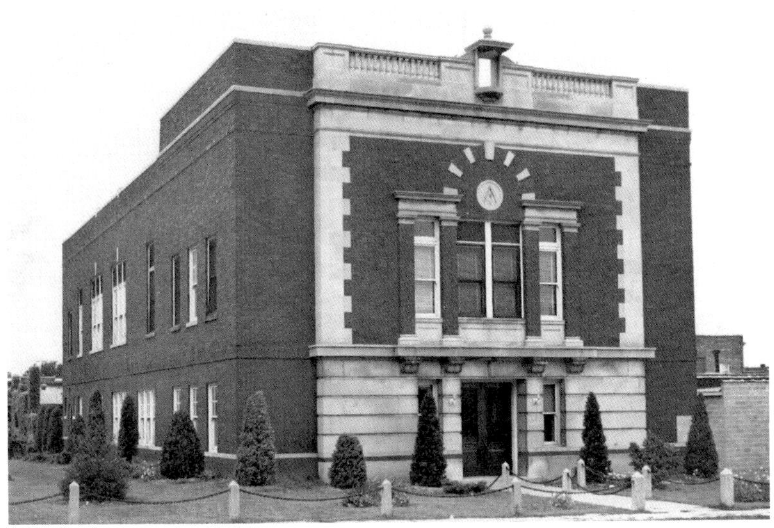

On April 10, the grocery store of mayoral candidate Marshall McCormack, stockholder in the defunct Klan paper and former Klansman, was bombed with dynamite. McCormack was running against the Klan's candidate, and the Herrin Fire Department, with its pro-Klan chief, arrived on the scene slowly.[263]

In April 1926, however, a series of township, school board, city, county and state elections were held, and in Herrin the Klan's preferred candidates were getting the votes. (Outside Herrin Township, Klan candidates didn't do well.) Both Klan and anti-Klan voters believed that "the election would decide the future of Williamson County before the curious eyes of the nation."[264]

Sheriff Galligan again deputized a large number of men to prevent violence at the polls, but they—again—included the Sheltons, Charlie Briggs (who'd been in the car that shot at Young and his wife) and "Blackie" Arms, a well-known gangster. On April 13, John Smith, a poll watcher and owner of the garage where the shootout had occurred six months earlier, challenged a longtime nun of Herrin for proof of citizenship. He was pistol-whipped by one of Galligan's deputies. At 2:30 p.m., gunmen shot up the Smith garage. Smith was present, but no one was injured. Within the hour, a full-on battle developed, with one hundred or more anti-Klan men shooting into the garage. My grandfather Sneed saw it happen from his office window and called for the National Guard, who arrived before another hour had passed.[265]

Twenty minutes after they got to town, three cars pulled up to the Masonic Temple, polling place for the fourth ward, where some Klan supporters lived. Gunmen got out and walked toward John Ford, now one of several Klan deputy constables meant to keep order. Accounts (again) vary, but almost certainly the anti-Klan men opened fire first. Three on each side were killed, including Harlan Ford (brother of John Ford) and Charlie Briggs.

Though it's called the "election-day riot," the attack was planned and carried out by gangsters who knew the Sheltons and Charlie Birger. Still, the coroner's jury attributed the deaths to gunshot wounds "at the hands of parties unknown." In nineteen Klan-war deaths from February 1924 to April 1926, no one had been punished.[266]

The National Guard left three months later in July.

The end of the Herrin Klan came officially when the Illinois Klan grand dragon arrived in Williamson County on August 7, 1926, and paid off the local Klan's debts, a symbolic act that "announced that the Invisible Empire had withdrawn from Williamson County."[267] Its stated mission had been law enforcement, but many of its members acted criminally. It was used to try to "dry out" the county and especially Herrin, but within five years of its founding, many of its members were working with bootleggers: Marshall McCormack (mayor of Herrin), Arlie Boswell (state's attorney) and George Bell (coroner) were all former Klansmen sentenced to terms in the penitentiary for conspiracy to violate the National Prohibition Act.[268] Boswell, according to gangster Art Newman, had a hand in the election day attack, too, though he was not investigated or prosecuted for it.[269]

CHAPTER 8

HOOLIGANS

The dissolution of the pro–law enforcement Klan in the summer of 1926 left Herrin and the rest of the county to the Shelton brothers and Charlie Birger. By all accounts, Herrin blew "wide-open" again as if the Klan had never been. Liquor was everywhere, along with brothels, gambling rooms and roadhouses that attracted both outside gangsters and "local boys who had come to hold the law in contempt."

With their common enemy out of the way, the professional bootlegger-criminals then turned their energies on one another. In summer 1926 in Herrin alone there were at least two beatings, five murders and an armed robbery in the European Hotel, with suspected ties to either the Sheltons or Birger.[270]

Mayor McCormack announced a campaign to drive the gangsters from town and even led one raid to the Palace Hotel with submachine gun in hand. Things quieted down a bit, though why is another question. According to his police chief, McCormack chose to enforce laws in his first term, but after reelection in 1926 began accepting bribes from bootleggers. The police stopped their raids.[271] It seems likely that McCormack drove out the Sheltons because he'd already sided with Birger.

Birger claimed that he first met Carl Shelton in the fall of 1923, when Birger was in the Herrin Hospital after being wounded in the gunfight at his Halfway saloon with "Whitey" Doering, a gangster in the Egan's Rats of St. Louis.[272] By the end of 1925, Birger and the Sheltons were partners in the slot machine business in Southern Illinois. Birger was treasurer, and though there were other reasons offered for their falling out, it seems likely he skimmed profits.[273]

In mid-September 1926, "Wild Bill" Holland, Pat Pulliam and his wife were shot getting into their car outside Grover's Place, a roadhouse near Herrin. The Sheltons were rumored to have been with them inside the roadhouse. Pulliam drove to Herrin Hospital, where he and his wife were treated. Holland was dead from a shotgun slug to the back of the head. Two days later, Pulliam was being taken in an ambulance to Benton for greater safety when a car full of armed men forced the ambulance to stop. Birger and his gang tried to shoot Pulliam, but Pulliam's mother lay across him and saved his life. They butt-stroked him unconscious and left.[274]

In late September, the bodies of Lyle "Shag" Worsham and another man were found, one in a burned farmhouse south of Marion, the other in a hog lot north of Shawneetown. Both murders were presumed to have something to do with the bootleggers.

On October 4, a deuce-and-a-half truck with homemade armor opened fire on gangster Art Newman and his wife on the road from Harrisburg to Birger's resort and flophouse called the Shady Rest. It was the Shelton gang. The Sheltons knew Newman well; they had lived in his hotel in East St. Louis years earlier, and Newman may have loaned them money to start running rum from Florida in the early days. But when Ora Thomas had been killed in the Young shootout, the Sheltons asked Art Newman to drive them to the funeral—as an alibi for robbing a mail messenger in Collinsville. Newman balked (but did it), and the Sheltons held it against him.

Carl Shelton had already introduced Art Newman and another man to Birger, back when Newman ran his East St. Louis flophouse.

"Boys, I want you to meet a high-class man," Shelton said. "If you ever need any help in Williamson County he's the one who can give it to you."[275] Now Newman became Birger's man.

Birger retaliated for the armored assault in mid-October by shooting up a Shelton roadhouse north of Herrin. On October 25, he and his men threatened Joe Adams—the West City mayor, a Stutz dealer, roadhouse operator and friend of the Sheltons—who wouldn't give them the Shelton "tank" he had in his garage.

On October 26, the body of Birger man William Burnett "High Pockets" McQuay was found between Herrin and Johnston City, as was the corpse of Ward "Casey" Jones, a Birger bartender and machine gunner, in a Saline County Creek. Both were pinned on the Sheltons, though some said

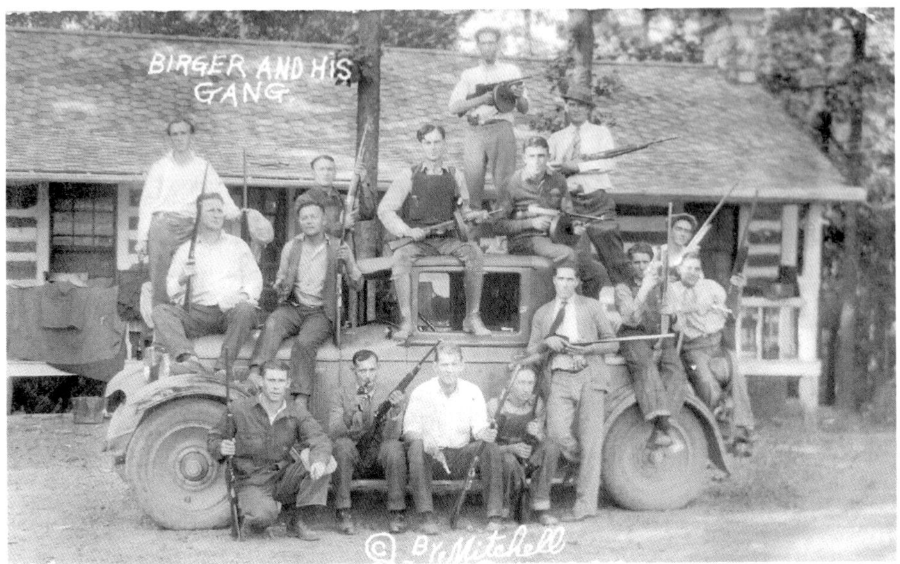

Charlie Birger (1881–1928) and his gang, spoiling for trouble. *Courtesy Williamson County Historical Society.*

that McQuay was killed by Connie Ritter, a Birger man. Two days later, a roadhouse near Johnston City said to belong to Birger was shot up and burned down. And a week after that, the mayor of Colp and another man were killed, and the Colp police chief wounded, in an attack, evidently by the Sheltons.[276]

On November 10, someone threw a powerful bomb at Birger's "Hut," the Shady Rest, but did little damage. Two days later, Joe Adams's house was machine-gunned, and a plane dropped homemade bombs on the Shady Rest. (It's been said that this was the first aerial bombing on U.S. soil, but the bombing of miners during the Battle of Blair Mountain, West Virginia, preceded it.) The next week, dynamite went off in front of Joe Adams's house. No one was hurt in all this.

But December 12, Joe Adams was murdered in his home by two young men working for Birger. On January 9, 1927, the Shady Rest exploded twice and burned down. Four bodies were found in the rubble.

The final straw was the murder of state highway patrolman Lory Price and his wife by Birger and his men. They took the two from their home north of Marion, shot and killed them and dumped their bodies—Ethel's in a mineshaft near Carterville, Lory's in a field in Washington County, thirty-five miles north of Herrin. According to testimony by gangster Art

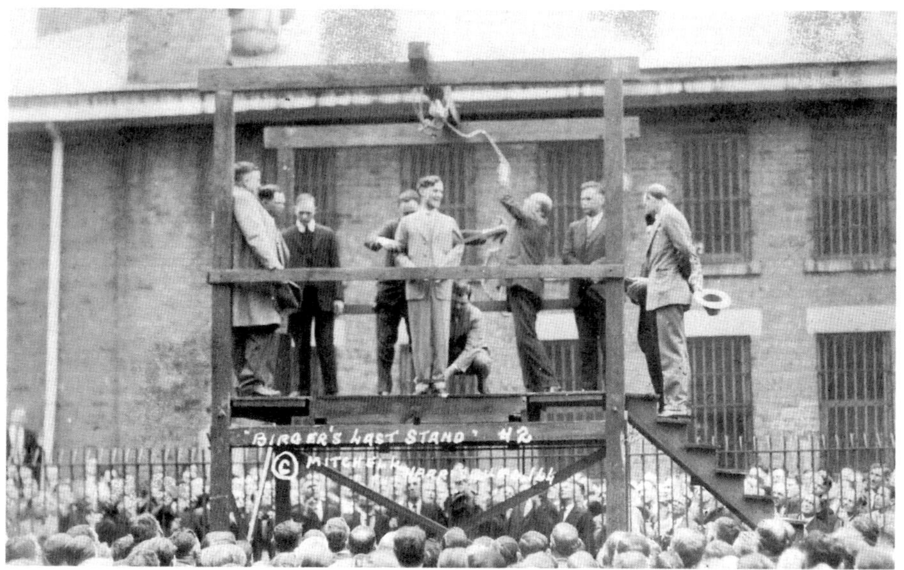

Birger on the gallows—pretty happy, all things considered. Angle says that Birger turned down a narcotic injection before the hanging in favor of his usual marijuana. "It *is* a beautiful world," he said before they slipped the hood over his head. *Courtesy Williamson County Historical Society.*

Newman, Price had been working a stolen car scam with Birger—and with Arlie Boswell, the state's attorney, who reputedly suggested Price be killed—but had threatened to snitch to Williamson County authorities. Birger also thought him to be a spy for the Sheltons.[277]

At the same time, Charlie Birger also got rid of his rivals in a similar manner as the Feds got rid of Capone—on a separate legal issue. Birger tipped off authorities and testified against the Sheltons for the Collinsville mail robbery. They were sentenced to twenty-five years at Leavenworth on February 5, 1927, the same day Lory Price's body was found. (They were released within four months when one of Birger's men who'd also testified against them admitted he perjured himself.)

Birger himself was arrested on April 29, 1927, for conspiracy to murder West City mayor Joe Adams. His accuser was teenager Harry Thomasson, one of the young men he'd told to shoot Adams. Thomasson had come to believe—correctly it seems—that Birger burned down his own Shady Rest, with Thomasson's brother, Elmo, inside. Elmo was the second gunman in the Adams murder and was shot, along with three others in the Shady Rest, for what they knew of Birger's operations, and

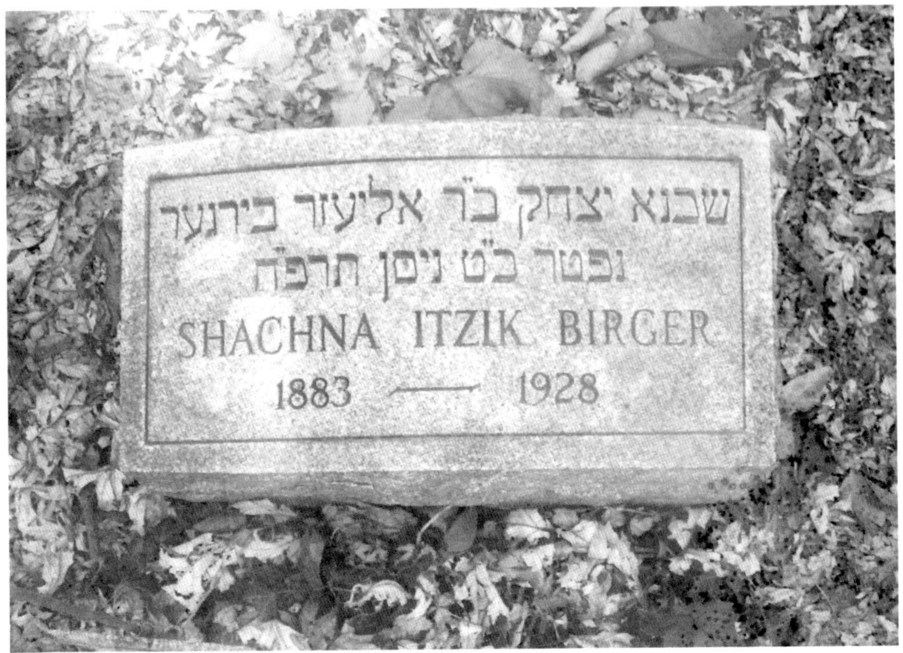

Birger's gravestone, Chesed Shel Emeth Cemetery, University City, Missouri. *Courtesy Williamson County Historical Society.*

so Birger could blame the Sheltons. Though Birger tried to twist his way out by various legal tactics and appeals, he twisted from the end of a rope in Benton on April 19, 1928.[278]

It was finally the end of the (large-scale) hooligan era in Herrin. The Klan was gone. Federal Prohibition was repealed at the end of 1933. Herrin now had a different kind of trial to face.

CHAPTER 9

AS HERRIN GOES, SO GOES AMERICA

A lot had gone right for a long time: White City had opened in 1924, with its enormous saltwater pool, rides, attractions and a dance hall for 500 couples, where the Dorseys, Benny Goodman, Duke Ellington and Guy Lombardo played to a seated crowd of nearly 1,700 more.[279] Businesses filled the downtown, and Herrin would remain the "trade center of Egypt" for decades.

It's hard to describe the feeling you get looking at old photos of the town. The buildings are heavy and snug with few gaps between them. Their offices are occupied, their windows painted with names. People are everywhere, choosing among eight cafés and restaurants, thirteen butchers, ten barbers and *seven* confectioners. The stores are trim and well stocked. There are soda fountains, a pool hall, theatres, bakeries, a roller rink and real hotels with real lobby bars. There's a lumberyard, a bottling plant and car dealerships. The Coal Belt Electric Railroad—the Interurban—ran up Park Avenue until 1926, and when it stopped running it was due to improved roads and more personal automobiles. You can see at a glance the density and amenities of town life.

There were at least ten newspapers (though not concurrently) in Herrin from its incorporation to World War II.[280] Hal W. Trovillion—editor, newspaperman and publisher of the *Herrin News* and the *Herrin Daily Journal*—also ran a small arts press for the first half of the century. It was called for a time America's oldest private press. (It wasn't the first, of course, but by the late 1950s it may have been the longest continuously running.)

Trovillion and his wife, Violet, traveled widely and knew many people, including type designer Frederick Goudy and writers John Cowper Powys

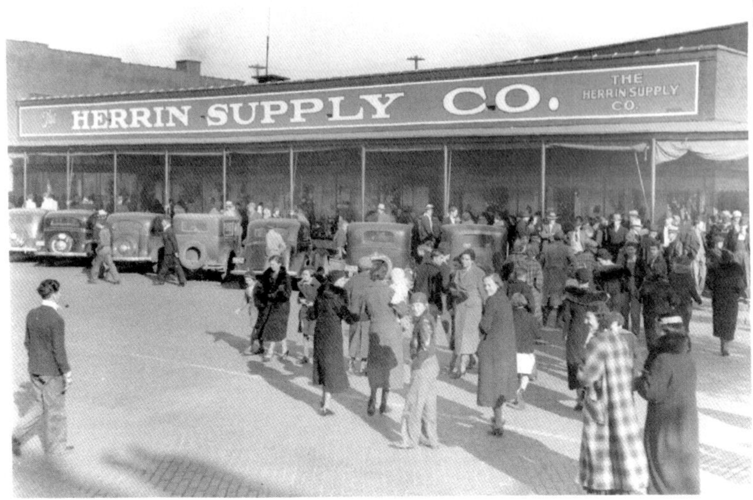

Busy downtown, circa 1940s. *Courtesy Herrin City Library.*

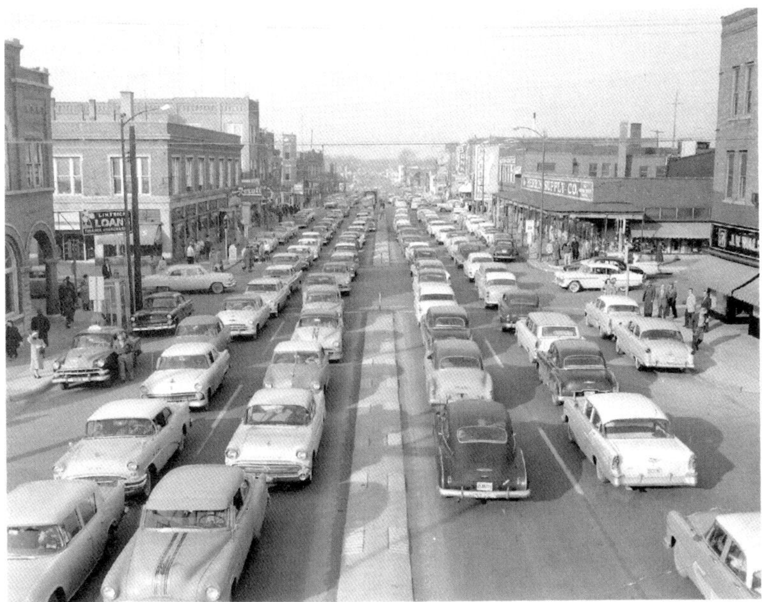

Busy downtown, circa 1950s. *Courtesy Herrin City Library.*

and Daphne du Maurier. They called their press the Trovillion Private Press at the Sign of the Silver Horse, but sometimes imprinted their books with "Thatchcot," after the odd (for Herrin) but lovely half-timbered cottage they built on South Thirteenth Street. Editions of their short books usually ran to about five hundred copies. They were printed on fine papers

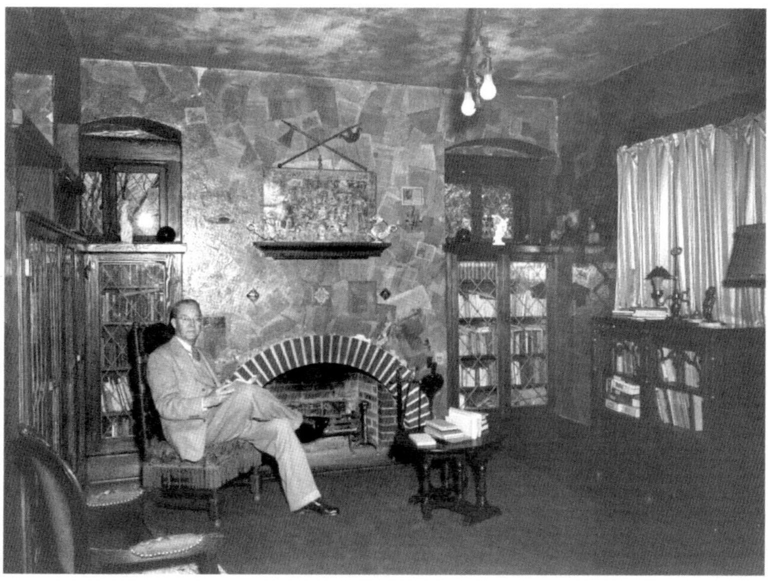

Newspaper editor and small press owner Hal Trovillion (1879–1967) in his home, Thatchcot, an important historical site. *Courtesy Herrin City Library.*

and often had gilt edges and elaborate covers. Many were reprints, such as *The Countrie Housewife's Garden* (1617), the *Love Letters of Henry VIII* or Oscar Wilde's *The Selfish Giant.*

Those days from the turn of the century to 1927 are the ones criticized as the "silk-shirt era." Workers' wages went up during and after the war, and they weren't afraid to spend them. Real estate boomed. Banks, building and loan associations and merchants thrived. All this was seen not only as "prosperity" but also as "soundness," and people who might never have trusted banks opened accounts. Bank deposits in the three counties of the Quality Circle went up $3 million in 1926 alone, when a miner made $50 to $60 every two weeks (and was happy to get it).[281]

In 1919, the state changed the assessment rate of all taxable property from one-third to one-half of full and true value, forcing coal operators, among others, to help support the communities they inhabited. It doubled the tax base in one year and made possible improvements to sidewalks, roads, sewage and water, as well as expansion of schools, police, fire and relief services.

The New Orient mine in Franklin County held world records for tonnage hoisted in a single shift and would become the biggest shaft coal mine in the world for a time. Even Europe began to buy Southern Illinois coal.[282]

"The thing for our people to do," one of the local papers editorialized, "is to settle down to a life of enjoyment and contentment."[283] Herrin *was* the American Dream, realized.

But as with portrayals of its frontier life (Indians noble or savage?), settler life (gander-pulling or servants leading the family to a Christmas feast?), the mine riot (primitive sadism or belief in a cause?) and the KKK (civic law enforcement or ethnic-religious persecution?), the picture of life in Herrin between the wars is split, as if we're looking at two different cities. After all, this was also the era of the Herrin Massacre, the Klan and the bootlegging wars, which developed side by side with domestic contentment.

Besides, the basis of the single-industry economy was not sound. Peak mine production was in 1923. In 1925, there was a national coal depression that anticipated the worldwide economic collapse to come, and "[w]ithin less than a decade the whole structure of prosperity lay in utter ruin" from overproduction, sporadic employment and underemployment, "cutthroat" competition and loss of markets. Mechanization in the mines; changing technologies elsewhere; rival fuels such as oil, natural gas and "smokeless" Pocahontas coal from West Virginia; and waves of fresh immigrant labor hadn't helped.[284]

In addition, the UMWA "began to lose agreements in one Appalachian coal field after another...There came a time at last when Illinois was the only leading coal-producing State with a strong miner's organization left intact."[285]

The union, organized for the best of reasons, had little to bargain with. What does a strike mean when your product is not in demand? The miners made a noble effort to keep all or none working, believing that they could will themselves through their difficulties if they stuck together.

But all this was just a microcosm of bigger forces, and the market crash of 1929, followed by the first effects of the Great Depression, meant disaster. Only one of sixteen Herrin mines remained open after a few years—the one with the most modern machinery, which reduced the need for workers. Thirty-four coal town banks collapsed by 1934, wiping out $7 million in savings. Building and loan associations failed, and hundreds of homes were torn down for their lumber. Small businesses closed by the dozens, and the tax system collapsed (71 percent of all lots in Herrin in 1937 had unpaid taxes).[286]

"A good, simple rule of thumb for evaluating the gravity of unemployment might be about as follows," a federal report just before World War II says:

> *When 10 percent of a community's labor force is unable to find a job, the community has begun to suffer appreciably. When unemployment climbs to 20 percent, a depression of serious consequences exists. And when unemployment reaches 30 percent—a figure rarely reached by most American communities and still more rarely maintained over any period of time—the community must be judged to be in extremely desperate circumstances. According to this scale, the predicament of southern*

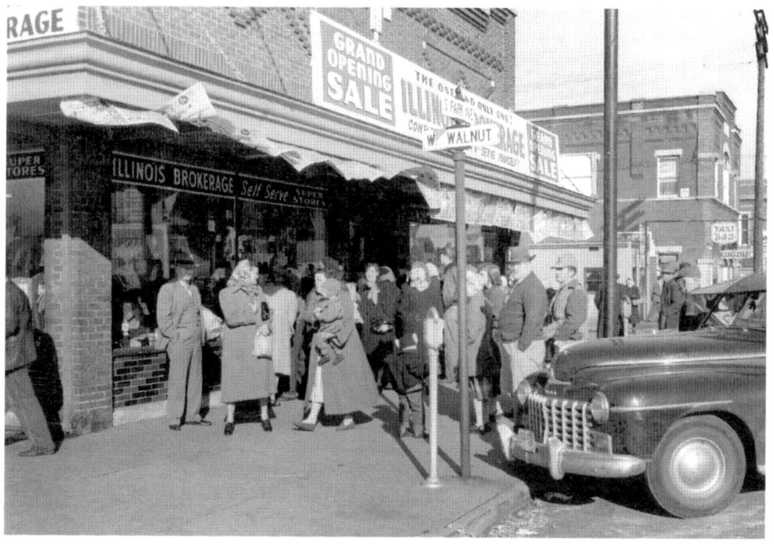

The self-service Illinois Brokerage had its grand opening in 1950. *Courtesy Herrin City Library.*

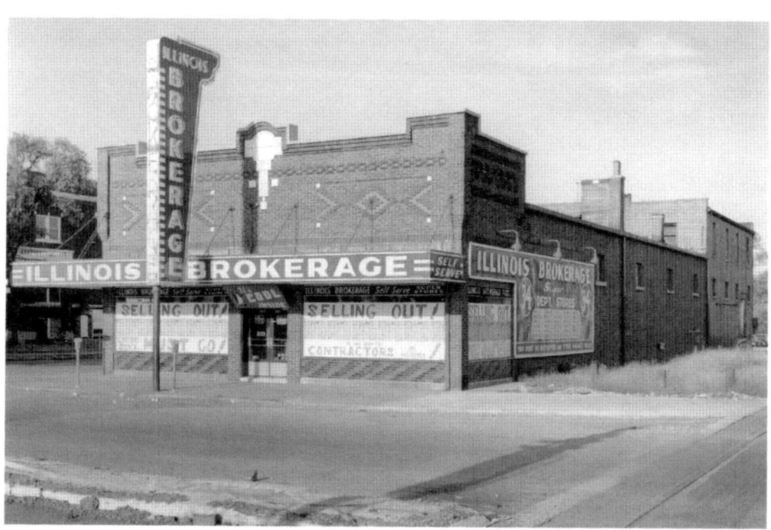

The Illinois Brokerage closed in 1956. *Courtesy Herrin City Library.*

> *Illinois will be clear; throughout the seven towns* [of this study, including Herrin,] *41 percent of all available workers had no jobs at the time of the census.*[287]

"[F]our out of every five unemployed families in the coal towns have had no work for a year or longer," the report says.[288]

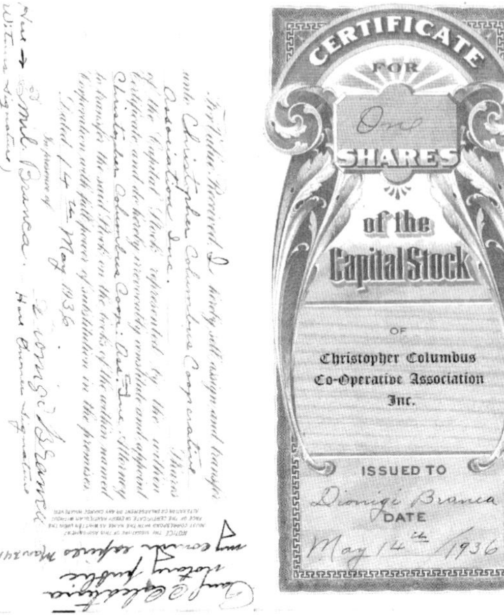

CERTIFICATE FOR One SHARES of the Capital Stock

OF

Christopher Columbus Co-Operative Association Inc.

ISSUED TO Dionigi Branca

DATE May 14th 1936

This page: Certificate Number 1 for the Christopher Columbus Co-Operative Association, issued to Dionigi Branca, 1936. The CC Club's annual dividend was one gallon of wine, one six-pack of beer and one bottle of whiskey. It closed in 1990. *Courtesy Herrin City Library*.

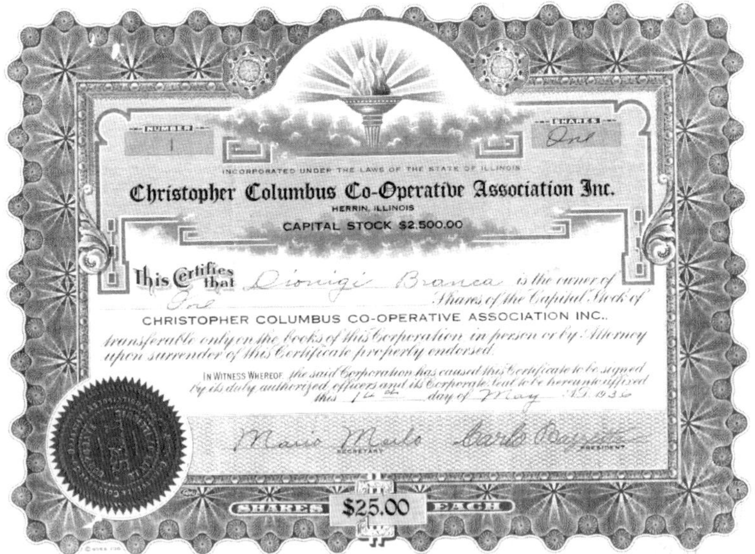

NUMBER 1

SHARES One

INCORPORATED UNDER THE LAWS OF THE STATE OF ILLINOIS

Christopher Columbus Co-Operative Association Inc.

HERRIN, ILLINOIS

CAPITAL STOCK $2.500.00

This Certifies that Dionigi Branca is the owner of One Shares of the Capital Stock of CHRISTOPHER COLUMBUS CO-OPERATIVE ASSOCIATION INC., transferable only on the books of this Corporation in person or by Attorney upon surrender of this Certificate properly endorsed.

IN WITNESS WHEREOF the said Corporation has caused this Certificate to be signed by its duly authorized officers and its Corporate Seal to be hereunto affixed this 14th day of May A.D. 1936

SECRETARY PRESIDENT

SHARES $25.00 EACH

CORPORATION SUPPLY CO. CHICAGO

Backyard gardens helped but "did not…solve the families' food problems—as outsiders so often suppose."[289] Neither did the activities suggested by helpful outsiders who believed the people should just pick themselves up by their bootstraps "selling magazine subscriptions, collecting coat hangers, cleaning tombstones, making flowerpots out of tin cans, and other 'ingenious' attempts to create services which no one wanted."[290]

It was also impossible for everyone to return to farming as had been practiced before the mines opened. The population had grown too much, and farmland had often been ruined by mineral salts from the mines, stripping or poor soil management. It had already been subdivided as far as possible, and many of the small plots couldn't even provide subsistence to a family, let alone income. "[N]ine-tenths of the new depression farms were enterprises on which an independent living was not possible," the report says.[291] (Even now, the USDA census shows agriculture in Williamson County is 96th of 102 counties in the state.[292])

The absentee mine owners "took little interest" in the problems of towns often far from where they lived. As far back as 1914, one of them had replied to a request from Illinois' governor to "relieve the suffering" of the unemployed with, "We can do nothing until…people begin to buy coal."[293]

Gopher (or rabbit) holes—small private mines employing a few men—continued to run seasonally for the local market but "had [little] appreciable effect upon the unemployment problem of the coal field." Besides, even the miners lucky to work them (at wages as low as one dollar per day) were "not self-supporting during the work season, let alone during the 7 idle months of the year."[294]

In times of economic crisis, someone always says that the unemployed should just move to where there are jobs. Some in Herrin did move away, but it was mostly "the young and the most able,"[295] and soon no one had "the reserves which might have financed migration."[296] Besides, people had been born in Herrin, and an entire generation of European immigrants had lived their entire adult lives there. To expect everyone to move to big cities (where work was also often impossible to find) is to expect a big change in a short period for a democracy founded by agrarians.

Was there a way to have changed Herrin's fate? Maybe if Teddy Roosevelt had won more Progressive victories for the mines by dissolving what were often effectively monopolies; maybe if the business and labor leaders of Southern Illinois had acted quickly enough to forestall land buyouts by absentee corporations when coal was discovered there; and maybe if the union had won more seats in national and state political offices…but no.

In my opinion, none of it would have helped in the end. Coal was a cheap way to fuel the growth of America—indeed, the industrialized world—but it was expendable in more ways than one, so the workers in its fields were, too. The town whose lifeblood is a single industry is a town bled dry when the industry is killed off (see Detroit in 2009, whose lifeblood was cheap petroleum).

It wasn't for lack of trying to diversify, though. "For two generations coal-town businessmen…campaigned ardently for 'outside industry' to supplant the declining coal industry," the Depression-era federal report says. "By 1941, however, these campaigns had still to win their first industry and to create their first lasting job in Franklin, Saline, and Williamson Counties."[297]

Say what you like about big government, but what finally kept much of Southern Illinois from starving to death were programs such as the federal Civil Works Administration in November 1933, which employed 6,500 people in the three counties. This was turned over one year later to a state agency under the Federal Emergency Work Relief Program. The Works Progress Administration and the Civilian Conservation Corps employed thousands (including my father, who worked and lived in a construction camp as a young man) and supported thousands more through them.[298]

> *By 1938…public-assistance programs had not only taken under care far more workers than were employed at the mines, but were also paying into the community a sum nearly equal to the annual mine pay roll itself…The coal field had indeed become, by 1938, a community with two industries instead of one; but the second industry was relief.*[299]

WPA workers employed in the county built three huge storage dams to alleviate summer water shortages, playgrounds, a pool, community buildings, parks, athletic fields and schools. They renovated libraries, gyms, parks, forty-six school buildings and two courthouses; they dug ditches to drain malarial marshes and laid sewers and water mains.[300]

The War Department bought twelve thousand acres of land at Crab Orchard, in addition to the thirty-two thousand acres the feds bought for the lake, and opened the Illinois Ordinance Plant (Ordill) at the start of World War II. At the height of the war it employed ten thousand people to make munitions such as 105mm and 155mm shells and five-hundred-pound bombs.[301]

Finally, with federal relief, the Ordill plant, a temporary spike in wartime mine employment and locals not only gone in the armed services but also earning its pay, the economy recovered.

Still, these factors didn't bring things back to previous levels, and even before the war was over, Herrin's leaders knew that they must plan for peace.

"We knew we were going to dry up around Herrin unless we did something," Leon Zwick said.

The Herrin Community Council was formed in 1944, and subscriptions to help bring new industry to Herrin were raised with events such as "Destiny Day." Through the further concerted efforts of well-known Herrin businessmen such as O.W. Lyerla, Clyde Brewster, John Marlow and others, the plants came this time.[302]

Borg-Warner opened Norge, a washing machine factory, in 1946, and Smoler Brothers started making dresses in 1947. Angle says that in all more than $800,000 was raised by the people of Herrin in mortgage notes to entice companies, and by the time he was writing in 1952, "most of these [notes had] already been returned."[303] Other companies that came to Herrin or the surrounding area, in what a newspaper headline in 1965 declared "an industrial boom," included Allen Industries (car liners and sound-deadening materials), Diagraph Bradley (stencil materials), the Sollami Company (mining equipment), Dura-Plex (modular homes), Dura-Container (cardboard boxes), Olin (propellants and munitions), Container Stapling (fasteners and machines) and U.S. Powder (explosives).[304]

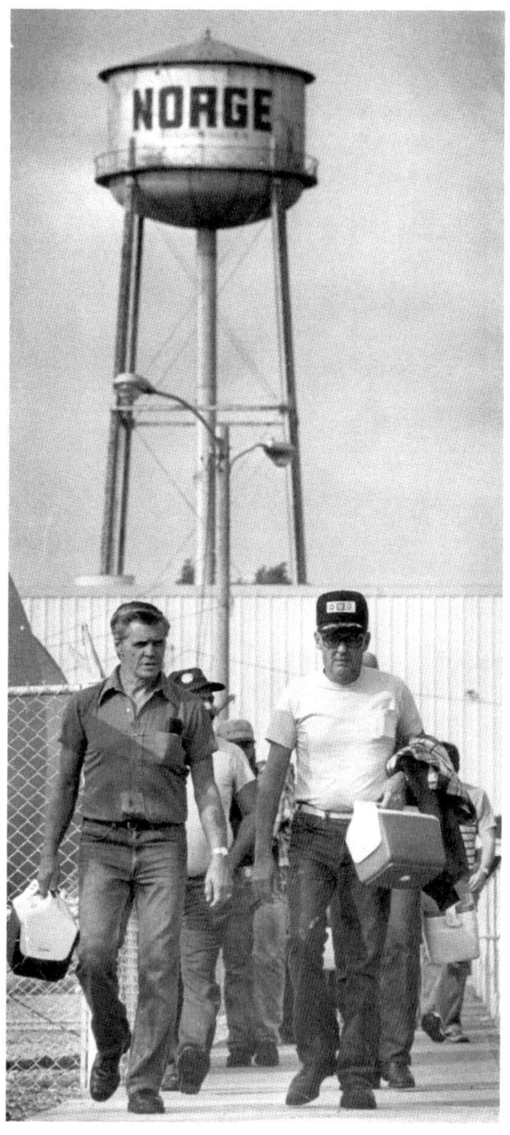

Workers leave Norge at the end of a shift. Though locals always called it Norge, it was owned by several companies over the years. Whirlpool Corp. shut the Maytag plant down for good on December 31, 2006. About one thousand jobs were lost. *Courtesy the* Southern Illinoisan.

When I was growing up in Herrin in the 1960s, the downtown was still going strong. My uncle Carl Sneed had his law office there, my sister worked at Herrin Supply, my mom shopped at the fabric store and the Woolworth's and I was allowed to peruse the toy store in Bailey's bus stop if I sat patiently through my haircut at Macmillan's barbershop next door. Herrin was a great place to be a boy. My boon companions and I rode our bikes from one end of the town to the other, built treehouses, played

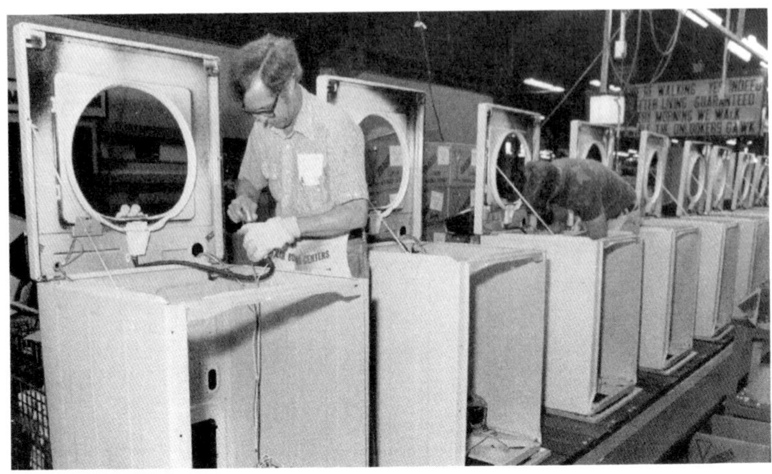

On the line at Norge. *Courtesy the* Southern Illinoisan.

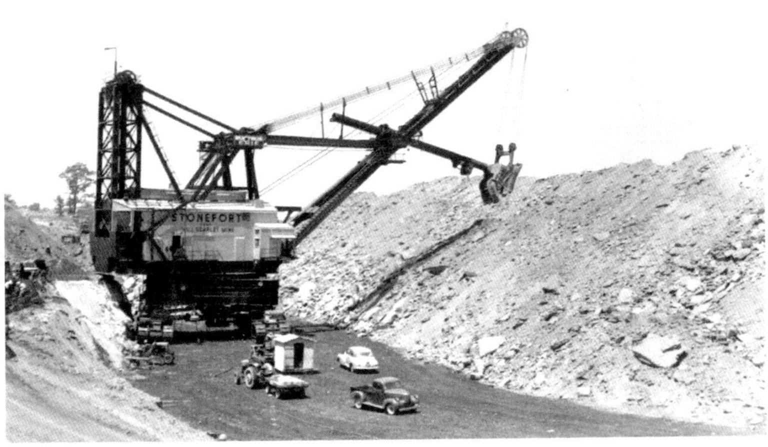

Will Scarlet strip mine, Williamson or Saline County, about 1955. The Bucyrus-Erie 1050-B shovel, designed for this mine and two-seam mining, removes overburden from the coal seams. *Courtesy Illinois State Geological Survey.*

tag on quarter horses, rode motorcycles in the strip pits and spent entire summers at the pool and the library.

By the time I was in high school, things were changing again. The mall had opened in Carbondale, and Marion was expanding around the highway, while businesses in Herrin struggled. I left for the army in 1982, feeling at the time that it could provide opportunities that Southern Illinois no longer could, and I never returned to stay. In the interval, most of the industrial employers have closed or been enticed elsewhere—another instance of

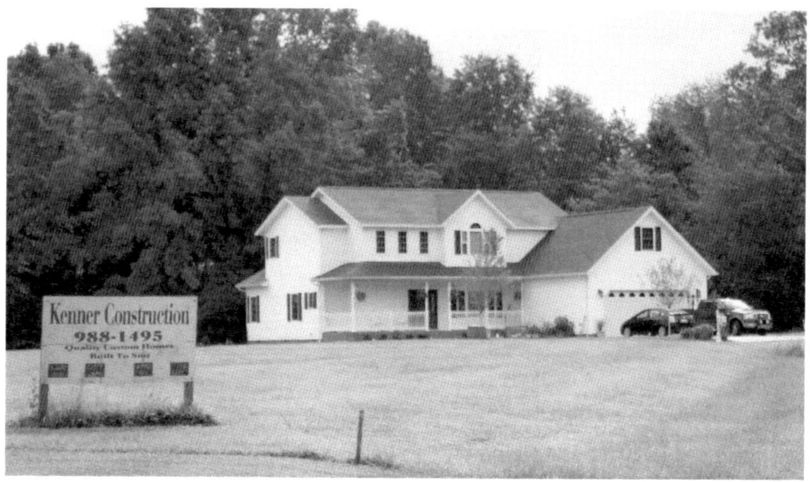

Despite global recession, new home construction continues, 2009. *Photo by the author.*

Herrin as a microcosm of America—and businesses and restaurants downtown have been replaced with the same chains, on the outskirts of town, that you can see anywhere in the country.

Still, I know that I'll always have what that federal report on "stranded coal towns" calls a "peculiar" attachment to Herrin, and even between visits I try to gauge how things are going. I've noted that people upstate seem to believe that Southern Illinois is a popular place to retire, and in August 2009 I asked Richard Pisoni, longtime real estate agent in Herrin, if that was true. He says that young people seem to be the ones buying houses in Herrin and that even in this economy sales in the county had slipped only 15 percent from January 2008 to January 2009.

"Even the closure of the Norge plant surprisingly didn't create a downturn in the market," he says. "My clients are able to get what they want for their homes."[305]

Mayor Vic Ritter says that ten years ago the city wasn't doing well economically. The landfill on the east side of town had closed, putting an end to $1 million of revenue each year. Herrin went "home rule" in response, to raise taxes independently of the state, and Ritter says that helped. But cleanup after the violent storm this spring took enormous resources, and Ritter has hopes that the Federal Emergency Management Agency will soon reimburse the city. I asked him about new subdivisions that seem to be going up every time I'm in town and how some say that Herrin has become a "bedroom" or "dormitory" community.

"We don't take 'bedroom community' as a bad thing," he said. "In addition to buying homes and paying taxes, people spend other money where they live. They shop in the stores, go to gas stations, eat at restaurants. They go

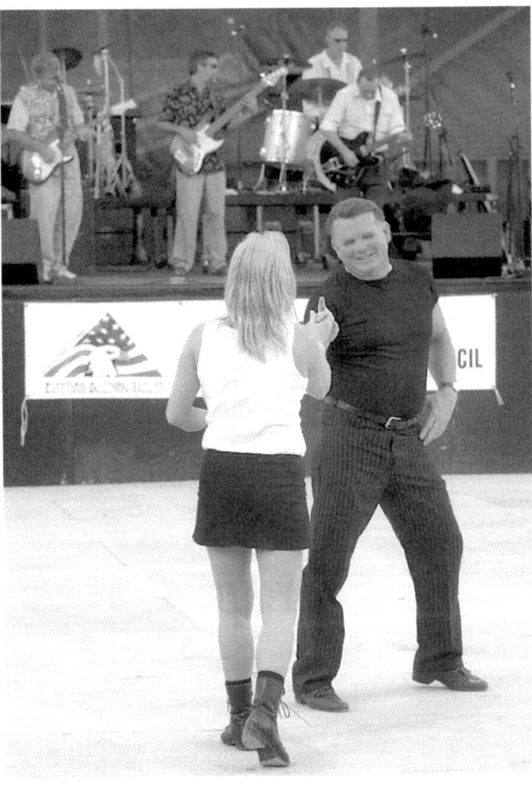

HerrinFesta Italiana celebrates the town's vibrant heritage. It started in 1991 as an extension of the carnival that had run every year for decades. It now brings thousands to Herrin each Memorial Day weekend. *Courtesy the* Southern Illinoisan.

to churches, join clubs and strengthen the community."

Unemployment in Herrin is currently about the national average—close to 10 percent—and is better than in many other Southern Illinois counties. Mayor Ritter said that the hospital is "a great asset" in this, as it employs eight hundred people, has bought a lot of property in town and has plans to build and expand. He also mentioned a food additive company that makes calcium supplements, and he said that after the EPA oversees cleanup of the Container Stapling property, which is owned by the city now, it will become part of a wholesale distributing business. The former Maytag/Norge plant rents, leases or sells portions of its property, and 330,000 square feet, or one-third of it, is currently used by Walgreen's for seasonal product storage. South Side Lumber will expand, as will McDonald's; Taco Bell is going in where the Burger King was.

"It's looking pretty good for us," the mayor said.[306]

Other residents worry about the town's infrastructure, the vitality of its downtown center, opportunities for significant employment, the quality of neighborhoods and the education of their children.

And what about coal? One hears rumors. Of course the Quality Circle that made the city of Herrin is mined out:

> *The most recent mining in the Herrin Quadrangle ended in 2003, when the…Cambria No. 1 Mine closed. Several other strip mines stripped coal up to the early 1980s, some mining both the Herrin* [No. 6] *and the Springfield* [Seam] *Coals. In many cases, they only took the pillars left from previous underground mining in the Herrin* [No. 6] *Coal.*

Statewide, "[m]ore than 7,400 coal mines have operated since commercial mining began…fewer than 30 are currently active."[307]

One reason (other than depletion of local seams) for the decline was that after the Clean Air Act of 1990 many power plants chose to buy from coal suppliers in the West rather than spend billions on sulfur-scrubbing units for their smokestacks. The number of mine jobs in the state dropped from fifteen thousand to four thousand.[308] But more recent regulations watch other emissions, too, like mercury, so all power plants will have to scrub their stacks anyway, and technologies are better. This could mean the "pendulum swings back" for Illinois coal.[309]

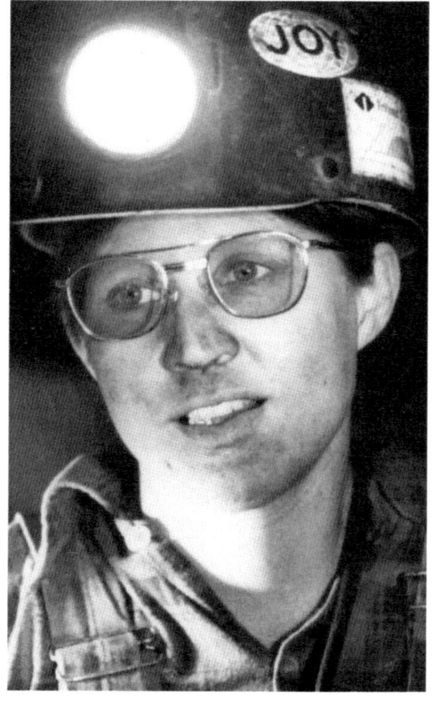

Women in Southern Illinois dig coal, too. The original caption read "Mary Sellers, mother, wife, and a face boss at Inland Steel Coal Co. Mine #1." *Courtesy the* Southern Illinoisan.

The use of coal is a complicated issue. When Barack Obama was running for the U.S. Senate, he blundered into the controversy on a trip to Benton by eagerly assuring its people their coal would prosper again. Later as a presidential candidate he was criticized for it. "[A] rookie mistake," someone said.[310]

But bituminous coal is relatively cheap and reliable, and Illinois has 100 billion tons of it still underground, one-fourth of America's reserves—enough, says Illinois' "top coal lobbyist," to power the country for two hundred years.[311] It's a nearly $1 billion industry[312] that's poised to grow again, which could provide jobs for some Herrin commuters.

"Prognostications in the coal rags, coal industry, [and] government energy agencies…all anticipate growth, possibly a doubling, in the Illinois coal industry over the next ten to fifteen years," says Scott Elrick of the Illinois State Geological Survey.

> [S]*ix permits for large, multiple-million ton coal mining operations* [are] *on file at the DNR Office of Mines and Minerals as we speak.*
>
> *A doubling of tons mined in the state would take us from approximately thirty million tons per year today, up to about sixty million tons per year*[, which] *would get us just beyond 1970–1980 levels, prior to the*

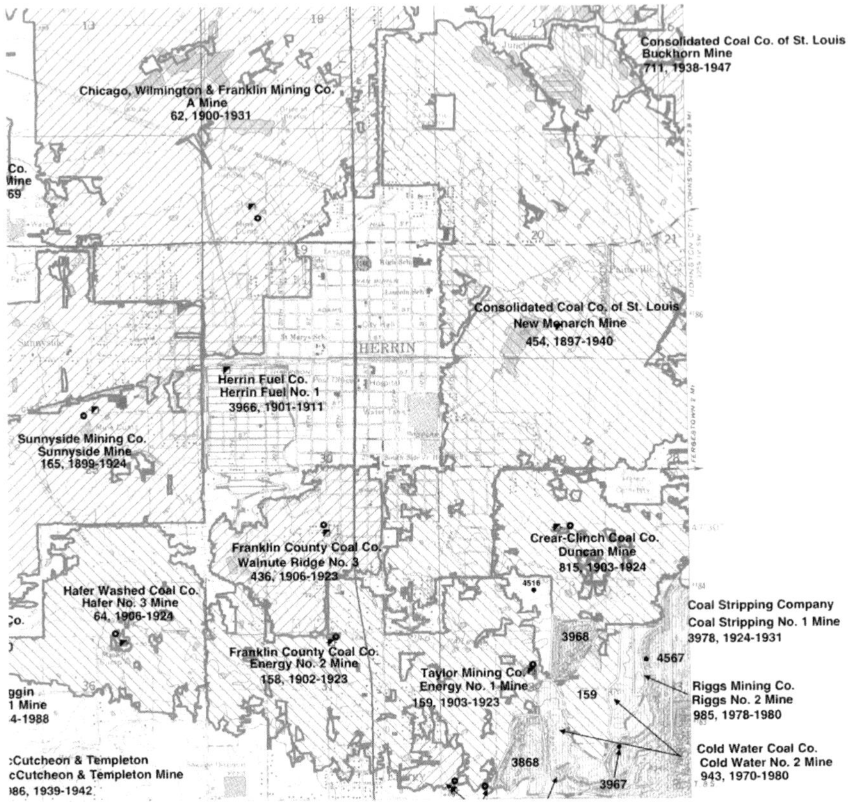

A map showing the extent of the mined-out land under Herrin. *Courtesy Illinois State Geological Survey.*

> *Clean Air Act…The new mines look to be located in both S*[outhern] *Illinois and in West Central Illinois…*
>
> *Consider also that the number of people employed by the mines today is nowhere…close to what it was back in the 1920s–30s. Consequently, I would think that a coal "boom" today in S*[outhern] *Illinois, while having a positive economic impact, would not have nearly the same impact as the growth of the coal industry* [there] *100 years ago.*[313]

Herrin, Illinois, has seen many things come and go in the nearly two hundred years since the land it now occupies was just a bell-shaped prairie on the Northwest frontier: settlement, farming, immigration, civic duty, two different industrial economies, class and cultural wars, boom, bust, growth and stagnation. In all these things, Herrin is part to the whole of the nation.

As I write this, America itself is in what some are calling the Great Recession, a time of trial and great change. How will we fare in the future? It's the same as asking what more Herrin can become.

NOTES

1. Stanley Kimmel is a little-remembered writer from Du Quoin who spent time in Paris with the "Lost Generation." He knew Hemingway and may have taken instruction from Ezra Pound. *The Kingdom of Smoke: Sketches of My People* (New York: Nicholas L. Brown, Inc., 1932).

Introduction

2. Ruby Duncan, née Sneed, was married to Wallace Duncan, a former state trooper, bar owner and vending machine concessionaire. As I was doing research for this book, someone said that he and his son, Billy Joe, "were into some dark stuff."
3. Clipping found in the Oldham Paisley Scrapbooks, various locations.
4. Six nonunion workers were marched past this spot by a mob during the Herrin Massacre.
5. William J. Sneed was also, at other times, a UMWA International organizer and interim president of UMWA District 12 (Illinois).
6. *A Democracy of Ghosts*, published by Wordcraft of Oregon, 2009, is set during the Herrin Massacre. The protagonist is based on my grandfather, who died fifteen years before I was born. My novel was an attempt to try on his and others' fictional lives, though one should never try to read that book as history. Truth wears many coats.
7. Paul M. Angle, *Bloody Williamson: A Chapter in American Lawlessness* (New York: Knopf, 1974), 199.
8. Angle, *Bloody Williamson*, 273.
9. Masatomo Ayabe, "The Ku Klux Klan Movement in Williamson County, Illinois, 1923–1926," PhD dissertation, University of Illinois at Urbana-Champaign, February 11, 2005, 416.

Chapter 1

10. I'm indebted in this chapter to Scott Elrick, staff member, Illinois State Geological Survey, Coal Section, who took time to explain terminology to me, show me a PowerPoint lecture and read this chapter.

11. David H. Swann, "A Summary Geologic History of the Illinois Basin," Indiana-Kentucky and Illinois Geological Societies, 1968. Reposted by Illinois Oil & Gas Association.

12. "Depositional History of the Pennsylvanian Rocks in Illinois," *GeoNote 2* (Champaign: Illinois State Geological Survey, Coal Section. Revised by Russell J. Jacobson, 2000).

13. Less than 2.5 percent sulfur, instead of the usual 3–5 percent. Herrin's low-sulfur coal was still high-sulfur compared to that of other areas.

14. W. John Nelson, *Geologic Disturbances in Illinois Coal Seams* (Champaign: Illinois State Geological Survey. Circular 530, 1983).

15. "Quaternary Glaciations in Illinois," *GeoNote 3* (Champaign: Illinois State Geological Survey, 2008).

16. Barbara Burr Hubbs, *Pioneer Folks and Places: An Historic Gazetteer of Williamson County, Illinois* (Herrin, IL: Herrin Daily Journal, 1939), 76.

17. Steven R. Hill, "Botanical Survey of the Herrin-Johnston City Highway (FAS 903 and FAU 9588), Williamson County, Illinois, Including the Discovery of Two Sedge Species New to Illinois," *Technical Report 2002 (21)* (Champaign, IL: Center for Biodiversity, Illinois Natural History Survey, 2002).

18. The main theories on where this name came from: 1) It was a land of milk and honey for Illinoisans north of Franklin County, who faced starvation after the severe winter of 1830–31 and a short growing season in 1831; and 2) It was named after the region and then community known as Goshen (now the southern part of Edwardsville) and the Bank of Cairo (which was actually in vanished Kaskaskia) by Bible-loving settlers. This use predates (1789–1800) the towns of Thebes (1818, failed; 1835), Cairo (1835) and Karnak (1905). See Edward Callary's *Place Names of Illinois* and John W. Allen's *Legends & Lore of Southern Illinois*, 40–42. I have also heard that "Egypt" was derogatory, a gaunt-cow-and-locust wasteland to northern Illinoisans who were rising in power over the once dominant southern part of the state.

Allen says that "Egypt" is the greater region on a line south of Vandalia or, alternately, below the line of latitude from east St. Louis to Vincennes. "Little Egypt," he says, refers to the eleven southernmost counties, with Benton at about the northern limit.

At least one writer has told me that "Little Egypt" is an erroneous term for the region and can only refer to a belly dancer. There was indeed a Syrian belly dancer, Farida Mazar Spyropoulos, at the 1893 World's Fair in Chicago who used the nickname Little Egypt. She was so popular that she inspired imitators, a film, the phrase "hootchy-kootchy" dancer and a song, "Little Egypt," by the Coasters. But everyone I knew as a boy called the region "Little Egypt" and "Egypt" interchangeably.

CHAPTER 2

19. Milo Erwin, *The History of Williamson County, Illinois* (Marion, IL, 1876), 3–7

20. I am at a loss as to the most sensitive term to use in this chapter: Native American, American Indian, indigenous peoples, etc. It's important to try to get it right, especially in a state where the biggest university in the Illinois system—where I teach—has had such controversy over its mascot. In the end, I'm going with a suggestion by John McKinn, the assistant director of the American Indian Studies Program at the University of Illinois at Urbana-Champaign, who writes to me: "I prefer the use of 'Indian' because that is how we are grouped together and written about in the US Constitution."

    Since that's the word that some of my historical sources use; since the prehistoric people are called "paleo-Indians" in archaeological literature; and since "Native Americans" is long, easily confused with "nativism" and has the same etymology problem that some Indian groups have protested in the word "Indian" (that it's a post-contact word for a world that long existed without whites), I'll use "Indian." McKinn points out how difficult the issue is, even for scholars, and says to see the first page of Shari M. Huhndorf's *Going Native* for an example of this word struggle. Huhndorf uses "Indian" in part because, as she points out, there are other indigenous peoples in native America, such as Native Hawaiians.

21. This new evidence, such as spear points found at Big Eddy, a site in southwestern Missouri, points to people before the Clovis people, whom scientists have long thought were the first to come over the Bering land bridge from Asia to North America. "Big Eddy" (Center for Archaeological Research, Missouri State University, May 18, 2006).

22. "The Midwestern United States 16,000 Years Ago," Illinois State Museum.

23. There was a renewed ice age at this time, after the big one had begun to wane. It lasted another 1,500 years and was known as the Younger Dryas. Some scientists think that it was brought about when Lake Agassiz—a body of glacial melt water in Canada, North Dakota and Minnesota bigger in total area (though not all at once) than the Great Lakes combined—drained into the North Atlantic and shut down the Gulf Stream temporarily.

24. Peter Tyson, "End of the Big Beasts," *Nova*.

25. A layer of "nanodiamonds" in the North American geologic record point to some event of great heat and pressure. Heather Pringle, "Did a Comet Wipe Out Prehistoric Americans?" *New Scientist* (May 22, 2007). But the theory has met resistance from the start, and new evidence quickly emerged to counter the theory. J.R. Marlon and others, "Wildfire Responses to Abrupt Climate Change in North America," *PNAS* 106, no. 8 (February 24, 2009): 2519–2524.

26. Other excavated sites in the region include the Black Bottom on the Ohio River, the Modoc Rock Shelter in the American Bottom on the Mississippi River, the Ferry site on the Saline River near its confluence with the Ohio, the Cache River Valley, the Duran Rock Shelter in Union County (a Carrier Mills Project), the West Harrisburg Project with three sites on the Bankston Fork of the Saline River and the Diana site

on Plum Creek, a southern tributary of the lower Kaskaskia River. Brian M. Butler, "Land Between the Rivers: The Archaic Period of Southernmost Illinois," *Archaic Societies: Diversity and Complexity Across the Midcontinent*, eds. Thomas E. Emerson and Dale L. McElrath (New York: State University of New York Press, 2009).

27. Jim Fay and Andrew C. Fortier, *The Tall Grass Prairie Peninsula: Its Role in Shaping American Culture* (Champaign, IL: Stipes Publishing, LLC), 7. The pockets of prairie opened and closed over time, so Herrin's Prairie may not have been a prairie long before settlers moved there.

28. Brian M. Butler, "Crab Orchard," *Archaeology of Prehistoric Native America: An Encyclopedia*, eds. Guy Gibbon and Kenneth M. Ames (Taylor & Francis, 1998), 180–81.

29. Some think the people disbanded and moved southward to become part of the Muskogean or Siouan group lower in the Mississippi River Valley, or stayed in the Midwest to become part of the Siouan and Algonquian people of the prairie. Robert L. Hall, "Cahokia Identity and Interaction Models of Cahokia Mississippian," *Cahokia and the Hinterlands: Middle Mississippian Cultures of the Midwest*, eds. Thomas E. Emerson and R. Barry Lewis (Urbana: University of Illinois Press, 1999).

30. Kaskaskia chief Jean-Baptiste Ducoigne (1725–1811) was half French and friendly to the Americans during the Revolution, serving George Rogers Clark as a scout and making subsequent treaties with the American government in the name of his people. Stu Fliege, *Tales and Trails of Illinois* (Urbana: University of Illinois Press, 2002), 31. He was buried in a Catholic cemetery. Since he died before the current town of Du Quoin was founded, it's been suggested that the town was named for his son, Chief Louis Jefferson Ducoigne. Michael Tow, "The Kaskaskia Reservation," *Illinois Heritage* 13 (2003). Northern Illinois University.

31. Lee Sulzman, "Illinois History," http://www.tolatsga.org/ill.html; "Illinois Indian History in the Context of Cultural and Political Events of the Time," Illinois State Museum; "Illinois," *Encyclopedia of Chicago*.

32. My grandfather Sneed, born in 1883, grew up in a village in Franklin County called The Diggins—apparently named for the gathering of traditional remedies. Glenn J. Sneed, *Ghost Towns of Southern Illinois* (Royalton, IL: G.J. Sneed, 1983). No relation, to my knowledge.

33. Erwin, *History of Williamson County*, 5–15.

34. The Kaskaskia had long held the territory from the Big Muddy River to the Mississippi; the Shawnee held it east of the Big Muddy to the Wabash. Their argument was partly over territory and perhaps partly due to Ducoigne being seen by the Shawnee as an appeaser to the whites. Fliege, *Tales and Trails*.

35. Erwin, *History of Williamson County*, 16. Fliege also tells (20–23) the story of "John Moredock, Indian Slayer." As a teen in 1786, Moredock witnessed the murder of his keelboat party by Indians in an ambush at what is now Grand Tower, Illinois, on the Mississippi. His six brothers, two sisters and mother ("singled out by the Indians for particularly cruel torture and mutilation") were among the dead. Moredock later became a sociopath, stalking and killing Indians who were often unarmed and

had surrendered to him, "regardless of intent or status." He served in the military and became a political figure with backers ready to make him governor.

36. Erwin, *History of Williamson County*, 22, 95.
37. Ibid., 11–17.
38 Both sides in the case referred to the Indians as "savage tribes" and "an inferior race" who could never own full, transferable title to the lands they had occupied. Robert J. Miller and Elizabeth Furse, *Native America, Discovered and Conquered* (Santa Barbara, CA: Praeger Publishers, 2006), 50–52.
39 This case continues to be the basis for landownership in the United States. And there continue to be challenges by tribes: the Miami tribe of Oklahoma sued for 2.6 million acres of private property in fifteen Illinois counties in 2000, claiming that they received them by treaty two hundred years ago. The state said that the federal Indian Claims Commission rejected tribal claims to Illinois land years ago, and the suit was withdrawn. *New York Times*, "Tribe Pulls Land Suit," June 16, 2001, 13.
40. Fliege, *Tales and Trails of Illinois*; "Indian Removal Act," *Primary Documents in American History*, Library of Congress, Virtual Programs & Services, July 6, 2009.

Chapter 3

41. Alexander B. Adams, *John James Audubon: A Biography* (New York: Putnam, 1966), 131–34. What could Audubon have meant when he said "used them as Regulators were wont to"? Beat them? Left them bound to die in the woods? Killed them outright?
42. An amateur historian disputes the standard sources and says that de Soto actually made it to the Herrin area, but that's not the accepted view. Donald E. Sheppard, "DeSoto's Midwestern Trail."
43. Erwin says that none of the waterways in Williamson County led to Kaskaskia, so it's unlikely that trappers came to the Herrin area. But with this much activity on both the Mississippi River and the Ohio, it seems likely they did. Crab Orchard and Pond Creeks, on the south and north edges of the prairie, were located in the Big Muddy watershed, and a tributary of the Saline runs along the east side of the county. Erwin, *History of Williamson County*, 8–9.
44. It's been mistakenly reported that bison didn't come to Illinois until the 1650s, but recent archaeological digs reveal that they were here well before the time of Christ. See Jeanne Townsend Handy, "A Day at Bison Beach," *IT Online* (October 13, 2005).
45. "Va Bache Tannery," *Southernmost Illinois History*.
46. Hubbs, *Pioneer Folks and Places*, 118. See also entries for Fredonia, Blairsville, Blairsville Township, and Big Muddy River.
47. Erwin, *History of Williamson County*, 17–18.
48. "Fort Massac State Park." Illinois Department of Natural Resources.
49. Hubbs, *Pioneer Folks and Places*, using those place names.

50. Erwin, *History of Williamson County*, 4. He also says (6) that later "the farmers stopped the hunters from burning the woods," with the result that woods grew up where prairie had been. Indians had burned the prairie for centuries, as well.
51. Fay and Fourtier, *Tall Grass Prairie Peninsula*, 13–19.
52. Erwin, *History of Williamson County*, 25, 45.
53. When wolves were "so common as to be a public nuisance" in the early 1800s, their "scalps" brought one dollar each, and several men made hunting them a business, Erwin says (46). A man might kill fifteen wolves in a day. Bison had been hunted to extinction in Illinois before 1830, elk within the next decade and bear by mid-century. Donald Frederick Hoffmeister, *Mammals of Illinois* (reprint, Champaign: University of Illinois Press, 2002), 29–31. Erwin, writing in 1876, even calls white-tailed deer "extinct."
54. Erwin, *History of Williamson County*, 42–47.
55. "MeasuringWorth," http://www.measuringworth.com/uscompare.
56. Erwin, *History of Williamson County*, 67–72.
57. Ibid., 6, 40–41.
58. Ibid., 29, 32.
59. Joseph Anthony Amato. *Rethinking Home: A Case for Writing Local History* (Berkeley: University of California Press, 2002), 191.
60. Erwin, *History of Williamson County*, 33–34.
61. Ibid., 47–48.
62. Mrs. John A. Logan, *Reminiscences of a Soldier's Wife* (New York: C. Scribner's Sons, 1913), 15.
63. *History of Gallatin, Saline, Hamilton, Franklin and Williamson Counties, Illinois, from the Earliest Time to the Present: Together with Sundry and Interesting Biographical Sketches, Notes, Reminiscences, Etc., Etc.* (Chicago: Goodspeed Publishing Co., 1887).
64. David Ruffin Harrison, "The Origin of Herrin's Prairie," reprinted in *Williamson County, Illinois, Sesquicentennial History* (Nashville, TN: Turner Publishing Company, 1989), 182–83.
65. Ruth C. Herrin, "A Story About Herrin's Prairie," *Williamson County, Illinois, Sesquicentennial History*, 184–85.
66. "Illinois Public Domain Land Tract Sales." Illinois State Archives.
67. Arthur Clinton Boggess, *The Settlement of Illinois, 1778–1830* (Chicago Historical Society, 1908), 80.
68. *History of Gallatin…*
69. This reflects neither squatters nor multiple or subsequent purchases by the same person that show up in the Land Tract Sales records in the state archives. David Herrin also has an earlier (1826) purchase listed. *History of Gallatin…*
70. Julia Bruce, "The George Henry Harrison Family," *Williamson County, Illinois, Sesquicentennial History*, 259. The durable names of Herrin often intermarried. Ruth C. Herrin says that Harrison met Delila when he went to Herrin's Prairie to talk shop with another miller. Hubbs implies (see her entry for "Harrison's mill") that he learned of Delila when the men of now Williamson County went north together

to fight Indians in the Black Hawk War. Julia Bruce, George H. Harrison's great-granddaughter, also says that he was a messmate of Abraham Lincoln during that war and that the two traveled back south together when mustered out.

71. Herrin, "A Story About Herrin's Prairie," 184–85; Hubbs, *Pioneer Folks and Places*, 145–48.
72. Erwin, *History of Williamson County*, 68–70.
73. Nannie Gray Parks, "The Story of Williamson County One Hundred Years Ago," *Souvenir Program of the Williamson County Centennial Celebration* (Herrin, IL: Herrin Daily Journal, 1939).
74. The Sunnyside mine, the second mine to open in the Herrin field in 1899, owned 1,360 acres of land but couldn't raise enough feed for its twenty-two mules. Hubbs, *Pioneer Folks and Places*, 76, 224.
75. *History of Gallatin…*
76. Harrison, "The Origin of Herrin's Prairie," 183.
77. Hubbs, *Pioneer Folks and Places*, 145.
78. "Past Illinois Capitols."
79. John W. Allen, *Legends & Lore of Southern Illinois* (Carbondale: Southern Illinois University Press, 1963), 43–44.

CHAPTER 4

80. "Historical Census Browser." University of Virginia Library.
81. Gordon Pruett, ed., *One Hundred Years of Herrin, Illinois* (Herrin, IL: Herrin Chamber of Commerce, 2000), 69.
82. Hubbs, *Pioneer Folks and Places*, 146–47.
83. "Deceased Veterans." *Williamson County, Illinois, Sesquicentennial History*, 65.
84. Hubbs, *Pioneer Folks and Places*, 150.
85. J.F. Wilcox, *Historical Souvenir of Williamson County, Illinois* (Effingham, IL: LeCrone Press, 1905), 44. From the second section, "Carterville, Herrin, Creal Springs, etc."
86. "Southern Illinois Now!" Facebook, http://www.facebook.com/group.php?gid=73547464267.
87. Catherine E. Breen and others, "Illinois Becomes a State: 1818 Compromise, Later Conflict," *Illinois Periodicals Online.*
88. Malcolm Brown and John N. Webb, *Seven Stranded Coal Towns: A Study of an American Depressed Area* (Washington, D.C.: U.S. Government Printing Office, 1941), 110.
89. Erwin, *History of Williamson County*, 247.
90. Ayabe, "The Ku Klux Klan Movement," 56.
91. "General John A. Logan," reprinted in *Williamson County, Illinois, Sesquicentennial History*, 57–58.
92. Logan, *Reminiscences of a Soldier's Wife*, 98–99.
93. Kellee Green Blake, "Aiding and Abetting Disloyalty Prosecutions in the Federal Civil Courts of Southern Illinois, 1861–1866," *Illinois Historical Journal* 87, no. 2 (Summer 1994): 95–108.

94. Ayabe, "The Ku Klux Klan Movement," 57.
95. Erwin, *History of Williamson County*, 282–83.
96. This was the case after World War I in Herrin, too, and arguably in America after the first soldiers began returning from Vietnam. Surely someone has written on the seeming link between the violence of warfare and violent domestic episodes in its wake.
97. *History of Gallatin…*, 475.
98. Erwin, *History of Williamson County*, 105.
99. Ibid., 108.
100. Hubbs, *Pioneer Folks and Places*, 94.
101. Angle, *Bloody Williamson*, 72–73.
102. Erwin, *History of Williamson County*, 228.
103. Ibid., 114–24, 183.
104. Angle, *Bloody Williamson*, 80.
105. Erwin, *History of Williamson County*, 72–79.
106. Ibid., 185.

CHAPTER 5

107. Fliege, *Tales and Trails of Illinois*, 36–39.
108. Angle, *Bloody Williamson*, 89–90.
109. Harrison, "The Origin of Herrin's Prairie," 182–83; Hubbs, *Pioneer Folks and Places*, 82; Wilcox, *Historical Souvenir of Williamson County*, 3; Angle, *Bloody Williamson*, 90; Alan R. Myers, *Directory of Coal Mines in Illinois. 7.5-Minute Quadrangle Series, Herrin Quadrangle, Williamson County* (N.p.: Department of Natural Resources, Illinois State Geological Survey, 2006).
110. Angle, *Bloody Williamson*, 90.
111. Erwin, *History of Williamson County*, 3.
112. While the coal became known as Herrin Coal, Energy's name remains in the "Energy shale unit," the Appalachian gray shale layer over the Herrin coal, which kept the ancient sea's sulfur out of the peat 300 million years ago in certain areas of Illinois, such as the Quality Circle under the town of Herrin. Scott Elrick, e-mail.
113. Harrison, "The Origin of Herrin's Prairie," 183.
114. Ibid.; Hubbs, *Pioneer Folks and Places*, 148–49.
115. Hal W. Trovillion, ed., "Brief History of City of Herrin," *Williamson County, Illinois, in the World War* (Herrin, IL: The Williamson County War History Society, 1919), 320.
116. Hubbs, *Pioneer Folks and Places*, 150–51.
117. Brown and Webb, *Seven Stranded Coal Towns*, 4–5, 103.
118. Ibid., 10.
119. As a good example of how the pioneer families not only made good but also kept the money in the family, note that D.R. Harrison was president; Ephraim Herrin, vice-president; John Herrin, cashier; and Cora Herrin, bookkeeper; its directors were

D.R. Harrison, George Harrison, Ephraim Herrin, Ed Elles and J.D. Peters. Wilcox, *Historical Souvenir of Williamson County*, 42.

120. E-mails with J. Fred Giertz, Department of Economics and Institute of Government and Public Affairs, University of Illinois at Urbana-Champaign, August 4 and 5, 2009.

121. Scholars need to look into this issue. Cheri Chenoweth of the ISGS Coal Section says that the records of ownership for these mines are impossibly tangled, making it difficult to straighten out who owners even were. E-mail to author, July 31, 2009.

122. Williamson County's population increased tenfold in the same time. Brown and Webb, *Seven Stranded Coal Towns*, 103.

123. Trovillion, "Brief History of City of Herrin," 320.

124. Ayabe, "The Ku Klux Klan Movement," 61.

125. Ibid., 66–67.

126. Hal W. Trovillion, ed., *Williamson County, Illinois, in the World War* (Herrin, IL: The Williamson County War History Society, 1919).

127. Hubbs, *Pioneer Folks and Places*, 151.

128. Trovillion, *Williamson County, Illinois, in the World War*, 342.

129. Hubbs, *Pioneer Folks and Places*, 152.

130. Trovillion, *Williamson County, Illinois, in the World War*. Compare numbers in two accounts on 320 and 350.

131. *Williamson County, Illinois, Sesquicentennial History*, 70.

132. Hubbs, *Pioneer Folks and Places*, 151; *Jubilee 2000: Our Lady of Mount Carmel, Herrin, Illinois*, Olan Mills Directories, 4. Father Hilgenberg, the first priest to say mass in Herrin, in 1898, was said to have heard confessions in eight languages and to conduct his sermon each Sunday in three.

133. Brown and Webb, *Seven Stranded Coal Towns*, 7.

134. Ibid., 23.

135. Trovillion, *Williamson County, Illinois, in the World War*, 120.

136. Ibid.

137. Brown and Webb, *Seven Stranded Coal Towns*, 1.

138. Trovillion, "Brief History of City of Herrin," 320.

139. Trovillion, *Williamson County, Illinois, in the World War*, 338.

140. The page from the phonebook is posted in the Herrin Library History Room.

141. Ayabe, "The Ku Klux Klan Movement," 62.

CHAPTER 6

142. The *Literary Digest* of October 14, 1922, summarized editorial views such as these from around the country. Quoted in Angle, *Bloody Williamson*, 56, n295.

143. In Illinois alone in the years after the Herrin Massacre, 54 died in a gas explosion in a Moweaqua Coal Company mine in 1932; 111 died in Centralia in a coal dust explosion in 1947; and 119 died in a gas explosion at Orient #2 in 1951. "Illinois Coal Industry Significant Dates."

144. David Ross, secretary, *Twenty-First Annual Coal Report of the Illinois Bureau of Labor Statistics… for the Year Ended Oct. 1, 1902* (Springfield, IL: Phillips Bros., State Printers, 1903).
145. "A History of the Colorado Coal Field War." *Colorado Coal Field War Project.* University of Denver.
146. John H.M. Laslett, "A Parting of the Ways: Immigrant Miners and the Rise of Politically Conscious Trade Unionism in Scotland and the American Midwest, 1865–1924," *The United Mine Workers of America: A Model of Industrial Solidarity?* (University Park: Pennsylvania State University Press, 1996), 418.
147. Brown and Webb, *Seven Stranded Coal Towns*, 5.
148. Angle, *Bloody Williamson*, 13.
149. "History of Mine Safety and Health Legislation," United States Department of Labor, Mine Safety & Health Administration.
150. Ross, *Twenty-First Annual Coal Report.*
151. Angle, *Bloody Williamson*, 92.
152. Walter C. Rucker and James N. Upton, *Encyclopedia of American Race Riots* (Santa Barbara, CA: Greenwood Publishing Group, 2007), 671–72.
153. Carl Weinberg, "'Hotter than San Juan Hill': The Battle of Virden, the UMWA and the Challenge of Solidarity," The Illinois Labor Society.
154. Franklin County Historical Society, ed., *Franklin County, Illinois, 1818–1997* (Nashville, TN: Turner Publishing Company, 1997), 27.
155. Angle, *Bloody Williamson*, 89–133.
156. "A History of the Colorado Coal Field War."
157. "Battle of Blair Mountain," Wikipedia, the free encyclopedia.
158. David Corbin, *Life, Work, and Rebellion in the Coal Fields: The Southern West Virginia Miners, 1880–1922* (Urbana: University of Illinois Press, 1989), 220.
159. "Pinks" was a generic term that included the Pinkerton Agency, the infamous Baldwin-Felts Agency and others. The Baldwin-Felts were involved in Colorado and West Virginia, two states where the situation was called "Hell and Repeat." Corbin, *Life, Work, and Rebellion*, 51.
160. The Battle of Blair Mountain, like the Herrin Massacre, would be public relations nightmares for the union. Corbin, *Life, Work, and Rebellion*, 51.
161. Angle, *Bloody Williamson*, 13.
162. Melvyn Dubofsky, *The State and Labor in Modern America* (Chapel Hill: University of North Carolina Press, 1994), 89.
163. Veritas [pseud.], *Life and Exploits of S. Glenn Young, World-Famous Law Enforcement Officer* (published originally by Mrs. S. Glenn Young, 1924, republished Herrin, IL: Crossfire Press, 1989), 219.
164. From *People of Coal Town*, an ethnography of Zeigler done in the 1950s by a team of researchers from SIU-C. It's an odd book, a cross between social science and what we'd now call creative nonfiction, and it lacks organization and sometimes sympathy. But it's still one of the very best sources of first-person voice and attitude of those early coal days in the county, and I highly recommend it for both entertainment and

education. Herman R. Lantz, *People of Coal Town* (New York: Columbia University Press, 1958), 99.

165. The current map that shows the position of the Lester mine is available as a free download: http://www.isgs.uiuc.edu/maps-data-pub/coal-maps/topo-mines/johnston_city.pdf. "The mine is in the southwest corner (lower left) and is part of the brown-shaded stuff. It looks [too] insignificant to have generated such controversy," says Cheri Chenoweth, Coal Section, Illinois State Geological Survey. E-mail with author.

166. Angle, *Bloody Williamson*, 11–15.

167. Paul Angle's version is easily read and has enough details to be meaningful, but some future scholar will no doubt deal in depth with those who may deserve the most blame for the actual murders: Fox Hughes, Hugh Willis, Melvin Thaxton, Otis Clark and others.

168. Angle, *Bloody Williamson*, 23–27.

169. This gravel road to the south currently has an old trailer at its entrance and a sign for Rhode Island hens.

170. On the northwest corner of that intersection, south of the transfer station there now.

171. Angle, *Bloody Williamson*, 6.

172. Ibid., 3–6.

173. When I was growing up, we believed one of the "hanging trees" from the massacre was on the south edge of the subdivision now in this remnant of woods. The tree went over in this year's "inland hurricane," which uprooted many old trees in town. Let me add a little to myth: A friend took me out to see it, and I reached in and ripped out a piece of its heartwood. It was riddled with infestation and charred from fire but was as heavy a piece of wood as I've ever felt. The same friend was told by crews helping the city clean up that they found bullets in trees they were cutting into pieces there. When queried more closely, they said they didn't think the bullets were deep enough—presumably judging by tree rings—to have been from the Herrin Massacre.

174. *Chicago Daily Tribune*, "Death Bullets Follow Taunts for Mine Victims," June 23, 1922, 2. Angle determined the number of dead at twenty-three: twenty nonunion and three union. Early reports varied wildly. Trovillion, Sneed, Farrington, Lewis, Lester and others—all at a distance from Herrin—were told different numbers by people on the scene. The Hargreaves Detective Agency that sent many of the strikebreakers had heard from only five of their thirty-three men the day after the massacre. I have much confidence in Angle, but it's still troubling to read, "The Associated Press correspondent and other newspapermen saw with their own eyes twenty-seven bodies in different parts of the county…freshly spaded piles of dirt were noticed in the woods." (From the *Daily Tribune* article listed above.) The Hargreaves agency information is from *New York Times*, "Mine Owners to Sue Union and County," June 24, 1922.

The *Chicago Daily Tribune*, fifteen years after the event, still put the number in question: "In all it was believed about thirty of the company workers and guards were killed. Nineteen bodies were given official burial, and eleven of the total group never have been accounted for." *Chicago Daily Tribune*, "The Herrin Mine Massacre—15 Years Ago," July 18, 1937.

175. While there must be extant records, no one seems to know where the graves are. One person working on a documentary believes that he's located them by comparing the photo shown here with aerial photos from the 1930s. Angle puts the potter's field graves "a few feet" from the grave of Ora Thomas—about the area where the filmmaker puts it. A volunteer at the Williamson County Historical Society has good theories about a different location, in the southwest corner, based on the dates of the stones and the number of seemingly family-less people buried there.

176. Angle, *Bloody Williamson*, 139–40.

177. Ibid., 51.

178. Ibid., 55.

179. Ayabe, "The Ku Klux Klan Movement," 104.

180. Oddly enough, both John L. Lewis and William J. Lester blamed "reds" or "bolsheviki." But that one instance of outside agreement came at the price of support for Herrin as a community.

181. Ayabe, "The Ku Klux Klan Movement," 102.

182. Ibid., 105.

183. Arthur Evans, "Terror Grips Law Abiding of 'Bloody' Herrin," *Chicago Daily Tribune*, July 2, 1922.

184. *The WPA Guide to Illinois: The Federal Writers' Project Guide to 1930s Illinois*, reprint of *Illinois, A Descriptive and Historical Guide* (1939) (New York: Pantheon Books, 1983), 453.

185. I can't remember the source, but someone suggested the split was encouraged by UMWA leaders, who hoped the more radical miners would take immigrants with them and become marginalized, leaving the "native" miners to better employment. I think the split ended (along with an attack on my grandfather by the KKK after he supported the non-Klan candidate in a local election) my grandfather's tenure in the state senate, after he went with John L. Lewis, who favored working with capital.

186. Laslett, "A Parting of the Ways," 419, 436–37.

187. Alan J. Singer, "Something of a Man: John L. Lewis, the UMWA, and the CIO, 1919–1943," *The United Mine Workers of America: A Model of Industrial Solidarity?* (University Park: Pennsylvania State University Press, 1996), 111.

CHAPTER 7

188. This will disappoint many, but according to Herrin native James Ballowe, who wrote the foreword for Gary DeNeal's *A Knight of Another Sort*, Charlie Birger was not the last man hanged in the state of Illinois. That honor evidently belonged to one

Charles Shader, who was hanged on October 10, 1928, at the Will County Jail in Joliet, Illinois, for the murder of a deputy warden. Gary DeNeal, *A Knight of Another Sort*, xxv.

189. Trovillion, *Williamson County, Illinois, in the World War*, 112.
190. Ayabe, "The Ku Klux Klan Movement," 22.
191. Ibid., n49.
192. Ibid., 205–6.
193. Trovillion, *Williamson County, Illinois, in the World War*, 111.
194. Ayabe, "The Ku Klux Klan Movement," 69.
195. William R. Tonso, in an introduction to the unpublished memoirs of his mother, Eva Tonso: "My Book of Memories: A Herrin Italian-American Memoir."
196. Ernest Hemingway, *A Moveable Feast* (New York: Bantam, 1965), 165.
197. Angle, *Bloody Williamson*, 139.
198. Ibid., 135–36.
199. Ayabe, "The Ku Klux Klan Movement," 82.
200. Ibid., 40.
201. Ibid., 268.
202. Ibid., 266.
203. Ibid., 138.
204. John M. Pico, an Italian Consular agent, came to Herrin to investigate. "The raiders made of Williamson county a little bit of Hell," he said. There's a good book title. Ayabe, "The Ku Klux Klan Movement," 177–78.
205. Angle, *Bloody Williamson*, 144–45.
206. I suspect the real story of immigrant-nativist relations remains to be written. It may not be written until the last of this generation, those born to immigrant parents, is gone, since it is one aspect of Herrin's history that could still raise tempers.
207. African Americans play little part in the history of Herrin, other than by their conspicuous absence historically. Several sources refer to Herrin as a "sundown town," a place where blacks were not permitted to stay after dark, let alone live. There appears to be no evidence of this, such as a law on old books, though that was always rumored to be the case. I also have seen no evidence of lynchings or other racially motivated murders of blacks, though that could be yet to be discovered.

Suffice it to say: 1) a separate town (Colp) housed most blacks in the immediate area; 2) the Madison No. 9 mine, which employed blacks, was referred to as the "nigger Nine"; and 3) the Excel sheet on James W. Loewen's site for his book *Sundown Towns: A Hidden Dimension of American Racism* shows no blacks in Herrin until 1950, when there was precisely 1. In 1990, the number went suddenly to 49, and in the 2000 census, of a total population of 11,298, there were 104 blacks. If true—Loewen's writing is less than scholarly—it's still a small fraction of the 12.8 percent average of blacks in the U.S. population. See Loewen and Ayabe. Loewen's website is at http://sundown.afro.illinois.edu/sundowntowns.php. Ayabe discusses this in conjunction with editor Hal W. Trovillion's "advocat[ing] the exclusion of African Americans from [Herrin]," 68.

208. Daniel Prosser, quoted in Ayabe, "The Ku Klux Klan Movement," 68.
209. The first business building erected in Marion was a "log shanty" saloon. In 1839, "Two members of the county court began to sell whiskey." Wilcox, *Historical Souvenir of Williamson County, Illinois*, 175.
210. Marion and Johnston City went dry in 1900. Carterville and Herrin joined them in 1907 (when Herrin had twenty-two saloons). But in 1910, Herrin, Marion and Johnston City went wet again. In 1914—the first year of the vote for women, who were predominately dry for the toll boozing took on families—the whole county went dry. Herrin went wet again two years later. Ayabe, "The Ku Klux Klan Movement," 72–73.
211. Angle, *Bloody Williamson*, 139; Ayabe, "The Ku Klux Klan Movement," 75.
212. Ayabe, "The Ku Klux Klan Movement," 115.
213. Ibid., 106–7.
214. Ibid., 1, 5–7.
215. Ibid., 17.
216. Ibid., 20–21.
217. Ibid., 23.
218. Ibid., 24, 38.
219. Ayabe calls S. Glenn Young both a lifelong devotee to enforcing the law and "a maniac and fanatic, even in the eyes of his sympathizers." Before Prohibition he'd worked as deputy U.S. marshal and investigator for the Department of Justice. As a Prohibition officer he'd already been charged with abusing the sixteen-year-old daughter of an Italian moonshiner near Staunton, and he did shoot to death a Croatian bootlegger near Granite City. After being acquitted, he was fired from the feds "for conduct unbecoming a government officer," 166–67 in Ayabe. Angle also includes charges of domestic violence and abandonment, "fictitious claim for auto hire," representation of himself as a prohibition agent after his suspension, never turning in cash and items from a gambler, nonpayment of debts and a rape charge for which he was acquitted and investigators found baseless, 160–61 in Angle.
220. Ayabe, "The Ku Klux Klan Movement," 87–88, 152.
221. Ibid., 134–36.
222. Ibid., 150–51.
223. Angle, *Bloody Williamson*, 141.
224. Ayabe, "The Ku Klux Klan Movement," 152.
225. Ibid., 156.
226. Angle, *Bloody Williamson*, 142; Ayabe, "The Ku Klux Klan Movement," 158.
227. Some have said that Southern Illinois' gangsters were Al Capone wannabes, but Capone didn't set up in Chicago until 1923. I'd say the influence was more in the American air: Manifest Destiny meets the jazz age. This era in Herrin's history coincided with the first real opportunity for hooligans across the country to air their egos by means of the relatively new public technologies such as radio and film.
228. Ayabe, "The Ku Klux Klan Movement," 172.

229. Angle, *Bloody Williamson*, 145–46.
230. Ayabe, "The Ku Klux Klan Movement," 172–73.
231. Angle, *Bloody Williamson*, 145–48.
232. Ayabe, "The Ku Klux Klan Movement," 154.
233. Ibid., 176.
234. Ibid., 192.
235. Ibid., 193–94.
236. Angle, *Bloody Williamson*, 150–51.
237. An "extra-legal vigilantism" Ayabe seems willing to condone, as Milo Erwin does "the law of the bush" in Williamson County's early days, when official law enforcement officers were often nonexistent.
238. Ayabe, "The Ku Klux Klan Movement," 197–99.
239. Angle, *Bloody Williamson*, 151–52; Ayabe, "The Ku Klux Klan Movement," 199.
240. Angle, *Bloody Williamson*, 153–54; Ayabe, "The Ku Klux Klan Movement," 200.
241. Angle, *Bloody Williamson*, 154–55, 168; Ayabe, "The Ku Klux Klan Movement," 200–202.
242. Ayabe, "The Ku Klux Klan Movement," 203–4.
243. Ayabe says that the Guardsmen said they had "a fine time" and "we wish we could have stayed a month." Among other things, they could see movies for free. All but one battalion left on February 14, 209 in Ayabe.
244. Ayabe, "The Ku Klux Klan Movement," 217.
245. Angle, *Bloody Williamson*, 163–67; Ayabe, "The Ku Klux Klan Movement," 206.
246. Angle, *Bloody Williamson*, 166–67.
247. Ibid., 170; Ayabe, "The Ku Klux Klan Movement," 228–29, 241, 247, 278–79. Herrinites curious about their families' involvement in any of these events should read Ayabe. Though "[n]o membership rosters survive for the Williamson County Klan…the local press provided sufficient information to allow us to identify Klan members and their supporters." Ayabe triangulates this with lists of those indicted in liquor raids and their bondsmen, as well as other sources (251). Wet or dry or in between, chances are you'll find a familiar name in his dissertation.
248. Angle, *Bloody Williamson*, 172–73; Ayabe, "The Ku Klux Klan Movement," 279–80, n335.
249. Ayabe, "The Ku Klux Klan Movement," 281–82.
250. Angle, *Bloody Williamson*, 174.
251. Ayabe, "The Ku Klux Klan Movement," 290.
252. Angle, *Bloody Williamson*, 177–80; Ayabe, "The Ku Klux Klan Movement," 296, 299.
253. Ayabe, "The Ku Klux Klan Movement," 300–3.
254. Angle, *Bloody Williamson*, 183; Ayabe, "The Ku Klux Klan Movement," 304, 308.
255. Angle, *Bloody Williamson*, 183–84; Ayabe, "The Ku Klux Klan Movement," 322–25.
256. Ayabe, "The Ku Klux Klan Movement," 327.
257. Angle, *Bloody Williamson*, 188–89; Ayabe, "The Ku Klux Klan Movement," 328–31.
258. Angle, *Bloody Williamson*, 189–91; Ayabe, "The Ku Klux Klan Movement," 332–34.

259. Ayabe, "The Ku Klux Klan Movement," 334.
260. Angle, *Bloody Williamson*, 197; Ayabe, "The Ku Klux Klan Movement," 381–82.
261. Ayabe, "The Ku Klux Klan Movement," 389.
262. Ibid., 363–65.
263. Ibid., 375.
264. Ibid., 366–69, 373.
265. Angle, *Bloody Williamson*, 200–201; Ayabe, "The Ku Klux Klan Movement," 393–94.
266. Angle, *Bloody Williamson*, 201–2; Ayabe, "The Ku Klux Klan Movement," 394–95. Ayabe revised the number of total deaths in this "war" from twenty to nineteen, e-mail from Ayabe to author, August 23, 2009.
267. Ayabe, "The Ku Klux Klan Movement," 397.
268. Ibid., 409–13.
269. Ayabe, e-mail to author, August 23, 2009.

CHAPTER 8

270. Angle, *Bloody Williamson*, 206–7.
271. Ayabe, "The Ku Klux Klan Movement," 398, 412.
272. Angle, *Bloody Williamson*, 213.
273. DeNeal, *A Knight of Another Sort*, 115.
274. Ibid., 119–20; Angle, *Bloody Williamson*, 207–8.
275. DeNeal, *A Knight of Another Sort*, 121–23; Angle, *Bloody Williamson*, 226–27.
276. DeNeal, *A Knight of Another Sort*, 130–31; Angle, *Bloody Williamson*, 209, 217–18.
277. DeNeal, *A Knight of Another Sort*, 243–45; Angle, *Bloody Williamson*, 236–37, 259.
278. DeNeal, *A Knight of Another Sort*, 250–54; Angle, *Bloody Williamson*, 231–32, 288–89.

CHAPTER 9

279. Many amusement parks of the time were called White City, after the famous White City at the 1893 Chicago World's Fair. In addition to the liberal use of electric light, its buildings were coated with plaster of Paris and whitewash. Chicago's White City Amusement Park opened in 1905, and there were others in Springfield (Missouri), Atlanta, Cleveland, New Haven, Syracuse, New Orleans, London, Sydney, Melbourne and so on. I've seen no reason to think Herrin's was named for anything else. "White City (Shrewsbury Amusement Park). Wikipedia, the free encyclopedia. More on Herrin's White City is available in *Williamson County, Illinois, Sesquicentennial History*, 99.
280. The most famous person no one knows is from Herrin has a newspaper connection, too. Writer Robert Coover, known internationally as a postmodern novelist, grew up for a time in Herrin, where his father was the managing editor of the *Herrin Daily Journal*. Coover's first novel, *The Origin of the Brunists* (1966), is set in a fictional Southern Illinois town, where a mine explosion has killed ninety-seven.

281. Brown and Webb, *Seven Stranded Coal Towns*, 18.
282. Ibid., 21.
283. Ibid., 24.
284. Ibid.
285. Ibid., 57.
286. Ibid., 15.
287. Ibid., 27.
288. Ibid., 45.
289. Ibid., 46–50.
290. Ibid., n89.
291. Ibid., 105.
292. *The Census of Agriculture, 2007.* United States Department of Agriculture.
293. Brown and Webb, *Seven Stranded Coal Towns*, 124.
294. Ibid., 95.
295. Ibid., xxvi.
296. Ibid., 113.
297. Ibid., iii.
298. Ibid., 139.
299. Ibid., 136–37.
300. Ibid., 139–40.
301. "Crab Orchard National Wildlife Refuge." U.S. Fish & Wildlife Service.
302. "Community Leaders, Citizens put Herrin Back on the Map." *Williamson County, Illinois, Sesquicentennial History*, 186.
303. Angle, *Bloody Williamson*, 270–72.
304. "Community Leaders," 186.
305. Phone conversation, August 11, 2009.
306. Phone conversation, August 12, 2009.
307. Myers, *Directory of Coal Mines in Illinois*.
308. Alec MacGillis and Steven Mufson, "Coal Fuels a Debate Over Obama," *Washington Post*, June 24, 2007, A01.
309. Scott Elrick, e-mail, June 6, 2009.
310. MacGillis and Mufson, "Coal Fuels a Debate Over Obama."
311. Ibid.
312. *FutureGen for Illinois: The World Needs FutureGen. FutureGen Needs Illinois.* Illinois Department of Commerce and Economic Opportunity.
313. Scott Elrick, e-mail, June 6, 2009.

BIBLIOGRAPHY

Adams, Alexander B. *John James Audubon: A Biography*. New York: Putnam, 1966.

Adams, Jane. *The Transformation of Rural Life: Southern Illinois, 1890–1990*. Chapel Hill: University of North Carolina Press, 1994.

Allen, John W. *Legends & Lore of Southern Illinois*. Carbondale: Southern Illinois University Press, 1963.

Amato, Joseph Anthony. *Rethinking Home: A Case for Writing Local History*. Berkeley: University of California Press, 2002.

Angle, Paul M. *Bloody Williamson: A Chapter in American Lawlessness*. New York: Knopf, 1974.

Ayabe, Masatomo. "The Ku Klux Klan Movement in Williamson County, Illinois, 1923–1926." PhD dissertation, University of Illinois at Urbana-Champaign, February 11, 2005.

———. Personal e-mail to author. August 23, 2009.

"Battle of Blair Mountain." Wikipedia, the free encyclopedia. http://en.wikipedia.org/wiki/Battle_of_Blair_Mountain.

Berggren, Dwain J., contr. "Quaternary Glaciations in Illinois." *GeoNote 3*. Illinois State Geological Survey, 2008. http://www.isgs.uiuc.edu/maps-data-pub/publications/geonotes/geonote3.shtml.

"Big Eddy." Center for Archaeological Research, Missouri State University. May 18, 2006. http://www.missouristate.edu/car/7707.htm.

Blake, Kellee Green. "Aiding and Abetting Disloyalty Prosecutions in the Federal Civil Courts of Southern Illinois, 1861–1866." *Illinois Historical Journal* 87, no. 2 (Summer 1994): 95–108.

Boggess, Arthur Clinton. *The Settlement of Illinois, 1778–1830*. Chicago Historical Society, 1908. http://books.google.com/books?id=j6zN_05Xq5kC&source=gbs_navlinks_s.

Breen, Catherine E., Gerald A. Danzer and Janet A. Lueby. "Illinois Becomes a State: 1818 Compromise, Later Conflict." Illinois Periodicals Online. http://www.lib.niu.edu/1995/iht29502.html.

Brestensky, Dennis F., Evelyn A. Hovanec and Albert N. Skomra. *Patch/Work Voices: The Culture and Lore of a Mining People*. Pittsburgh, PA: University Center for International Studies Publications, University of Pittsburgh, 1978.

Brownell, Baker. *The Other Illinois*. New York: Duell, Sloan and Pearce, 1958.

Brown, Malcolm, and John N. Webb. *Seven Stranded Coal Towns: A Study of an American Depressed Area*. Washington, D.C.: U.S. Government Printing Office, 1941.

Bruce, Julia. "The George Henry Harrison Family." *Williamson County, Illinois, Sesquicentennial History*. Nashville, TN: Turner Publishing Company, 1989.

Butler, Brian M. "Crab Orchard." *Archaeology of Prehistoric Native America: An Encyclopedia*. Edited by Guy Gibbon and Kenneth M. Ames. London: Taylor & Francis, 1998.

———. "Land Between the Rivers: The Archaic Period of Southernmost Illinois." *Archaic Societies: Diversity and Complexity Across the Midcontinent*. Edited by Thomas E. Emerson and Dale L. McElrath. New York: SUNY Press, 2009.

Butler, Brian M., and Mark J. Wagner. "Land Between the Rivers: The Late Woodland Period of Southernmost Illinois." *Late Woodland Societies: Tradition and Transformation Across the Midcontinent*. Edited by Thomas E. Emerson and others. Lincoln: University of Nebraska Press, 2000.

Callary, Edward. *Place Names of Illinois*. Urbana: University of Illinois Press, 2008.

The Census of Agriculture, 2007. United States Department of Agriculture. http://www.agcensus.usda.gov/Publications/2007/Online_Highlights/County_Profiles/Illinois/index.asp.

"Charles Juchereau, VaBache Tannery: French exploration in Illinois." Southernmost Illinois History. http://www.southernmostillinoishistory.net/juchereau.htm.

Chenoweth, Cheri, staff member, Coal Section, Illinois State Geological Survey. Personal e-mails with author.

Chenoweth, Cheri, Alan R. Meyers and Jennifer M. Obrad. *Photographic History of Coal Mining Practices in Illinois*. Illinois State Geological Survey Circular 572, 2008. Available at https://shop.isgs.illinois.edu/circulars.html.

Chicago Daily Tribune. "Death Bullets Follow Taunts for Mine Victims." June 23, 1922.

———. "The Herrin Mine Massacre—15 Years Ago." July 18, 1937.

Coal Section. "Depositional History of the Pennsylvanian Rocks in Illinois." *GeoNote 2*. Champaign: Illinois State Geological Survey, Coal Section. Revised by Russell J. Jacobson, 2000.

"Crab Orchard National Wildlife Refuge." U.S. Fish & Wildlife Service. http://www.fws.gov/midwest/CrabOrchard/history.html.

Crawford, Joe. "Crab Orchard Home to Wildlife, Industry." Shawnee Forest Convergence Project. http://journal.siu.edu/shawnee/index.php?option=com_content&task=view&id=69&Itemid=117.

"Deceased Veterans." *Williamson County, Illinois, Sesquicentennial History*. Nashville, TN: Turner Publishing Company, 1989.

DeNeal, Gary. *A Knight of Another Sort: Prohibition Days and Charlie Birger*. Second edition. Carbondale: Southern Illinois University Press, 1998.

Dix, Keith. *What's a Coal Miner to Do?: The Mechanization of Coal Mining*. Pittsburgh, PA: University of Pittsburgh Press, 1988.

Dubofsky, Melvyn. *The State and Labor in Modern America*. Chapel Hill: University of North Carolina Press, 1994.

Elrick, Scott, staff member, Coal Section, Illinois State Geological Survey. E-mails to author, June 3 and 6, and personal discussion, 2009.

Erwin, Milo. *The History of Williamson County, Illinois*. Marion, IL: [self-published?], 1876.

Evans, Arthur. "Terror Grips Law Abiding of 'Bloody' Herrin." *Chicago Daily Tribune*, July 2, 1922.

Fay, Jim, and Andrew C. Fortier. *The Tall Grass Prairie Peninsula: Its Role in Shaping American Culture*. Champaign, IL: Stipes Publishing, 2007.

Federal Writers' Project. *The WPA Guide to Illinois: The Federal Writers' Project Guide to 1930s Illinois*. Reprint of *Illinois, A Descriptive and Historical Guide*, 1939. New York: Pantheon Books, 1983.

Fliege, Stu. *Tales and Trails of Illinois*. Urbana: University of Illinois Press, 2002.

"Fort Massac State Park." Illinois Department of Natural Resources. http://dnr.state.il.us/lands/LANDMGT/parks/r5/frmindex.htm.

Franklin County Historical Society, ed. *Franklin County, Illinois, 1818–1997*. Nashville, TN: Turner Publishing Company, 1997.

FutureGen for Illinois: The World Needs FutureGen. FutureGen Needs Illinois. Illinois Department of Commerce and Economic Opportunity. http://www.illinoisbiz.biz/dceo/Bureaus/Coal.

"General John A. Logan." Reprinted in *Williamson County, Illinois, Sesquicentennial History*. Nashville, TN: Turner Publishing Company, 1989.

Giertz, J. Fred, Department of Economics and Institute of Government and Public Affairs, University of Illinois at Urbana-Champaign. E-mails to author, August 4 and 5, 2009.

Hale, Stan J., ed. *Williamson County, Illinois, Sesquicentennial History*. Nashville, TN: Turner Publishing Company, 1989.

Hall, Robert L. "Cahokia Identity and Interaction Models of Cahokia Mississippian." *Cahokia and the Hinterlands: Middle Mississippian Cultures of the Midwest*. Edited by Thomas E. Emerson and R. Barry Lewis. Urbana: University of Illinois Press, 1999.

Handy, Jeanne Townsend. "A Day at Bison Beach." *IT Online*. October 13, 2005. http://www.illinoistimes.com/gyrobase/Content?oid=oid%3A4761.

Harrison, David Ruffin. "The Origin of Herrin's Prairie." Reprinted in *Williamson County, Illinois, Sesquicentennial History*, from a text written 1907–8, transcribed twice over the years. Nashville, TN: Turner Publishing Company, 1989.

Hawse, Mara Lou, and Dianne Throgmorton, eds. *Tell Me a Story: Memories of Early Life Around the Coal Fields of Illinois*. Carbondale: Coal Research Center, Southern Illinois University, 1992.

Hemingway, Ernest. *A Moveable Feast*. New York: Bantam, 1965.

"Herrin, Illinois. Sperling's Best Places." http://www.bestplaces.net/City/Herrin-Illinois.aspx.

Herrin, Ruth C. "A Story About Herrin's Prairie." *Williamson County, Illinois, Sesquicentennial History*. Nashville, TN: Turner Publishing Company, 1989.

Hill, Steven R. "Botanical Survey of the Herrin-Johnston City Highway (FAS 903 and FAU 9588), Williamson County, Illinois, Including the Discovery of Two Sedge Species New to Illinois." *Technical Report 2002 (21)*. Champaign: Center for Biodiversity, Illinois Natural History Survey, 2002.

"Historical Census Browser." University of Virginia Library. http://fisher.lib.virginia.edu/collections/stats/histcensus/php/county.php.

History of Gallatin, Saline, Hamilton, Franklin and Williamson Counties, Illinois, from the Earliest Time to the Present: Together with Sundry and Interesting Biographical Sketches, Notes, Reminiscences, Etc., Etc. Chicago: Goodspeed Publishing Co., 1887. Accessed online http://www.archive.org/stream/historyofgallati00chic/historyofgallati00chic_djvu.txt.

"A History of the Colorado Coal Field War." *Colorado Coal Field War Project*. University of Denver. http://www.du.edu/ludlow/cfhist.html.

Hoffmeister, Donald Frederick. *Mammals of Illinois*. Reprint. Champaign: University of Illinois Press, 2002.

Hubbs, Barbara Burr. *Pioneer Folks and Places: An Historic Gazetteer of Williamson County, Illinois*. Herrin, IL: Herrin Daily Journal, 1939.

Huhndorf, Shari M. *Going Native: Indians in the American Cultural Imagination*. Ithaca, NY: Cornell University Press, 2001.

"Illinois Coal Industry Significant Dates." http://www.commerce.state.il.us/NR/rdonlyres/0C25B98A-C4CA-4BD9-B61E-860AC7965164/0/IllinoisCoalIndustryHistorytimeline.pdf.

"Illinois Public Domain Land Tract Sales." Illinois State Archives. http://www.cyberdriveillinois.com/departments/archives/data_lan.html#location.

"Indian Removal Act." *Primary Documents in American History*. Library of Congress, Virtual Programs & Services, July 6, 2009. http://www.loc.gov/rr/program/bib/ourdocs/Indian.html.

Jacobson, Russell L., and Christopher Korose. "Coal Geology of Illinois." *2003 Keystone Coal Industry Manual*. http://www.isgs.uiuc.edu/maps-data-pub/coal-maps.shtml.

Jubilee 2000: Our Lady of Mount Carmel, Herrin, Illinois. 2001 Directory. Olan Mills Church Directories. Our Lady of Mount Carmel, Herrin, Illinois.

Lantz, Herman R. *People of Coal Town*. New York: Columbia University Press, 1958.

Laslett, John H.M. "A Parting of the Ways: Immigrant Miners and the Rise of Politically Conscious Trade Unionism in Scotland and the American Midwest, 1865–1924."

The United Mine Workers of America: A Model of Industrial Solidarity? University Park: Pennsylvania State University Press, 1996.

Loewen, James W. *Sundown Towns: A Hidden Dimension of American Racism*. New York: New Press, 2005.

Logan, John A., Mrs. *Reminiscences of a Soldier's Wife: An Autobiography*. New York: C. Scribner's Sons, 1913.

Long, Priscilla. *Where the Sun Never Shines: A History of America's Bloody Coal Industry*. New York: Paragon House, 1991.

MacGillis, Alec, and Steven Mufson. "Coal Fuels a Debate Over Obama." *Washington Post*, June 24, 2007, A01. http://www.washingtonpost.com/wp-dyn/content/article/2007/06/23/AR2007062301424.html.

Marlon, J.R., P.J. Bartlein, M.K. Walsh, et al. "Wildfire Responses to Abrupt Climate Change in North America." *PNAS* 106, no. 8 (February 24, 2009): 2519–2524.

"Measuring Worth—Relative Value of US Dollars." http://www.measuringworth.com/uscompare.

"The Midwestern United States 16,000 Years Ago." Illinois State Museum. http://www.museum.state.il.us/exhibits/larson/index.html.

Miller, Robert J., and Elizabeth Furse. *Native America, Discovered and Conquered*. Santa Barbara, CA: Praeger Publishers, 2006.

Myers, Alan R. *Directory of Coal Mines in Illinois. 7.5-Minute Quadrangle Series, Herrin Quadrangle, Williamson County*. Champaign: Department of Natural Resources, Illinois State Geological Survey, 2006.

Nelson, W. John. *Geologic Disturbances in Illinois Coal Seams*. Circular 530. Champaign: Illinois State Geological Survey, 1983.

New York Times. "Mine Owners to Sue Union and County." June 24, 1922.

———. "Tribe Pulls Land Suit." June 16, 2001.

Paisley, Oldham. Scrapbooks of articles he clipped on national coverage of the Herrin Massacre of 1922. Various locations, including the Chicago History Museum and University of Illinois.

Parks, Nannie Gray. "The Story of Williamson County One Hundred Years Ago." *Souvenir Program of the Williamson County Centennial Celebration*. Herrin, IL: Herrin Daily Journal, 1939.

"Past Illinois Capitols." http://www.ilstatehouse.com/past_capitols.htm.

Pensoneau, Taylor. *Brothers Notorious: The Sheltons: Southern Illinois' Legendary Gangsters*. New Berlin, IL: Downstate Publications, 2002.

Pisoni, Richard. Phone conversation, August 11, 2009.

Pringle, Heather. "Did a Comet Wipe Out Prehistoric Americans?" *New Scientist* (May 22, 2007). http://www.newscientist.com/article/dn11909.

Prosser, Daniel J. "Coal Towns in Egypt: Portrait of an Illinois Mining Region, 1890–1930." PhD dissertation, Northwestern University, 1973.

Pruett, Gordon, and Michael D. Covell, eds. *A History of Herrin, Illinois*. Video, 40 minutes. Available from the Herrin Chamber of Commerce.

Pruett, Gordon, ed. *Old Times in Herrin*. 2nd ed. Herrin, IL: Herrin Chamber of Commerce, 2002. Pruett has cleaned up and reissued Hal Trovillion's classic collection of memories by early residents and added photos from his own postcard collection.

———. *One Hundred Years of Herrin, Illinois*. Herrin, IL: Herrin Chamber of Commerce, 2000. Companion book of photos to the video *A History of Herrin, Illinois*.

Ritter, Vic. Phone conversation, August 12, 2009.

"A Rock That Burns." Illinois State Museum. http://www.museum.state.il.us/exhibits/changes/con_trPE_mc.swf.

Ross, David, Secretary. *Twenty-First Annual Coal Report of the Illinois Bureau of Labor Statistics…for the Year Ended Oct. 1, 1902*. Springfield, IL: Phillips Bros., State Printers, 1903.

Rucker, Walter C., and James N. Upton. *Encyclopedia of American Race Riots*. Santa Barbara, CA: Greenwood Publishing Group, 2007.

Sheppard, Donald E. "DeSoto's Midwestern Trail." http://www.1st-history-of-the.us/illinois2.html.

Singer, Alan J. "Something of a Man: John L. Lewis, the UMWA, and the CIO, 1919–1943." *The United Mine Workers of America: A Model of Industrial Solidarity?* University Park: Pennsylvania State University Press, 1996.

Sneed, Glenn J. *Ghost Towns of Southern Illinois*. Royalton, IL: self-published, 1983.

Sulzman, Lee. "Illinois History." http://www.tolatsga.org/ill.html. Revised July 17, 1997.

Swann, David H. "A Summary Geologic History of the Illinois Basin." Indiana-Kentucky and Illinois Geological Societies, 1968. Reposted by Illinois Oil & Gas Association. http://www.ioga.com/Geohist.htm.

Temple, Wayne C. *Indian Villages of the Illinois Country*. Springfield, Illinois State Museum Scientific Papers, vol. 2, part 2. 1966.

Tonso, William R. Introduction to "My Book of Memories: A Herrin Italian-American Memoir," by Eva Tonso. Unpublished.

Tow, Michael. "The Kaskaskia Reservation." *Illinois Heritage* 13 (2003). Northern Illinois University. http://www.perrycountyillinois.net/sub107.htm.

Treworgy, Colin G., and Russell J. Jacobson. *Paleoenvironments and Distribution of Low-Sulfur Coal in Illinois*. Illinois Department of Energy and Natural Resources, State Geological Survey Division, Reprint 1986E. From *Compte Rendu* of Ninth International Congress on Carboniferous Stratigraphy and Geology, Washington, D.C., and Champaign-Urbana, vol. 4, *Economic Geology: Coal, Oil and Gas*, by A.T. Cross, ed., 349–59. Carbondale: Southern Illinois University Press, 1985.

Treworgy, Colin G., Christopher P. Korose and Christine L. Wiscombe. *Availability of the Herrin Coal for Mining in Illinois*. Illinois Minerals 120. Champaign: Illinois State Geological Survey, 2000.

Trovillion, Hal W., ed. *Old Times in Herrin*. Herrin, IL: *Herrin News*, 1922.

———. *Souvenir Program: Williamson County Centennial.* Herrin, IL: Herrin Daily Journal, 1939.

———. *Williamson County, Illinois, in the World War.* Herrin, IL: Williamson County War History Society, 1919.

Tyson, Peter. "End of the Big Beasts." *Nova.* http://www.pbs.org/wgbh/nova/clovis/megafauna.html.

Veritas [pseud.]. *Life and Exploits of S. Glenn Young, World-Famous Law Enforcement Officer.* Originally published by Mrs. S. Glenn Young, 1924. Republished Herrin, IL: Crossfire Press, 1989. Masatomo Ayabe says that Reverend Herbert Bryce was the ghostwriter.

Weinberg, Carl. *Labor, Loyalty and Rebellion: Southwestern Illinois Coal Miners and World War I.* Carbondale: Southern Illinois University Press, 2005.

"White City (Shrewsbury [MA] Amusement Park)." Wikipedia, the free encyclopedia. http://en.wikipedia.org/wiki/White_City_(Shrewsbury_amusement_park).

Wilcox, J.F., ed. *Historical Souvenir of Williamson County, Illinois.* Effingham, IL: LeCrone Press, 1905.

Williamson County, Illinois, Sesquicentennial History. "Community Leaders, Citizens Put Herrin Back on the Map." Nashville, TN: Turner Publishing Company, 1989.

INDEX

ABOUT THE AUTHOR

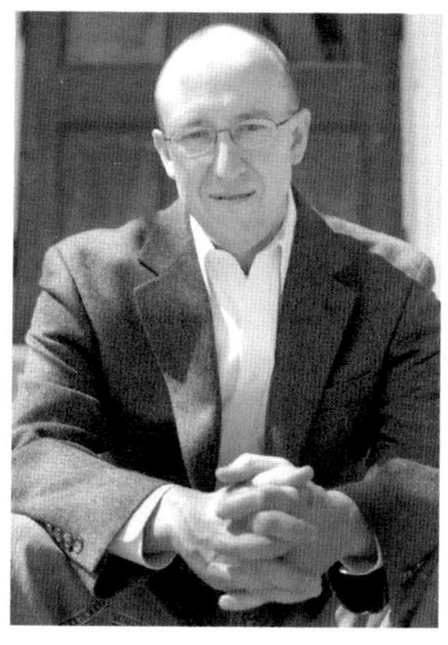

John Griswold, a 1981 graduate of Herrin High School, is the author of *A Democracy of Ghosts*, a novel set during the Herrin Massacre of 1922. His writing has appeared in many literary journals, such as *Natural Bridge*, which nominated his short story about the aerial bombing of Shady Rest for the Pushcart Prize. His essays on downstate Illinois have appeared in *Ninth Letter* and the third volume of the W.W. Norton anthology *The Best Creative Nonfiction*. In 2009, he won the Delta Award from the Friends of Morris Library, Southern Illinois University-Carbondale, for "writing with distinction on southern Illinois."

John is also a contributing writer for *Inside Higher Ed* and a columnist for McSweeney's Internet Tendency. He has taught creative writing, literature and rhetoric at the University of Illinois, Urbana-Champaign, since 2000. Read more at www.johngriswold.net.